Evaluating Planned
Organizational Change

ORGANIZATIONAL AND OCCUPATIONAL PSYCHOLOGY

Series Editor: PETER WARR

MRC/ESRC Social and Applied Psychology Unit, Department of Psychology, The University, Sheffield, England

A complete list of titles appears at the end of this volume.

Evaluating Planned
Organizational Change

K. Legge

Department of Social and Economic Studies
Imperial College of Science and Technology
London

1984

ACADEMIC PRESS

(Harcourt Brace Jovanovich, Publishers)
London   Orlando   San Diego   San Francisco   New York
Toronto   Montreal   Sydney   Tokyo

ACADEMIC PRESS INC. (LONDON) LTD.
24/28 Oval Road
London NW1

United States Edition published by
ACADEMIC PRESS INC.
(Harcourt Brace Jovanovich, Inc)
Orlando, Florida 32887

British Library Cataloguing in Publication Data
Legge, Karen
    Evaluating planned organizational change. —
    (Organizational and occupational psychology)
    1. Organizational change — Evaluation
    I. Title
    658.4'06   HD58.8

    ISBN 0-12-440980-6
    LCCCN 83-73564

Phototypeset by Dobbie Typesetting Service, Plymouth, Devon
Printed by St Edmundsbury Press, Bury St Edmunds, Suffolk

Preface

Changes in our organizations and society as a whole have become a way of life. But increasing awareness of the scarcity of resources demands that we evaluate the changes we make and allocate resources in the directions we believe to be most fruitful. Applied normative research into the impact and experience of programmes of planned change is now a major social science activity.

However, in this book, it is argued that such "evaluation research" has been beset by three crises: of verification/methods, accreditation/values, and utilization/functions. Briefly, researchers are questioning the validity of traditional positivistic research methods for establishing the effects of change programmes; the acceptability of the values that permeate much evaluative research; and even its usefulness to decision-makers and society generally. The result is a crisis of confidence among researchers and potential users alike.

The question, of course, is whether, and how, these crises might be resolved. In the chapters that follow their nature is explored and a strategy to cope with them is presented. In a nutshell, it is argued that the crises may be ameliorated by undertaking a "matching" process to achieve compatibility between the evaluation functions sought (by potential users, and those participating in a change programme) and the research design employed, *within the constraints imposed by the nature and conceptualization of the change process*. Associated organizational design questions are also considered. But while this strategy may alleviate the crises in methods and utilization, it cannot deal with the underlying crisis in values. The way round this dilemma, it is suggested, lies in a complete re-examination and redefinition of the evaluator's role.

The terms "ameliorate" and "alleviate" are used deliberately. Basically it is considered that there are no complete answers to these crises *because they are expressions of five fundamental paradoxes embedded in the different paradigmatic positions through which the evaluation of change programmes may be approached* (and which are summarized in the concluding chapter on p.216).

v

These paradoxes emerged when the attempt was made, in considering the crisis in verification/methods, to assess the full logical implications of adopting particular ontological and epistemological positions in conducting research. Too often researchers appear unwilling to confront the "impractical" implications of their assumptions about reality and the grounds of knowledge for the research designs and methods they may employ. Inconsistencies resulting in an abstracted empiricism appear to pass unrecognized or be shrugged off without a qualm. A major concern of this book is to highlight where the logic of different paradigmatic positions lead, rather than to fudge what are often uncomfortable realizations. To those who might say (as one valued colleague and critic has already done) that drawing extreme distinctions and contrasts increase the danger that one may not be discussing groups and behaviours in reality, I can only echo Wagner's (1981, p.xix) comment, in reaction to a similar criticism:

> Have I, then, artificially exaggerated the polarities of human symbolization by imposing extreme contrasts and oppositions upon usages that are most often only relatively opposable, and even then debatedly so? Of course I have, hoping that, like the tracery of semi-visible geometry that Cézanne introduced into his landscapes, this 'imagery' would help us to see the landscape better . . .

Put another way, exploring the three crises that confront evaluation research through a series of paradoxes, may be seen as a sort of exercise in "deconstruction" (to use a literary analogy), whereby paradoxes are used "as a positive technique for making trouble; an affront to every normal and comfortable habit of thought" (Norris, 1982, p.xi).

Regrettably, "normal and comfortable habits of thought", in spite of conscious efforts at avoidance, may have crept in to this book, with the impersonal use of the masculine pronoun. Where the use of "he or she" became cumbersome (and why not "she or he"?) an unconscious reversion to the conventional masculine usage seems to have triumphed over any exercise in consciousness-raising — an unfortunate contradiction, in the light of earlier comments perhaps!

In the course of writing this book, I have incurred many debts. In particular I would like to thank my colleagues and friends at the MRC/ESRC Social and Applied Psychology Unit, University of Sheffield, for their stimulating company, helpful comments and constructive criticisms and, at Imperial College, for their forebearance during the manuscript's gestation period. To Professor Peter Warr, MRC/ESRC SAPU, I owe very special thanks for a most careful persual of chapter drafts and much encouragement towards completion. Above all, though, my debt is to Dan Gowler, whose presence permeates this book to an extent that will be most evident to those who know us both. Last, but not least, my very grateful thanks go to Mrs. Joan Wright, Imperial College, whose patience and good humour in typing drafts of chapters gave me the courage to give her, undeservedly, more.

Karen Legge

Imperial College
May, 1984

Contents

Chapter 1

Evaluation in Crisis

In modern industrialized societies we are faced with two clichéd images of change. The first, Utopian image is that we live and will live with ever accelerating rates of benign technological change, accompanied by progressive changes in social values (Beer, 1972; Bennis, 1966; Bennis *et al.*, 1976; Schön, 1971). The second, Malthusian image, born of energy crises and accompanying recessions of the 1970s and 1980s, is that we live in a world of increasingly scarce resources, and that our technological achievements, in part, only serve to aggravate this situation through their extravagant consumption of natural resources and potential for polluting and even destroying our physical and moral environments.

The first image is mainly optimistic, that man is capable of, and indeed, should attempt to be master rather than servant of his environment. The picture of man manipulating, controlling and changing his environment for the general betterment of his fellows was symbolized by such typically "1960s" events and aspirations as landing a man on the moon ("A small step for man, a giant leap for mankind"), the first human organ transplants, and "Equal Rights". Less dramatic, but possibly more significant, was the use of technology to translate the erstwhile luxuries of the rich—automatic washing machines, colour T.V.s and cars into the everyday conveniences of broad sections of society. Today it is conventional to define both organizational and managerial effectiveness in change related terms. For example, organizational effectiveness is generally defined in terms of an organization's capacity to anticipate and adapt functionally (i.e. in the light of its goals, or for survival and growth) to the turbulence and uncertainties of a changing environment (Emery and Trist, 1965; Lawrence and Lorsch, 1967; Steers, 1977; Yuchtman and Seashore, 1967). Likewise, managerial or administrative effectiveness is often equated with an individual's or group's ability to make appropriate decisions, in the light of specified success criteria, in conditions of change-induced risk and uncertainty. And it is consistent with the "man as master of his environment" facet of this image that it has increasingly become the convention that managers and administrators

1

should not be merely *reactive* to *unplanned change* (as was characteristic of the traditional "maintenance" and "breakdown" roles of line management and administration) but proactive, capable of *anticipating, planning and implementing* their own change programmes in response to perceived changes, internal and external to the organization, in order to control crucial sectors of their environments (Morris and Burgoyne, 1973). The growth of matrix organization structure through which to manage the design and development of planned technological and product innovation, as in the case of the American Space Agency (NASA), the introduction of organizational development consultants to initiate and develop social change in organizations, as in the large multinational companies, not to mention the development of "social engineering" programmes in the U.S. in the 1960s and early 1970s — all are illustrative of this demand (Beckhard, 1969; Bennis *et al.*, 1976; French and Bell, 1973; Galbraith, 1973; Kingdon, 1973; Knight, 1977; Sayles and Chandler, 1971).

But this is to ignore the other mainly pessimistic image of change — of a society constrained by increasingly scarce natural resources, requiring man to be the servant or victim of the environment, rather than its master or exploiter. This image of society, which has become increasingly prevalent throughout the 1970s and 1980s, as energy crises and economic recessions have walked hand in hand, has been symbolized by such movements as "Friends of the Earth" and "Green Peace" and by protests against costly prestige technological development (as in military hardware, or in high technology medicine). Moreover, this unhappy perspective has been sharpened by the opinion that the rapidity of change generates its own problems, e.g. "future shock" (Toffler, 1970).

As both inflation and unemployment rise together, and the conventional post-Keynsian economic models seem no longer "to work", as awareness grows that high technology brings not only material benefits but potential social disasters (Three Mile Island, Seveso, the implications for employment of the micro-processing revolution), the image of man controlling the environment has come increasingly under question. The environment of opportunity of the 1960s, in 1970s and early 1980s, is being recast in popular imagery as one of constraint. In place of ambitious industrial expansion and innovatory social programmes, the climate is one of retrenchment and cutbacks, of justifications and accountability, rather than experimentation and risk.

It is against the background of these two contrasting images of change that the rapid rise of evaluation research, in the late 1960s and throughout the 1970s can best be understood. Thus, this book presents evaluation research, or the systematic assessment of programmes of planned change, as an activity whereby managers and administrators *attempt to control and reconcile these two images of immanent change.* To clarify and elaborate upon this comment, it is necessary to establish just what is "evaluation research".

Characteristics of evaluation research

We all evaluate, that is assess, against implicit or explicit criteria, the value or worth of individuals, objects, situations and outcomes, informally and often unconsciously every day of our lives. The reasons we do this are a source of considerable controversy, but it appears that we require a rationale for the choices that are supposed to shape our actions. We have to make choices because both our own resources and those of our environment are not infinite—we have not the time, energy or ability to do everything, nor can our environment allow everyone an infinite amount of everything. In other words, *any act of evaluation, however informal, rests on the assumption of scarce resources*, behind which assumption lies a system of categorization and related views about the proper order of things (Foucault, 1970).

Acts of evaluation span the whole continuum of informality—formality (Gowler and Legge, 1980; Joyce, 1980). But at the "formality" end of the continuum are explicit acts of evaluation, systematic, planned activities, formally distinct and separate from the on-going acts of evaluation that form part of everyday life or even the core of high discretion tasks. These are dignified by the title of "evaluation *research*" when they possess two characteristics: the use of "*scientific*" method, by *professional* "evaluation researchers".

Suchman (1967, p.45) along with many others (e.g. Rossi *et al.*, 1979; Weiss, 1972a) has defined evaluation research solely as "the use of the scientific method of collecting data concerning the degree to which some specified activity achieves some desired effect". But what is meant by scientific? Some clues are dropped by Suchman's reference to "activity" effectiveness being judged in terms of demonstrable attainment of stated objectives—in other words in terms of the "impact" or effect (and effectiveness) of the change programme, the independent variable, on specified dependent variables. Such "impact" studies suggest that evaluation researchers would conventionally define "scientific" very much in terms of conformity to the rules of the positivistic paradigm, with its emphasis on a hypothetico-deductive rationality, expressed through an insistence on an experimental or quasi experimental approach. This, until recently, has proved to be the case. "The classic design for evaluations has been the experimental model" (Weiss, 1972a, p.9)—an assertion endorsed by many evaluation researchers (Bernstein and Freeman, 1975; Campbell and Stanley, 1963; Wholey *et al.*, 1970). Assumptions about what constitutes a "proper" scientific approach (i.e. that the evaluation should contain both "experimental" and "control" groups) underlies a more limited and specific use of the term evaluation research. As Nicholas (1979, p.27) put it, "some writers chose to distinguish between evaluation research, as studies of programs across various settings, from single setting studies which they term 'programme evaluation'." Belief that the latter can degenerate into "the weakest of all study designs — the case study in which a program is analyzed without comparing it with any sort of control" (Rossi and Wright, 1977, pp.16–17) has led some evaluation researchers to make this distinction, although the grounds on which they do so is simply a reassertion of their commitment to the positivistic paradigm, rather than the assertion of any new criteria by which to differentiate evaluation research from other forms of evaluation.

The second characteristic of "evaluation research" is that it has been developed by, and is giving rise to distinct bodies of professional evaluation researchers. Three major groups are identifiable, but membership is often overlapping. The first comprises those researchers who are engaged in the evaluation of federally funded U.S. social change programmes. Members of this group are possibly the most self-conscious and articulate about their identity as professional *evaluation* researchers (as opposed to just "applied" social scientists). These professional evaluators tend to have academic training as applied social scientists (for example, in the field of education) and to work either from university departments, university affiliated institutes, government departments, or independent research/consultancy organizations. Further, they meet at jointly run conferences, contribute to their own academic/professional journals, such as *Evaluation Quarterly*, *Evaluation Comment* and *Evaluation* and, as will be discussed later, bear all the characteristics of an emergent professional group.

In industry, the comparable group of professional evaluators (in the sense of their explicit awareness of their evaluatory function) tend either to be drawn from the ranks of commercial consultancy agencies or to occupy an "internal consultant's role" within a large organization. Either way, the role incumbent invariably has some relevant professional qualification, e.g. in accountancy, personnel management or organizational development.

A third group of evaluation researchers comprise those applied social scientists, working in university departments and research institutions, who are interested in organizational analysis. While some would flatly deny the title of "evaluation researcher" — arguing that their research is descriptive rather than normative, and cross-sectional rather than dealing with the dynamics of change — many would recognize at least the normative nature of their work. For example, included in this group might be those concerned with how to design organizational structures to cope with different and changing environments (e.g. Galbraith, 1973; Knight, 1977; Lawrence and Lorsch, 1967); with the effectiveness of different payment systems in enhancing motivation or controlling productivity drift (e.g. Lawler, 1971; Lupton and Bowey, 1974); or with the relationship between job design, productivity and satisfaction (e.g. Hackman and Lawler, 1971; Kelly and Clegg, 1982); or with the effectiveness of different management and leadership styles (e.g. Fiedler, 1967; Vroom and Yetton, 1973). As will be discussed in more detail later, these are the researchers who are committed to the "normative" contingency theories (see Legge, 1978, pp.96–98) or other forms of action research and organizational development and who, as a result, work closely with an organization's members in implementing as well as evaluating change programmes (e.g. Argyris, 1970; Argyris and Schön, 1974; Blake and Mouton, 1964). As such, they may undertake "research consultancy" assignments for organizations. In my view, such applied social scientists join the ranks of evaluation researchers when (a) their work has normative overtones (over and above the values implicit in choice of research subject and method) (b) they are concerned that their findings should be used by organizational members or other decision-makers (c) they recognize obligations to their funders and sponsors. To label as evaluation researchers, those applied social scientists whose concerns are exclusively with descriptive and explanatory research (Mohr, 1982), designed solely to increase knowledge for the consumption of fellow academics, seems overly inclusive.

Taking the two characteristics together, then, evaluation research may be typified as a "scientific" activity undertaken by "professional" evaluators.

It is against this background that I now turn to the major focus of this book. In a world that desires to exploit opportunities for change and development, but in a context of competing interests and diminishing resources, evaluation research would appear to be an eminently worthwhile and useful activity. For it both supports the necessity of change whilst admitting the existence of constraints. The reconciliation of the two, it suggests, lies in developing informed decision-making about the selective allocation of scarce resources, so that change programmes may be supported which carry a high probability of cost-effectiveness (however defined). It is to this activity that evaluation research seeks to contribute by providing decision-makers, directly or indirectly, with an objective and reliable information base to facilitate such decision-making. Furthermore, it is assumed to contribute to the maintenance of a dynamic equilibrium, i.e. change without disintegration. *Yet it is confronted by three crises which threaten its future development and even, some would argue, its survival.* The nature of these crises and their implications for the development of the evaluation of planned change will be discussed throughout this book. But, first, what are the crises to which I refer? The remainder of this chapter will introduce the crises in evaluation research concerning problems of (1) *utilization*, (2) *verification* and (3) *accredition*. But, as will be indicated, and developed in later chapters, these crises, in reality, are surface symptoms of deeper dilemmas concerning the *functions*, *methods* and *values* of evaluation.

The crisis of utilization

Whether concerning the evaluation of social change programmes or programmes of change in industrial organizations, "the consensus in the evaluation literature is that research findings are ignored in program decision-making" (Patton, 1978, p.22). These comments, in relation to social change programmes are echoed in Weiss (1972a), Wholey *et al.* (1970) and Williams and Evans (1969), while the experience of applied and action researchers in industrial organizations appears little different (Blackler and Brown, 1980; Carnall, 1979; Klein, 1976). For example, Burgoyne (1973, p.40), commenting on attempts to evaluate management development programmes in industry, concludes that

> There are very few people in the world of management development who have not acknowledged the need to evaluate their attempts to influence managers . . . but there is a general feeling that evaluation research has failed to provide the breakthrough in management development that was expected of it.

The evidence we have of the circumstances in which evaluation findings are most likely to be used by decision-makers is hardly reassuring: findings tend to be listened to when they "confirm what decision-makers already believe or disclose what they are predisposed to accept" (Weiss, 1975, p.23); when they lend support to facts already known, or confirm suspicions already entertained (Patton, 1978, pp.29–30). What seems rarely to happen is decision-makers acting upon findings that *disconfirm* their existing beliefs, or which suggest a radical and politically or ideologically unpalatable change in direction.

Why then are evaluation findings often ignored by the planners, public administrators and industrial managers to whom they are directed? The simple answer—because the latter often do not wish, or are unable to use them—begs the question of "why not?" It is at this point that issues of relevancy tend to be raised by researchers and organizational decision-makers alike. Researchers often suggest that the lack of utilization of their findings stems from the fact that the individuals and groups to whom such findings are officially addressed are frequently the "wrong" people. Either they are not directly involved in implementing the change programme which is the subject of the research and therefore cannot fully appreciate the potential utility of the findings, or perhaps they are not really interested, or sufficiently committed to use them. Or, if they are directly involved, may have their own "political" axes to grind and be appreciative only of the "right" set of findings. Managerial turnover may result in the individuals who commissioned the study having left the organization before it is presented (Klein, 1976).

In their turn, managers and administrators often accuse evaluators of producing irrelevant findings in academic gobbledy-gook, that either do not answer the questions in which they are really interested, or which come too late to improve the programme, or are trivial and only provide information that the administrators knew instinctively anyway.

Clearly, these issues of irrelevancy are mutually and negatively reinforcing. "Uninterested" administrators are unlikely to be sufficiently committed to work with the evaluator in establishing useful evaluation questions (i.e. questions on which they both want, need and can get information) and hence may be landed with irrelevant or trivial answers. Evaluators who do not match the time-span of their proposed study to administrators' time-spans of decision-making should not be surprised when their findings are considered to have arrived too late to influence related decisions.

However, behind these overt criticisms and mismatches evaluators and administrators are likely to hold covert positions that impede the potential utilization of evaluation findings. Evaluators may in reality be more interested in the extent to which their evaluation designs conform to the canons of the positivistic paradigm and meet with their professional colleagues' approval than in the extent to which they satisfy the administrators' needs. Their desire to increase the body of knowledge of their academic discipline may take priority over any desire to assist an organization's members. This attitude may be reinforced if the evaluator believes that "in any case" the administrators will not use the findings of the evaluation—in which circumstances she may just as well satisfy her own research interests and reputation first. The administrators involved in running the change programme may not have wanted the evaluation to take place at all, fearing that "evaluation . . . may be a threat, the execution warrant to admit the fiscal axeman, an exposé of failure and a mode of accountability" (Jenkins, 1978). They may be reluctant participants at the dictate of their Head Office, or, particularly in the case of social programmes, constrained by the conditions attached to their funding. (Many of the Affirmative Action programmes in the U.S. carried with them a legislative requirement and resourcing for independent researchers to evaluate their effectiveness.) In these circumstances, rejecting evaluators' findings on the grounds of their irrelevancy, triviality or lateness, may constitute a defence mechanism, irrespective of the justice or injustice of the charge.

All these accusations and counter accusations, however, point to an underlying problem in the utilization of evaluation findings—that is, what function is the evaluation to serve? For information to be perceived as "relevant" to decision-makers it must meet their needs—in other words, fulfil whatever functions they require of the evaluation. The problem is that the different stakeholders in the evaluation are likely to see its purpose differently and to have very different, and often incompatible requirements of it. *The crisis in utilization reflects a deeper problem—the question of what functions an evaluation design can and should fulfil.* This question and the problems it generates for evaluation research will be dealt with in Chapter 3.

However, the assumption here—that if managers and administrators are to use evaluation findings, these findings must be the product of evaluation designs that are compatible with the purposes they wish the evaluation to serve—leads on to the second crisis, that of verification.

The crisis of verification

"Evaluation", being the assessment of value or worth, has obvious normative and functional connotations. "Verification", "the action of establishing or testing the truth or correctness of a fact, theory, statement, etc., by means of special investigation or comparison of data" (to give it its *Shorter Oxford English Dictionary* definition), in contrast has positive or descriptive connotations. Verification cannot therefore be equated directly with evaluation, but obviously is central to evaluation *research*, as the latter generally purports to provide decision-makers with "objective" "hard" "established" facts on which to base their future decisions. This gap, yet interdependence, between verification and evaluation raises a number of important methodological dilemmas for the evaluation researcher.

First, there is the question of what is meant by the "truth or correctness of a fact, theory or statement". In principle, evaluation researchers, along with most other empiricists, do not seek to verify facts or theories (in the sense of carrying out all possible tests, since a test not carried out might refute the theory) but to design studies by which propositions are capable of "being refuted (i.e. falsified) by experience" (i.e. by empirical testing) (Popper, 1959, p.41). (Admittedly, the extent to which researchers, *in practice*, actually seek to falsify a proposition, as opposed to finding evidence to support it is open to question, and will be considered further in Chapter 5.)

Given that the overt, rational purpose of evaluating change programmes is to establish their effectiveness in achieving specified objectives, in order to assist decision-makers in the formulation of future policy and resource allocation, testing a hypothesis in evaluation research is conventionally directed at establishing "enduring truths" (Burgoyne and Cooper, 1975) about the capacity of an independent variable (the change programme) to cause changes in the behaviour of specified dependent variables (e.g. workers' attitudes about X, Y or Z, machine utilization levels, pregnant mothers use of antenatal clinics) in specified circumstances. To do this involves first establishing that a casual relationship does exist between the independent variable and observed changes in the dependent variables, secondly, establishing the magnitude of the effect of the independent variable upon dependent variables and, thirdly, the circumstances in which the causal relationship and the degree of impact will obtain. To achieve this also requires that the evaluation design controls for major threats to *internal validity* (the degree to which a design allows the evaluation to rule out alternative explanations for the effects observed) and to *external validity* (the degree to which the findings are capable of generalization). Thus, testing facts and theories, in these terms, as indicated earlier, inevitably directs the evaluation researcher toward a hypothetico-deductive approach and experimental or quasi- (i.e. approximately) experimental designs.

However, serious objections have been raised about the adequacies of this approach to evaluation. First, there is the practical problem that, in real life organizations, experimental or even quasi-experimental evaluation designs may prove unacceptable and/or impractical to implement. Secondly, there is the methodological problem that the design requirements for internal validity may be incompatible with those directed at achieving external validity, although the latter, in practice, may be of more interest to the manager who wishes to translate the change programme to another plant, or the administrator who wants to know if a curriculum will work in another school, if not to the evaluation researcher. Thirdly, there is the practical problem that experimental designs, if undertheorized, are often of less use in establishing *why* the observed phenomena or relationships exist, than of establishing the fact of their existence. These questions will be dealt with in Chapter 4.

The third dilemma raises a broader theoretical point. To be useful to administrators and managers, it is not enough for evaluation findings to be "true" or "valid" — they must also be "meaningful". That is, an administrator needs to know not just that a fact or relationship exists, but what its existence means for future decision-making and policy-making. Because the evaluation "findings" generated by experimental or quasi-experimental methods have often proved of little meaning to administrators, questions are now being raised as to whether methods of non-positivistic paradigms (for example, the ethogenic analysis of the interpretive, reflexive paradigms) might be more productive of meaningful data (e.g. Argyris, 1980; Reason and Rowan, 1981). This issue, which will be discussed in detail in Chapter 5, is, of course, directly related to the earlier discussion about the utilization crisis in evaluation research, and in turn, to the question of what function(s) an evaluation is to serve.

Finally, researchers are increasingly questioning whether the emphasis on measurement and quantification, which are associated with the hypothetico-deductive approach, is misplaced. Given the complexity of interrelationships in the real world, social scientists sometimes joke that everything is correlated with everything else at about 0·3. Moreover even when significant correlations are established they explain relatively little of the variance in the relationships of the variables tested. This can result in the manager being presented with a series of apparently weak findings about the measured effects of his or her change programme on the subject population or other dependent variables (Elinson, 1967; Ward and Kassebaum, 1972; Weiss, 1972a). Yet both practically and psychologically, most administrators are more interested in what their change programme did do (even if it was not what was planned or even anticipated) than what it did not do (even if a planned result did not materialize) (Rossi, 1972, p.22). In the political environment in which most administrators or managers work, information that their change programmes did not achieve the objectives sought is likely to be of interest only if it is accompanied by information about why this was so—particularly if scapegoats for failures can be identified. But it is this sort of information that the experimental method, in particular, often fails to produce. In other words, the crisis in verification points to underlying concerns about the power and appropriateness of different methodological approaches to evaluation research. In particular the ascendancy of positivistic approaches, irrespective of evaluation's function or situation is coming increasingly under attack (cf. Mitroff and Kilmann, 1978). These issues, and the whole question of the status and utility of various evaluation research *methods* will be considered in detail in Chapters 4 and 5.

I have already mentioned that a gap exists between evaluation as a normative activity and verification, on which evaluation research rests, as a positive and descriptive exercise. Whereas an administrator may wish to be "guided by the facts" in his judgement of the value of a particular change programme, the facts cannot make the judgement for him. Not only do issues of value enter the selection of the criteria against which the programme, on the basis of the facts, is to be judged, but, also, the importance placed on the facts themselves. Evaluation is therefore a different and broader activity than verification. This brings us to the third crisis in evaluation research—the accreditation crisis.

The crisis of accreditation

Obviously, if evaluation researchers' findings are ignored by the managers and administrators to whom they are addressed and if practical, methodological and theoretical doubts are expressed about their professionally favoured "best" research method, it is not surprising if a crisis of credibility about the utility and validity of the activity develops. But, the problem of credibility goes deeper than that, raising *important issues of professional and social values.*

As Weiss (1975, p.23) points out, evaluation researchers', particularly those involved in the evaluation of "social" change programmes, tend to be "liberal, reformist (and) humanitarian". In my experience, managers—and the public at large—make a similar claim about many applied social scientists working in industrial organizations: that they are "pro-union", "left-wing", "sweetness and light merchants" (Blackler and Brown, 1980). If evaluation research is seen to have a liberal bias, it can threaten its credibility with officialdom. Weiss (1975, pp.21–22) quotes the comment of one administrative official (Lynn, 1973, p.57):

> . . . The choice of conceptual frameworks, assumptions, output measures, variables, hypotheses, and data provide wide latitude for judgement, and values of researchers often guide the decisions to at least some degree . . . To the extent that this is true, the evaluator becomes another special interest or advocate rather than the purveyor of objectively developed evidence and insights, and the credibility of his work can be challenged.

She goes on to make the point "the message that comes through is that 'objectively developed evidence' is that which develops only out of government sanctioned assumptions and values" (1975, p.22).

These comments raise an important issue that confronts any evaluation researcher. Several commentators (e.g. Sjöberg, 1975; Weiss, 1975) have suggested that evaluation research tends to have a conservative bias. When evaluation research asks how effective a change programme was in achieving its goals, it implictly accepts the desirability of achieving those goals, and with it, therefore, the assumptions underlying the programme (Weiss, 1975, p.19). Yet this may be far from the case—particularly if the change programme is designed and implemented with a greater view to its latent rather than manifest functions (for example, to show that the management is "doing something" about health and safety, or is "interested in" increasing worker participation, rather than what the change programme is designed to achieve). "But when the social scientist agrees to evaluate a program, he gives it an aura of legitmacy" (Weiss, 1975, p.19).

Furthermore, as Warren (1973) has pointed out, if the research design is experimental, and the researcher limits his study to the effects of the experimental variables alone, he conveys the message that other contextual factors are either unimportant or unchangeable. In doing this, he implicitly adopts an ameliorative and, therefore, essentially conservative posture, rather than a radical one. Deutscher (1976) makes the same point when he suggests that many change programmes define the situation as one in which individuals need to be developed or helped to adjust better to their environment, rather than the environment being adjusted by societal reform, to better meet the needs of the individual. And these observations are equally relevant to the evaluations undertaken in industrial organizations. For example, the experiments designed to test whether supportive or task centred supervision is most likely to increase worker productivity (Stogdill, 1974), do not question whether such hierarchical relationships are necessary nor that productivity is a worthwhile objective.

Two other factors exercise a conservative influence on evaluation research. First, evaluation studies tend to be commissioned by those who are responsible (whether as funders, designers or implementers) for the change programme, rather than those at whom it is directed. A result is that even if the subjects of the programme consider that it should have different objectives or priorities, it is unlikely that their views will influence the programme. Furthermore, because those responsible for the programme are the evaluator's direct clients, and therefore first recipients of the report, they have the initiative in controlling its distribution or influencing its interpretation. This can greatly modify the potentially reformist impact of negative findings, and be used to protect the administrators' conservative position (Weiss, 1975).

Secondly, evaluators' own desire that their findings are used can lead to a conservative bias. In order to improve their findings' acceptability, evaluators are sometimes tempted to develop what Stake (1974) has called "responsive evaluation", i.e. an evaluation that attempts to be highly relevant and "credible" to the needs of decision-makers, providing information directed at the questions the decision-makers wanted answering. The problem here is that, by identifying as a particular client of the evaluation those decision-makers whether in a school, hospital or factory who have the power to "get things done", who *can* change the design or implementation of a change programme in the light of the evaluator's findings, "the evaluator is merely aligning himself with the most powerful group which is most opposed to any radical change in the programme" (Joyce, 1980, p.184).

Evaluators, then, face the crisis of frequently being caught in a cleft stick. If they take an overtly radical position in their evaluation designs they may lose credibility with the decision-makers (Weiss, 1975). If, on the other hand, they seek to maximize the utility of their evaluations for the decision-makers (after all, they might argue, what is the point of doing it, if it is not used) they run the risk of adopting a far more conservative stance than they might either desire or even be aware of. These issues are considered further in Chapter 6.

Implications of the crises

From the outset researchers have recognized that their role in evaluating organizational change is not an easy one. Weiss, (1972a, p.9) speaks from personal experience when she writes that

> to make research work when it is coping with the complexities of real people in real programs run by real organizations takes skill—and some guts.

The crises in evaluation both reflect and contribute to the difficulties of an action setting. Moreover, because of the interrelated and mutually reinforcing nature of the crises, they tend to present the professional evaluator with a series of "double binds" (Bateson, 1973).

If evaluators perceive professionalism pre-eminently in terms of a professional/client relationship, emphasizing the "first duty is to the client" aspect of the role, the utilization crisis is likely to be a major concern. But, if they attempt to resolve this by providing decision-makers with useful, relevant information, it may be at the expense of tailoring the research design to match an evaluation function to which they have ethical objections. For example, to take an extreme case, for information to be relevant to a manager who sees the only function of an evaluation of his or her change programme as being one of bearing the good news, it may have to be the product of an "eyewash" or a "whitewash" research design (Suchman, 1970). That is, a design which selects (post facto) only those aspects of a weak programme that look good on the surface (eyewash), or one which attempts to cover up failure by avoiding any objective appraisal (whitewash). To achieve this, scientifically spurious or dubious subjective measures may have to be employed, for example, the use of the "grateful testimonial", confounding of selection with treatment, capitalizing on regression artifacts and so on (Campbell, 1969). In such circumstances, evaluators are faced with a difficult dilemma; if they respond to their clients' need in their role as professionals, they violate their role as scientists, and sin against the positivistic canons of testing. This is to present the potential conflict in extreme terms, but most evaluation researchers face some problem in reconciling their desire as professionals to meet the clients' needs which places constraints on research design, with their desire as scientists to do methodologically acceptable research. Nor does the potential conflict end here. Even when evaluators feel they can *legitimately* reconcile the two roles through the adoption of valid research approaches outside the straitjacket of the positivistic paradigm, they run the risk of being accused by the die-hard positivists among them of compromising their integrity in a corrupt world (Weiss, 1972a, p.9).

In responding to the utilization crisis, evaluation researchers are confronted by another dilemma. As already suggested, for findings to be used at all, the recipient must have some power to influence people and to get decisions changed. Evaluators, not unnaturally then, find there are advantages in accepting as their immediate clients those who have the power to make decisions about the change programme (for example, funders, policy-makers, senior management). However, in practice, this may involve accepting a less radical value position than the evaluator on ethical grounds might consider desirable. In particular, if the key decision-makers desire evaluation to fulfil covert functions of which they disapprove, evaluators may well feel that they are providing the wrong service for the wrong client. Furthermore, when the client has the upper hand and can define the nature of the service, the situation is ripe for "obligation to the client" to conflict with more universalistic professional values, such as expertise and altruism (Gowler and Legge, 1980).

Not only then does evaluation have a role in mediating between optimistic and pessimistic images of the future but, if this is to continue and maintain credibility, evaluation researchers themselves must mediate the potentially conflicting demands of these crises.

Summary and conclusion

In this chapter I have discussed both why evaluation research came into being and the three crises that are undermining its present credibility and constraining its future development.

Not only does evaluation research have to surmount these crises—and how this might be approached is a major theme of this book—it has also to accommodate itself routinely to the different types of planned change it seeks to evaluate. The question then arises, do different types of change place different constraints upon—and allow different opportunities for—evaluation design? What ground rules can be suggested for matching different evaluation design to different types, or models of change? And, to what extent does the magic of evaluation help us cope with the uncertainties created by a rack fashioned out of the opposing demands of the optimistic and pessimistic images of change commented upon above? These questions, which are often neglected in evaluation studies, are considered in the next and subsequent chapters. Not only are they central to the development of evaluation research, but their lack of systematic consideration in the past has contributed much to the evaluation crises I have identified.

Chapter 2

Perspectives on "Planned Social and Organizational Change"

At the end of Chapter 1, it was suggested that an evaluator's choice of evaluation design might be constrained by—and should be matched to— the type of planned change he or she seeks to evaluate. Perhaps, more precisely, it should have been said that such constraints and opportunities will arise from the way those involved actually plan, design and implement the change, and, consequently, from the normative and descriptive models they explicitly or implicitly hold about the "proper" and "real" nature of these processes. The evaluator's examination of planned changes will equally be guided by his or her own conceptualization of the nature of change. Hence, before attempting to match models of planned change with evaluation designs, it may be useful to identify and explicate conventional perspectives on the nature of planned social and organizational change.

The nature of "change"

Dictionary definitions of what constitutes change, for example, "the substitution or succession of one thing in place of another", or "to become different, alter" (*Shorter Oxford English Dictionary*) at first sight are no more than truisms. However, they do raise interesting issues. When something or someone is identified as becoming different or altering, how can we be sure that the change is really taking place in the phenomenon observed and not in the mind of the observer? Similarly, if, for example, the standard of living has improved over the years (as measured on objective indices), but due to the rise in individuals' expectations, it is perceived by them not to have improved, but to have remained exactly the same, in what sense can change be said to have taken place at all? Also, if change is about "becoming different" is its central meaning to be found in the processes involved (the "becoming") or in the outcomes achieved (the "different")? These issues lie at the heart of choices which may be made in conceptualizing change.

There is a choice about whether change may be viewed as a subjective or objective reality. There is a further choice about whether a normative perspective is adopted—about how best to achieve different outcomes, or a descriptive one—about the dynamics of becoming.

The first choice, about whether to view change as an objective or subjective reality is often not presented as a choice at all. Much of the literature about social and organizational change assumes without question that change is an objective phenomenon, that occurs outside the mind, that it is a "fact" of life that can be planned, initiated and managed, or if unplanned, can be "reacted to", "contained" and so forth. If asked to justify this position, naive adopters might assert that it was "commonsense" and "obvious", while the epistemologically more sophisticated might argue that its objectivity could be verified by recognized procedures for demonstrating intersubjective agreement. The extent to which the real meaning of individuals' actions as opposed to the facts of their behaviour can be verified in this way, is the subject of much discussion in later chapters. Suffice to say at this point that most people involved in the design and management of programmes of planned change do not question its objective nature, and, until very recently, the same could be said of most evaluation researchers. *But this choice—or taken-for-granted assumption about the nature of reality—is the most fundamental in conceptualizing change.* As such it has far reaching implications not only for how a change programme might be evaluated, but whether, logically, it is appropriate to evaluate it at all. While this is not the place to anticipate later arguments about evaluation design, two assumptions must be recognized at the outset: an evaluator cannot reasonably regard change from an objectivist ontological position and then seek to evaluate it from even a qualified subjectivist one—or vice versa; extreme subjectivist (i.e. nominalist and "social construction") views of reality are totally incompatible with evaluation research (see Chapter 5).

As for the second choice, while the evaluator may himself adopt either perspective in analysing a change programme, he should be aware that those planning, designing and implementing it are, as change-agents, most likely to be holding some form of normative model of change, if with an awareness of alternative descriptive models. What then are the conventional normative and descriptive models of change? First let us clarify their empirical focus, and consider what constitute planned programmes of *social* and *organizational* change.

Social and organizational change

It should be made clear at the outset that while my focus is on evaluating *organizational* change (and, in particular, change programmes in industrial organizations) I consider that many of the programmes conventionally labelled as social change, analytically speaking, are not dissimilar, and, hence, should not be ignored. How do I justify this position?

Clearly the content and recipients of programmes of planned social change differ from those conventionally labelled as organizational change. For example their recipients are usually either members of "disadvantaged" groups, racial minorities, the materially deprived, the sick, etc. or "problem" groups, such as drunk drivers, delinquents, the elderly infirm (or both!). "Head Start" in the U.S., whereby special pre-school educational programmes and facilities were aimed at deprived minority children, in order to compensate for their potential educational deficiencies, is a prime example of a programme aimed at the disadvantaged. In contrast, the focus of what are usually termed programmes of "planned organizational change", seems to be industrial or administrative organizations, the recipients being their employees. The Volvo experiments in factory and job design at Kalmar, "to improve the quality of working life" (Duncan *et al.*, 1980) or the restructuring of the British Steel Corporation in order to effect cost reductions and greater employee productivity are typical examples. But if this descriptive distinction holds, analytical ones are more debatable. This is evident when looking at ambiguous cases, such as the re-organization of the British school system on comprehensive lines or the introduction into the health service of a three-tier structure—both organizational changes with social objectives. Should they be classified as programmes of social or organizational change?

Some might argue that social and organizational change programmes *can* be differentiated by the nature of their goals and objectives. But, as will be discussed later in this chapter, the goal concept, both theoretically and empirically, is something of a chimera. And, even if it was easy and meaningful to identify programme goals, it is by no means clear that social change programme goals would always be directed at some social good (i.e. the good of society as a whole) and organizational change programmes at a non-social good (i.e. self-interested, sectional good). An argument can be made that the values that underpin most change programmes are ultimately utilitarian (see Chapter 6), in whatever coinage they are expressed. Even this coinage becomes increasingly undifferentiated as industrial organizations use the rhetoric of "improving the quality of (working) life", and increasing "(industrial) democracy".

Conversely the similarity between many examples of planned social and organizational change emerges when we consider the focus of analysis and action in organizational change. Conventionally it is on tasks (organizational raison d'être) technology (raw materials, equipment, plant and buildings) and structure (systems of authority, workflow, information systems, established methods of problem-solving, co-ordination and communication systems) that shape organizational roles and, consequently, the behaviour of individuals as organizational members (Katz and Kahn, 1966; Leavitt, 1964; Perrow, 1970). If this form of classification is accepted then many conventionally termed "social change" programmes could just as well be termed "organizational change" programmes, i.e. when the focus is on changing a social institution, or some aspect of it (task, technology or structure) in order to *indirectly* modify the behaviour of its members/clients. The examples quoted earlier of the re-organization of the school system and the National Health Service in Britain would then be classified as organizational changes—as would Head Start and much of the social change programmes in education in the U.S. (curriculum reform would count as a change in the organization's, the school's, technology), prison reforms, hospital programmes and so on. Programmes of social change that would still not be classified as organizational change would be those which involved manipulating discrete variables in individuals' general economic/social/legal environment in order to *directly* modify their behaviour as a general social category (the "low tax payers", O.A.P.s, racial minorities) *not* as organizational members. The famous New Jersey/Pennsylvania Negative Income Tax Experiment or the introduction of breathalyser tests, would fall into this category.

Having outlined what I understand by organizational and social change programmes, normative and descriptive models of change can now be considered.

Normative models of change

Normative models of change are those which prescribe a change strategy as a means of achieving a desired future state. The change strategy is "planned" if conscious efforts are made on the part of those responsible for its initiation and implementation, to increase its validity in terms of the present and future environment (Faludi, 1973; Glennester, 1975). Thus, in considering normative models of change, it is necessary to deal with three aspects of "changing": *planning, strategies of change, desired outcomes or effectiveness.* Each of these aspects are vast subjects—and involve models—in their own right. However, brief summaries of these issues must suffice.

Planning change

The "rational comprehensive" model
Let us start by considering three definitions of planning.
(a)   Planning is concerned with deliberatively achieving some objective, and its proceeds by assembling actions in some orderly sequence (Hall, 1974, p.4).
(b)   (Planning is) a process of strategic choice, requiring a capacity to anticipate the future and yet also to adapt to the unforeseen (Friend and Jessop, 1969).

(c)   (Planning is) the process of preparing a set of decisions for action in
       the future, directed at achieving goals by preferable means (Dror, 1973).
    Most well known definitions of planning suggest that it involves *choices*
or *decisions* about *goals* and *objectives* and the course of *actions* necessary
to achieve them. Permeating these definitions and the concepts they comprise
is an assumption of *rationality*: choice will be deliberate and actions taken
in an "orderly" sequence. Also, although these definitions state that
"planning is", it is clear that these statements are normative—they are about
what planning aims to be, not necessarily about what those involved in
planning change actually do or achieve.
    Planning, in terms of these definitions, comes very close to the "rational"
model of decision-making. Such a model assumes that the best decisions (or
plans) are made rationally, and that for rationality to be achieved the
following requirements must be met:
(1)   Decision-makers make clear their values and express them as a consistent
       set of goals and objectives.
(2)   Decision-makers then generate and examine all the alternatives available
       for maximizing goal achievement.
(3)   Decision-makers then predict and assess the utility and probability of
       all the consequences that would follow from the adoption of each
       alternative.
(4)   Decision-makers then compare the consequences in relation to the
       agreed set of goals and objectives.
(5)   Decision-makers then select the alternative whose consequences
       correspond to a greater degree with goals and objectives.
This basic model of the choice process underlies what has been termed
"rational comprehensive planning" (Friedmann and Hudson, 1974) and is
an examplar in the planning models developed, for example, by Davidoff
and Reiner (1960), Hart (1976) and Delbecq and Van de Ven (1971). The
latter, the "program planning method" is typical of such approaches in its
prescription of five iterative planning steps—problem exploration, knowledge
exploration, priority development, programme control and evaluation. The
work of corporate strategists such as Ansoff and Argenti is similarly
rationalistic in tone.
    Even so, most would be compelled to recognize that purely rationalistic
planning is an unrealistic aspiration in an uncertain world. It is unrealistic
to assume that decision-makers can *agree* on an objective they wish to
maximize, or even a set of coherent objectives. It is unrealistic to expect them
to be completely informed about all alternatives, each alternative's
consequences and the probabilities of these consequences occurring. It is
certainly completely unrealistic to assume that decision-makers are capable
of absorbing all alternatives, of determining the utility of each consequence,

of multiplying each utility by its probability, of summing across all consequences for each alternative in turn and finally, of choosing one which will maximize the expected utility. In real life, this model of taking decisions can only obtain where decisions are highly routine—where means–ends relationships are already known and consensus exists about outcome preferences. But most planning decisions are exactly the opposite.

Many planners who aim for rationality in planning would admit that the models they adhere to at best represent a form of "bounded rationality" (Simon 1957). In other words when planning change they do not seek to maximize (as they would if purely rational) but, because of problems in reaching a consensus over which value to maximize, they are content to satisfice, that is make choices that are "good enough" to satisfy a range of interests. Bounded rationality assumes too that in most circumstances planners are likely to lack full knowledge of all alternatives, of the consequence of each alternative and of the probabilities of each consequence. They therefore have to construct a simplified model of reality and behave rationally with respect to this model.

How they *actually* do this, Cyert and March (1963) suggest is by employing four strategies: the "quasi-resolution of conflict", "uncertainty avoidance", "problemistic search" and "organizational learning". Briefly, conflict among different priorities is never fully resolved but contained by using "local rationality" (letting subunits look after their own "bit" of a problem, which can then be dealt with in terms of one goal), by dealing with problems sequentially, and by being content to satisfice rather than optimize across units. Uncertainty is avoided by focusing on pressing problems, rather than on long-term possibilities, and by negotiating the environment (e.g. price-setting externally, budgets internally). Search is limited by reacting only to pressing problems and then aiming only for a satisfactory solution. It is "simple-minded", in that, in the first instance, it is restricted to seeking a cause "near" its effect, and a new solution near those previously adopted—radically new alternatives are thereby eliminated. Finally organizations—and decision-makers—learn and adapt—in the light of experience, priorities are changed, attention shifts and search and standard operating procedures are revised.

The "disjointed incrementalism" model

Not all planners would advocate the use of a rationalistic model, even as an examplar. It has been argued that not only are such models (including the "bounded" version) unrealistic, but they are actually inappropriate for complex planning. Lindblom (1959) and Braybrooke and Lindblom (1963) present an alternative model of the planning process which they claim to be both a descriptive account of how planners or managers actually make decisions, and also a normative/prescriptive model of how they *ought* to proceed. This model suggests that decision-makers make a series of "successive limited comparisons", a series of "disjointed" and "incremental" decisions by which they "muddle through" — and that this in fact is the best way to make complex decisions in an uncertain puralistic world. For example, people planning change do not, and should not, clarify objectives prior to evaluating alternative programmes in the light of these objectives, because of the practical problems of ascertaining and reconciling the value positions of all interested parties; they tend to choose directly (and should choose directly) among alternative strategies that offer marginal "improvements" without specifying precise objectives first. Because means and ends are not clearly distinguished — for the statement of objectives takes the form of a description of the chosen policy or some alternative to it — the test of a "good" change programme is not that it can be shown to be the most appropriate means to desired ends, but that the most powerful interested parties are willing to agree to it and support it in preference to alternatives (without their agreeing that it is the most appropriate means to an agreed objective). The analysis of alternative strategies makes, and should make, no attempt to be comprehensive: resources do not permit a fundamental inquiry into a range of hypothetical alternatives "unthought of" by the interested parties, when all that is "required" is an analysis of the marginal differences among marginally differing initiatives, in order to assess which is likely to produce consequences most acceptable to the parties involved. In a nutshell, the guiding spirit of planning is, and should be, to achieve marginal improvements on the existing state of affairs, "to identify situations or ills from which to move *away* rather than goals *towards* which to move" (Braybrooke and Lindbolm, 1963, p.102).

Similarly, systematic monitoring and modification of the programme during implementation is less likely than "off-the-cuff" *ad hoc* tinkering in reaction to the unanticipated emergence of "unacceptable" outcomes.

While many managers and administrators involved in planning change would accept that this is a good *descriptive* model of the processes involved, they would not accept its *prescriptive* validity. Many would concur with Boulding's (1964, p.931) epigrammatic criticism that even if in real life it may regrettably occur, planning should not resemble "stagger(ing) through history like a drunk putting one disjointed incremental foot after another". Others have argued that, prescriptively speaking, the model is problematic not because it implies a lack of planning direction, but because the direction is inherently conservative. The intermingling of descriptive and normative statements only results in equating "what is" with "what ought to be", with planning decisions reflecting the interests of the most powerful groups in the organization and society (Etzioni, 1968). Furthermore it is anti-innovatory as a basic element in the strategy is to maximize security in making changes. All reliable knowledge is based on the past, thus "the only way to proceed without risk is by continuing in the same direction" (Etzioni, 1968, p.273).

In response to the criticisms of both the "rational comprehensive" and "disjointed incrementalism" models of planning a compromise prescriptive model has emerged, and which has found acceptance among many involved in planning (see, for example, Faludi, 1973) that is "mixed-scanning".

The "mixed-scanning" model

The essence of the mixed scanning approach to planning change is contained in an example Etzioni (1973, pp.223–224) uses to illustrate his model—that of setting up a "worldwide weather observation system using weather satellites". While "rationalism" would try to examine "the entire sky" as exhaustively as possible, and "incrementalism . . . would focus on those areas in which similar patterns developed in the recent past and, perhaps, on a few nearby regions", mixed scanning would use two types of camera: "a broad angle . . . that would cover all parts of the sky but not in great detail" and "one which would zero in on those areas revealed by the first camera to require a more in-depth examination". "While mixed-scanning might miss areas in which only a detailed camera could reveal trouble, it is less likely than incrementalism to miss obvious trouble spots in unfamiliar areas".

Mixed scanning, Etzioni points out, essentially provides prescriptions about collecting information ("scanning"), about allocating resources, and about the relations between the two by dichotomizing the planning process. On the one hand there are fundamental decisions to be made, on the other there are incremental decisions derived from them. Fundamental decisions involve scanning at an "all-encompassing level"—that is "exploring the main alternatives" in the light of basic "values/goals", but omitting "details and specifications . . . so that an overview is feasible". Incremental decisions made within the contexts set by the fundamental decisions, involve scanning at "a highly detailed level" and selecting alternatives in the light of objectives derived from goals. The relative investment in the two types of scanning depends on cost-benefit assessments. To clarify his approach Etzioni translated the mixed scanning planning strategy into a series of steps which decision-makers should follow, and which have been summarized by Camhis (1979, pp.58–59).

While Etzioni advocates a set of iterative steps as the way planning ought to be done, he also suggests that in broad outline—getting a broad overview before looking at the detail—mixed scanning represents "a realistic description of the strategy used by actors in a large variety of fields"

(Etzioni, 1973, p.223). Like Lindblom, then, he conflates the normative with the descriptive. The four planning models discussed here comprise the core of conventional wisdom about how change *should* be and sometimes, it is claimed, *is* planned. The full implications for evaluation design, of change-agents adherence to these models, will be discussed in the conclusion to this chapter, when related issues can be drawn together. I now turn to consider change strategies.

Change strategies

What are the conventionally advocated strategies for achieving change in the behaviour of organizational members (and, ultimately, desired outcomes)? So much has been written on this subject that it is impossible in the space available to attempt more than an outline sketch of dominant themes and popular models. Basically though, I suggest that prescriptions about change strategies focus on three issues: *leverage point*—where should you intervene? *mode*—what style of intervention should you adopt? and *tactics*—what steps should the intervention involve?

Leverage point

Perhaps the most commonly cited model in identifying the leverage points in changing the behaviour of organizational members is that of Leavitt (1964). Leavitt argues that a change agent might find it useful to view organizations as multivariate systems comprised of four key and interdependent variables, viz:

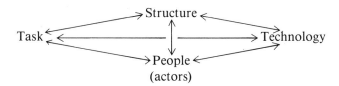

(actors)

(The definitions adopted for these variables are essentially those referred to at the beginning of the chapter.) To effect change, depending on his or her objectives and theory of action, the change agent may intervene in any one of these areas (indeed, he or she can hardly avoid so doing). Where Leavitt's model becomes useful prescriptively, though, is through its corollary that because of their interdependence, "planned" change in any one area will most probably result in "compensatory" or "retaliatory" unplanned changes in another—unless, that is, these changes are anticipated and themselves planned for. The implication is that they should be.

Popular change strategies may be classified in terms of Leavitt's four variables (see Table I).

Reference to different strategies in Table I will be made in subsequent chapters. Most of the examples cited show clearly that although a change programme may focus on one "leverage point", it will have repercussions throughout the system. For example the introduction of a new product (e.g. British Leyland's small car — the "Metro" — a market-oriented strategy) has

Table I

Task	("raison d'être", "sub tasks")	e.g.	*Market Oriented Strategies* Develop new products/ services Enter new markets Service new client groups
Technology	("technical tools", 'problem-solving' inventions")	e.g.	*Technological Strategies* Introduce the "new" micro-electronic technologies Introduce a new curriculum Redesign the physical layout of a hospital ward
Structure	("systems of communication", "authority" and "workflow")	e.g.	*Organizational Design Strategies* Introduce "matrix organization", "functional organization", "divisionalization", "regionalization", "centralization", "decentralization" Introduce "employee participation" structures Introduce job and work system redesign Introduce a new reward system, appraisal system, system of budgetary control
People	("actors" or members)	e.g.	*Organizational Development Strategies* T-Group training Survey feedback Team Building Process consultation Grid O.D.

implications for technology (the use of robots on the new production lines at Longbridge—a technological change) and for organizational design (product division re-organization). It is well known how a radically new product (e.g. NASA space programmes) may call forth new organizational forms (matrix organization) (Sayles and Chandler, 1971). Similarly organizational development strategies may have major implications for authority structures and communication patterns (see for example, the account of Berg, 1979). Leavitt's model prescribes that a management should be aware of, and plan for, these repercussions.

There is another side of the coin to planning for "repercussions". Precisely because change strategies in one area will have implications for the others, a strategy may be used as a means to a further change rather than as an end in itself. Thus, as will be seen in the next section, organizational design and development strategies are often advocated as the means of facilitating market-oriented and technological changes. For example, organizational development may be treated as an end in itself, with the general objective of "improving organizational climate", but it may also be used specifically, to overcome resistance to, say, a technological change. In particular when organizational design and development strategies are used as vehicles for market and "technological changes" they embody assumptions about the best style for managing change.

An alternative to these change strategies, and which also has implications for the best style for managing change, is that advocated by Peters (1978). He suggests that because the management of change is "inextricably bound up with the mundane occurrences that fill an executive's calendar" change can best be achieved by the use of similarly "mundane tools" rather than through "grand" forms of intervention such as those outlined above. These tools are symbols (e.g. calendars, reports, agendas, physical settings, public statements), patterns (e.g. positive reinforcement, frequency and consistency of behaviour) and settings (e.g. role of modelling, location, agenda control, deadline management, use of minutes) that are part of daily work activities. Peters examines how manipulation of these daily activities as symbols can be a valuable strategy in creating change in organizations.

Mode

Various approaches to the style of intervention have been advocated, but all rest on two related assumptions. One is that desired programme outcomes are more likely to be achieved if those affected by the programme co-operate in its implementation. The other, its corollary, is that if co-operation is unlikely to be obtained, at least resistance to the programme must be overcome. (Indeed, "resistance to change" may be seen as one "unplanned" repercussion involving the "people" variable in Leavitt's model).

The approaches advocated tend to reflect more general prescriptions about managerial style. In other words the focus is on whether a participative or authoritarian style is more effective. Greiner's (1967) classification of styles of intervention is a well-known model. He suggests that change-agents tend to adopt one of three styles: "unilateral action", "sharing power" and "delegated authority". He argues that a sharing power strategy should be adopted: while unilateral action fails to generate commitment, and a delegated approach fails to provide guidance and support, a shared participative approach should avoid both dangers and may even unleash "new surges of energy and creativity not previously imagined" due to the "exchange of influence between upper and lower levels".

However, not all change agents would adhere to this prescription. It has been argued (Hage, 1974, 1980; Zaltman *et al.*, 1973) that if a radical change programme is planned, "sharing power" may only serve to vitiate its radicalism. In other words, the price of gaining acceptance and commitment to implementation, is that the programme is watered down and little of the initial conception is implemented. If this appears likely, a strategy of strategic replacement — recruiting a team of new occupational specialities and individuals with a pro-change value set (Hage, 1980, p.243) may be more effective. Carrying the "strategic replacement" approach to its logical conclusion, Hage (1980, p.244–245) argues that perhaps the best approach to achieving a radical change programme is to create a new organizational unit, with new personnel, its own source of resources, and only "loosely-coupled" (Weick, 1976) to other parts of the organization.

Whether a participative or authoritarian style is advocated in part rests on the change agent's assumptions about whether those involved are predisposed to co-operate or resist. If co-operation is envisaged, re-educative and persuasive strategies, within a framework of participation are often urged; if intransigent resistance is feared, the basically authoritarian approaches of manipulation and outright coercion may be deemed more appropriate. Assumptions about why those involved are resisting change, are also likely to influence which approach is used. For example, if it is assumed that people resist change because they dislike change *per se*, then a reeducative and participative approach might seem the "right" style; if it is assumed resistance is due to a calculation that personal costs may outweigh benefits, then a negotiating style may seem right to achieve a "bargained acceptance".

As with general prescriptions about managerial style the current orthodoxy, and one to which many change agents would subscribe, is that a contingent approach is necessary, in which the costs and benefits of different ways of introducing change are weighed up in the light of organizational circumstances (Kotter and Schlesinger, 1979). There is some agreement (Hage, 1980; Zaltman *et al.*, 1973) that an authoritarian style is most likely to be effective when the organization faces a major crisis and its members agree that "something has to be done".

Tactics

What steps should the intervention involve? It has been argued (Greiner, 1967) that change programmes are more likely to achieve success when their initiation, implementation and routinization follow a distinct series of steps, in the following logical sequence: pressure and arousal ⟶ intervention and reorientation ⟶ diagnosis and recognition ⟶ invention and commitment ⟶ experimentation and search ⟶ reinforcement and acceptance.

From an analysis of these steps, which Greiner (1967) derived from comparing successful with unsuccessful programmes of planned changes, the following prescriptions for managing change programmes are drawn:

(1)   Do not attempt to introduce a change programme unless there exists a widely felt need for it.

(2)   Follow each step of the change process in the logical order, described above — do not skip initial stages, such as encouraging an unskilled newcomer to make quick and drastic changes.

(3)   Always involve top management.

(4)   Always pilot a proprosed programme.

(5)   Use a participative approach.

The stages advocated by Greiner, in essence, follow the action research model of managing change. This model, which explicitly underlies all organizational development change strategies (and implicitly some of the market, technological and organizational design strategies, depending on the intervention style deemed appropriate by those managing the change) suggests that a change strategy should follow a set sequence of events, in an iterative cycle:

(1)   Key executives perceive a problem and consult with a 'behavioural scientist' consultant.

(2)   Data gathering and diagnosis by consultant.

(3)   Further data gathering.

(4)   Feedback to client group.

(5)   Joint setting of objectives and designing programme of activities to achieve them.

(6)   Implementation.

(7)   Joint data gathering and evaluation.

(8)   Joint diagnosis of further problems.

                    (repeat the cycle) (French and Bell, 1973)

Blake and Mouton's (1964) "Grid" approach is a classic example of prescriptions about managing change based on such a model, and many further examples may be found in the *Journal of Applied Behavioral Science*, or in Golembiewski (1979).

Explicit in these "tactic" or "stage" prescriptions is the assumption that planned change should be managed in a participative style. However, those advocating an authoritarian approach do not deny the validity of the problem recognition —→ diagnosis —→ programme planning —→ implementation —→ evaluation stages. Where they differ is in their prescription about who should be involved in these activities, i.e. the dominant coalition rather than all potential stakeholders.

Finally, Cohen and March (1974) propose a set of eight rules for managing change that contain prescriptions about both the style and tactics of intervention, viz: spend time, persist, exchange status for substance, facilitate opposition participation, overload the system, provide garbage cans (throwaway issues to absorb debate), manage unobtrusively and interpret history.

Managing change through such stages and tactics, so proponents argue, will enhance a change programme's chance of "success". So how should the success or effectiveness of a change programme be assessed?

Assessing effectiveness — in principle

Normative models of planned change generally define success in terms of goal attainment. French and Bell (1973, p.81), for example, in discussing organizational development strategies, assert "both organizations and individuals need to manage their affairs against goals — explicit, measurable, obtainable goals". So, many would suggest, strategies of change should be selected in the light of the goals the change-agents wish to achieve, and the success of these strategies measured in terms of the degree to which they are achieved.

However, even advocates of this approach recognize that it involves many operational problems, and some alternatives suggested — the systems resource approach (Yuchtman and Seashore, 1967) and participant–satisfaction approach (Barnard, 1938) — raise equal difficulties. In the interests of avoiding repetition, the problems associated with the goal attainment approach, and these attempts to side-step them, will be discussed in the following section on descriptive models of change.

Summary

The models discussed here — whether relating to planning, strategies of change, or assessment of the outcomes of change — are normative. That is, they are about what commentators believe *should be* done to manage programmes of change *"successfully"*. Being common-place to the point of cliché, the evaluator should be aware that any of these models may form part of the taken-for-granted assumptions that are guiding those involved in designing and implementing the change programme with which he or she is involved. Failing that, they may hold normative models of their own, which the evaluator will need to uncover for their influence on programme design, implementation and, ultimately, evaluation. The implications of the models discussed here, for evaluation design, will be considered at the end of the chapter.

But, first, it is necessary to look at *descriptive* and explanatory models of organizational change. Whereas normative models guide what should be done, descriptive models focus on what *actually happens*. As such, their importance in evaluation design is two-fold. First, the normative models that change-agents hold may be derived from descriptive models. Beliefs about what should be done, often rest on ideas about how an organization or the individuals within it actually behave, what their characteristics are, and so on. Greiner's (1967) prescriptions about the importance of a participatory style in designing and implementing change were derived from case-study observations about the lack of success of change programmes characterized by an authoritarian style. The style adopted also rests on the change agent's assumptions about why individuals may be predisposed to either co-operate with, or resist change. Secondly, the evaluator needs to be aware of descriptive models of change, to alert himself to likely gaps between the change agent's rhetoric about what he hopes will take place and what actually does take place—the gap "twixt cup and lip" as Weiss (1973) has put it. To assume that what "should be" will equate with what "is" can lead to serious errors in evaluation design, which, also, will be discussed at the end of the chapter.

Descriptive models of change

What do we know about change *actually* takes place—bearing in mind the recognized gap between "espoused" theories and "theories-in-use" (Argyris and Schön, 1974)? It may be useful, by way of comparison with the normative models, to discuss well-known theories under similar headings: how change is planned, how change occurs and planned change programmes are implemented, assessing their outcomes.

How change is planned

How are change programmes actually planned? How are decisions about programme design actually made? As already stated, the "disjointed incrementalism" and "mixed scanning" models of Lindblom and Etzioni respectively, are claimed by their authors to represent what actually occurs during decision-making, quite apart from being models of how decisions ought to be made. Certainly, empirical examples of "disjointed incrementalism" can be found in budgetary decisions, such as those discussed by Wildavsky (1975) and Pfeffer and Salancik (1974). Simon (1957) and Cyert and March (1963) make similar claims for the validity of the "bounded rationality" model. Given that there are points of overlap between all three models, it is reasonable to recognize that each may possess some descriptive validity, depending on the precise nature of the decision to be made. But, before outlining the circumstances in which each of these descriptive models would appear to be a valid representation of change programme planning, it is necessary to introduce a further model of how decisions are actually made: the "garbage can" model, so called because its authors conceptualize decision-making situations as "a garbage can into which various problems and solutions are dumped by participants" (Cohen *et al.*, 1976, p.26).

"Garbage can" model of decision-making

Briefly, Cohen *et al.* argue that in many choice situations (including planning change programmes) although it is assumed that the main concern is with "making decisions" in fact other activities seem equally important, such as fulfilling earlier commitments, justifying past actions, scapegoating or cementing loyalties, recruiting and socializing and game playing. As a result, a "choice situation", rather than being regarded as an opportunity for rational problem-solving, may be more realistically conceptualized as

> . . . a meeting place for issues and feelings looking for decision situations in which they may be aired, solutions looking for issues to which they may be an answer, and participants looking for problems or pleasure. (Cohen *et al.*, 1976, p.25)

The key concepts in the garbage can model are, then, problems, solutions, participants and choice opportunities. In a garbage can situation a decision is an outcome of the interaction of these four factors or relatively independent "streams". It is a highly contextual event, "depending substantially on the pattern of flows in the several streams" (Cohen *et al.*, 1976, p.27).

The reason why planning processes frequently bear more resemblance to the garbage can than to the orderly, logical procedures specified in the rationalistic normative models, is because goals are often problematic, means–ends relationships are often unclear, and participation often fluid (Cohen *et al.*, 1976, p.25). In these circumstances "criteria of relevance" — of what issues and solutions are associated with what problems, what problems are associated with what choices, what people appropriately participate in what choices — are unclear. Hence what actually happens "is often the almost fortuitous result of the intermeshing of loosely-coupled processes" (Cohen *et al.*, 1976, p.26) during which decisions are as likely to emerge by oversight and flight as by resolution.

Cohen *et al.* (1976, pp.34–35) suggest that garbage can decision processes reveal eight characteristic properties. First, resolution of problems is the least common decision-making style. Secondly, the process is highly sensitive to variations in load—as load increases problems are less likely to be solved, decision-makers are likely to shift from one problem to another more frequently, choices take longer to make. Thirdly, decision-makers and problems tend to "track" each other through choices and, as a result, decision-makers tend "to feel that they are always working on the same problems in somewhat different contexts, mostly without results". Fourthly, there is the question of the relationship between "problem activity" ("the amount of time unresolved problems are actively attached to choice situations"), "problem latency" ("the amount of time that problems spend activated but not linked to choices") and "decision time" ("persistence of choices"). A garbage can process is typified by an inability to optimize the relationship between these factors. Instead of problem activity and latency being kept low through rapid problem solution, the number of active unresolved problems might be reduced but at the cost of increasing the latency period of problems and the time devoted to reaching decisions. Or, if problem latency is decreased, it is at the cost of increasing problem activity and decision time. Fifthly, the decision-making process is highly interactive, in that "many of the outcomes are produced by distinct consequences of the particular time phasing of choices, problems, and participant availability". Sixthly, the process produces a queue of problems in terms of their importance—late arrivals, relatively unimportant problems are less likely to be resolved than important, early arriving ones, particularly when the load is heavy. Seventhly important choices tend to be made by oversight and flight, while unimportant choices are made by resolution. Eighth, and finally, when choice failures occur, they are concentrated among the most important and least important choices, "choices of intermediate importance are virtually always made".

In relation to planning social and organizational change programmes, this model highlights two possibilities about the process. The first is that a change programme is not necessarily a carefully designed answer in response to a particular problem—even if it is represented as such. It is just as likely to be its protagonist's pet solution to a wide range of problems, its design antedating the problem to which it is conveniently attached. As March (1981, p.569) has pointed out, organizational change is often solution, rather than problem driven, and for very practical reasons:

> Organizations face a large number of problems of about equal importance, but only a few solutions. Thus, the chance of finding a solution to a particular problem is small; if one begins with a solution, however, there is a good chance that the solution will match some problem facing the organization ... [Also] the linkage between individual solutions and individual problems is often

difficult to make unambiguously. Then, almost any solution can be linked to almost any problem, provided they arise at approximately the same time . . . [Finally] . . . change is stimulated not by adversity but by success, less by a sense of problems than by a sense of competence . . . When a major stimulus for change comes from a sense of competence, problems are created in order to solve them, and solutions and opportunities stimulate awareness of previously unsalient or unnoticed problems or preferences.

The second possibility is that the change programme eventually arrived at may have no close relation with the explicit intentions of participants: it "emerges" but may be presented as "planned" after the event. In this case there is the danger that "differences between what happens and what does not happen (may appear) deceptively significant" (Cohen *et al.*, 1976, p.37). The implications of both these possibilities, for evaluation design, that so-called "planned" change programmes may, in a sense, be fortuitous, will be discussed at the end of this chapter.

Cohen *et al.* (1976) suggest that their garbage can model of decision-making represents how decisions are made when goals and means–ends relationships (that is, *how* to achieve the goals) are problematic. This echoes Thompson and Tuden's (1959) earlier analysis, which conceptualized the decision-making environment in terms of the extent to which decision-makers could agree on the ends they sought and the extent to which they understood how to achieve the ends. Following this approach I would suggest that the models discussed in this chapter are likely to approximate to what *actually* takes place, in the following situations:

(1) Goals	—	negotiated agreement	potential for some rational analysis	"Mixed scanning"
Means–ends	—	moderately well understood		
(2) Goals	—	moderate disagreement	potential for reasoned compromise	"Bounded rationality"
Means–ends	—	moderately well understood		
(3) Goals	—	high disagreement	potential for bargained compromise	"Disjointed incrementalism"
Means–ends	—	less well understood		
(4) Goals	—	high disagreement	potential for "inspiration"	"Garbage can"
Means–ends	—	not well understood		

Planning decisions about change programmes might fall into any of these categories, although the more "political" the environment the more likely it is that planning will resemble the "disjointed incrementalism" and "garbage can" models.

But, before concluding this section, there are two further points. First, are there any circumstances in which the normative "rational comprehensive" model might be accepted as representing the reality of planning change? In principle, when there is a complete consensus about ends and where means–ends relationships are so well understood that the evaluation of alternatives is non-problematic, a highly rational model may come close to representing how certain decisions are actually made. However, the model's maximization and comprehensive search prescriptions limit its applicability to such highly routine, "technical" decisions (e.g. scheduling) that its empirical relevance to all but the most trivial of change programmes is dubious.

Secondly, there is the theoretical situation, which I have not discussed, where there is consensus about ends, but where means–ends relationships are not well understood (for example, reducing unemployment without increasing inflation). Are change programmes likely to be planned in this decision environment and if so, what model of decision-making adequately represents the process that take place? I would suggest that this decision environment is somewhat unreal, as, with the exception of highly routine decisions, consensus about ends usually dissolves when broad aims are translated into operative targets, and priorities have to be assigned. In these circumstances, the planning process, once initiated, may rapidly resemble the disjointed incrementalism or the garbage can model depending on just how little is known about means–ends relationships.

How change occurs

How does change take place in and to organizations? Two underlying perspectives may be identified. There are those who consider change to be a distinguishable behaviour, that may be characterized (e.g. evolutionary vs revolutionary) and about which theories of causation may be developed. Theories about the process of innovation, for example, would fall into this category (see, for example, Zaltman et al., 1973). There are others, though, who see change, as an integral part of an organization's adaptive behaviour and theories of change, in consequence, as "not remarkably different from a theory of ordinary action" (March, 1981, p.564). From this perspective, change may be conceptualized, analyzed and explained from the same theoretical stance as any other episode of organizational behaviour that the analyst—whether change agent, client or evaluator—holds. For example, the assumptions about the processes that embody the decision-making models already discussed—conflicts of interest, power relations, uncertainty avoidance—could be applied to all aspects of the process of change. So, I will consider first change as "ordinary" adaptive behaviour.

Change as "ordinary action"
It is, of course, impossible here to discuss the many different approaches to analyzing organizational behaviour—and hence organizational change— that can be adopted. However, some broad distinctions may be drawn. In theory, following Burrell and Morgan (1979) the approach adopted will derive from where one stands on two dimensions—the subjective–objective nature of the reality continuum, mentioned at the beginning of this chapter, and the regulation–radical change continuum. The latter refers to whether one is concerned to provide explanations of society (or organizations) in terms of its underlying unity and cohesiveness, in which change is viewed as adaptive, and basically preservative of the status quo (regulation) or in terms of deep-seated structural conflict, modes of domination and structural contradiction (radical change). Within the four resulting paradigms, the approaches that theoretically are available would include, for example, "systems theory" (regulative/objectivist paradigm), "ethnomethodology" and symbolic interactionism (regulative/subjectivist paradigm), "radical organization theory" (radical change/objectivist paradigm) and "anti-organization theory" (radical change/subjectivist paradigm). Which of these perspectives on change are most prevalent in guiding organizational analysis, and hence might be expected to most influence change-agents and evaluators alike?

By a process of elimination I suggest that most change agents managing programmes of planned change in an organizational setting—and to a marginally lesser extent—most evaluators, conceptualize change processes from positions firmly within the regulative/objectivist paradigm, or at most, within the regulative paradigm, but on the borders of the objectivist/ subjectivisit continuum. In other words, while the vast majority would adhere to some form of the systems perspective, a minority may adopt an action frame of reference or even a watered down form of symbolic interactionism. Why is this?

Briefly, both those committed to the design and management of programmes of planned social and organizational change and those who evaluate them, whether they are fully conscious of it or not, are acting in defence of the status quo. The reasons for this are discussed in detail in Chapter 6 and will not be repeated here. Suffice to say this places change-agents and evaluators alike firmly within a regulative paradigm (1). Furthermore, as already suggested, change-agents, interested in "variables" they can manipulate, generally do not even question the objective nature of reality, while evaluators who do so, even to a modest extent, are likely to confront many epistemological problems in evaluation design. These problems are discussed extensively in Chapter 5. However, by way of an introduction to later chapters, it may be useful to outline the key elements of a systems approach to organizational action—including change—and contrast it briefly with the action and symbolic interactionism approaches.

The "systems" approach to analyzing ordinary action

This perspective represents the current management orthodoxy about organizational processes. Briefly, as applied in organizational analysis, it rests on the following assumptions. First that the organization, as a system, can be identified by some sort of boundary that differentiates it from its environment. Secondly, that the organization is processual, and, as an open system, survives by interacting with its environment through a series of basic input, conversion, output and feedback processes. Thirdly, that it comprises a series of mutually interactive subsystems whose "purpose" is to contribute to the satisfaction of overall system needs. Change, in the light of these assumptions, is essentially a process of adaptation to the environment and adjustment of sub-systems in order to maintain the organization's dynamic equilibrium. Finally that the operation of the organization can be observed in terms of the behaviour of its constituent sub-systems (Buckley, 1967; Katz and Khan, 1966; Miller and Rice, 1967).

Translated into a model for organizational analysis, these assumptions have given rise to what has been termed a "contingency approach". Because the organization is dependent on the environment, organizational analysis, at the macro level, should be centrally concerned with identifying and explaining the key associations which characterize relationships between the organization and its environment (e.g. Lawrence and Lorsch, 1967). Much debate surrounds the degree of constraint in such relationships. Child (1972), opposing environmental determinism, argues that managers can and do, through the exercise of "strategic choice", influence how their organizations adapt to—indeed mould—the environment. Pfeffer and Salancik (1978), developing a "resource dependence" perspective, suggest that managers can influence their environment (through mergers, diversification and co-optation) but that there are real contingencies that must be adapted to. Aldrich's (1979) "population ecology" model, on the other hand, argues that it is the environment that "selects" certain organizational structures, from a wider population of structural variations, for survival.

Given that a central concern is with organizational survival—and by implication—organizational effectiveness, explanations of its determinants are stressed (e.g. Burns and Stalker, 1961; Hage and Aiken, 1967; Pugh and Hickson, 1976; Woodward, 1965, 1970). Contingency theorists have looked for explanations in the key subsystems—technology, task and structure—and have developed a central tenet that an organization's effectiveness in coping with the demands of its environment is contingent upon the elements of the various subsystems being designed in accordance with the demands of the environment with which they interact. In practice, this means securing a degree of subsystem differentiation appropriate to the nature of the environment, characterized by a congruency between subsystem elements, and the achievement of an appropriate state of integration. Organizational analysis focuses on defining what is appropriate in the light of environmental characteristics.

A tool in operationalizing this basic approach at the micro level, is socio-technical systems analysis. This identifies two subsystems—the "technical" and the "social" as central to the organization's conversion processes and hence in determining organizational effectiveness. Because these subsystems are interactive and interdependent, the nature of their interrelationships is examined in order to analyse how their "joint optimization" might be achieved, and hence the contribution of the socio-technical system to organizational effectiveness enhanced. It is this perspective that has informed much of the recent work on job and work system redesign (Clegg, 1979, 1982; Fitter, 1982; Mumford, 1976; Wall, 1980; Wall and Clegg, 1981; Warmington *et al.*, 1977). A good summary of the systems approach applied to the modelling and analysis of adaptive behaviour in organizations may be found in Hage (1980, Chapter 8).

It is not difficult to see why a systems approach to analyzing organizational action is likely to be *the* model adopted by many change agents. That it is the predominant model for organizational development practitioners and those managing technical change—insofar as they consciously hold an explicated model—is well attested (see for example, French and Bell, 1973; Margulies and Raia, 1972; Mumford, 1976, 1981; Schmuck and Miles, 1971). Margulies and Raia (1972) go so far as to state "planned organizational change, by its very nature, must consider the potential impact on *all* elements of the system when one of its elements or subsystems is changed". The reasons for its predominance is that its descriptive statements are easily transposed into normative prescriptions (Legge, 1978). It is the systems approach that identifies variables (subsystems) which may be manipulated (changed) in order to achieve changes in people and in their own, and ultimately, organizational performance. From a managerial point of view it is convenient to be able to treat people as a "factor" or independent variable that may be manipulated to effect changes in other subsystems, or as a dependent variable, whose responses to manipulations elsewhere in the system can be measured and subsequently evaluated. The interactive nature of the system can also alert the manager to the possibility of "effects" that might otherwise have surprised him ("unplanned change"). Finally, the functionalist orientation of the approach (given its assumption that organizations are systems with a need to survive and adjust to their environments) highlights organizational effectiveness as a key concern.

Interestingly, criticisms of this perspective on organizational action have come mainly from academics not managers or administrators (e.g. Child, 1972; Silverman, 1970; Wood, 1979). The nub of the criticisms is that the approach tends to view individuals as passively reacting to a deterministic organization and environment, rather than actively defining, manipulating and constructing the world in which they live. It is a view which sees individuals largely moulded by the norms and values of their culture (the determining environment) and hence as essentially conformist. This, allied with the functionalist perspective, so it is argued, makes the systems approach inherently conservative and inadequate in explaining deviance and change, outside the confines of adaptation. It is out of such criticisms that the two alternative approaches to analyzing organizational action, consistent with an essentially regulative perspective, have emerged—namely the "action frame of reference" and "symbolic interactionism".

Action frame of reference and symbolic interactionism approaches to analyzing "ordinary action"

Very briefly, both these approaches see individuals not simply as responding to stimuli, but as constructing a meaning for that with which they are confronted, and acting in accordance with that meaning. Where the two approaches differ though, is in the extent to which they move towards a subjectivist view of reality. The action frame of reference, as propounded by Silverman (1970) see the meanings of stimuli "given to men by society". "Shared orientations become institutionalized and are experienced by later generations as social facts". But, these shared meanings only remain "facts" if continually reaffirmed by peoples' everyday actions, as "through their interaction men also modify, change, and transform social meanings". In essence "while society defines man, man in turn defines society". This view of social—and organizational—action, therefore hovers on the middle of the objectivist–subjectivist continuum. Statements that "society defines man" and that shared meanings, becoming institutionalized, are experienced as "social facts" suggests the existence of an environment external to and prior to the individual, while statements about man defining society, and social facts surviving only through their reaffirmation suggests a subjectivist world, in which the "outside world" is no more than a set of shared meanings attributed to observed behaviour. Putting the two positions together we are left with a picture of ordinary action as a "contextual field of information" (Morgan and Smircich, 1980) in which individuals are engaged in a continual process of interaction and exchange with their environment, in which they both reaffirm and redefine it and are redefined by it.

This position represents the world in slightly more concrete terms than what has been termed "behavioural" (as opposed to "phenomenological") interactionism. This form of symbolic interactionism is well represented by dramaturgical forms of analysis, in which individuals are seen as engaged in a theatrical performance, a process of impression management in the creation and acting out of social, including, occupational roles (e.g. Goffman, 1959; Mangham, 1978). The essence of this approach is that the essential concepts of symbolic interactionism are interpreted within a framework which acknowledges the "stage", or backdrop of a realist world of physical and symbolic objects. Thus, within this world, individuals are seen as acting towards things, such as events, on the basis of the meanings they have for them. The meanings though are themselves the products of social interaction, and therefore open to modification through an interpretive process used by each individual in dealing with situations encountered. Mangham (1978, p.14) offers a good example of this process:

> The meaning of the office or role of managing director, for example, is given by the way people behave towards that role or function: reverentially, subserviently, or whatever . . . Given my particular set of experiences, I may ascribe a different meaning to the role of the managing director and behave accordingly, behaviour which, in turn, may modify the interpretations of others and thus affect their behaviour which influences my interpretation, and so on.

The result of such interpretations, definitions and acts is the establishment between individuals and groups, of patterns of "taken-for-granted behaviour". This "negotiated order" (Strauss, 1963) reflects their tacit and temporary agreement about the meaning of a situation and the appropriate and complementary behaviour to be enacted within it (Mangham, 1978).

Although this is not the dominant perspective on adaptive behaviour, increasingly it is influencing the prescriptions of such academically oriented change agents as Mangham (1979) and Peters (1978). From this perspective, change and adaptation come about by managers applying different languages and rituals, using different settings and so on, to modify organizational members' shared meanings (Pfeffer, 1981). This is a perspective on ordinary action which Morgan and Smircich (1980) term "symbolic discourse", and which, along with the "action" or "contextual field of information" perspective, will be discussed in far more detail in Chapter 5.

Taking together these different approaches to analyzing change as "ordinary action", one important contrast should be drawn. This concerns their respective approaches to those issues of interests, conflict and power which implicitly, or often explicitly, permeate the change process (Burrell and Morgan, 1979).

In relation to these issues two contrasting views of organization have been drawn: the unitary and the pluralist (Fox, 1966). Following Burrell and Morgan (1979, p.204) the unitary view places emphasis on organizations as goal-directed, adaptive systems, where its members strive for the achievement of common goals in the manner of a well integrated team. Conflict is regarded as unnatural, largely the creation of troublemakers, and can be "removed through appropriate managerial action". Power tends to be ignored in favour of notions of authority, leadership and control, whereby managers exercise their prerogatives of "guiding the organization towards the achievement of common interests". The pluralist view, in contrast, places emphasis on the diversity of individuals' and group interests and downplays the status of organizational goals as being "little more than a legitimizing facade, an umbrella under which a host of individual and group interests are pursued as ends in themselves" (Burrell and Morgan, 1979, p.203). Conflict is seen as an inevitable characteristic of organizational action which may have a constructive role to play. Power is identified as the medium through which conflicts of interest are resolved. The organization, as a whole, is viewed as a plurality of power holders, each of which draw upon different sources of power, in order to pursue objectives which they value, through processes of bargaining and mutual adjustment.

These perspectives are somewhat caricatured in order to highlight the contrast. However, as Burrell and Morgan point out, the systems approach, by highlighting authority and control over the organization as a goal directed system comes closer to the unitary perspective than do action and symbolic interactionism approaches. The latter perspectives, with their emphasis on the different meanings held by different groups, on their differing attachment to rules, and on the relative ability of different actors to impose their definition of the situation upon others, are more clearly within a pluralist framework. The implication of this, debatably, is that those who view change from a systems perspective may be less prepared for the emergence of conflicts and power struggles during change than those who view action from an interactionist perspective.

The implications for evaluation design of these different perspectives in analyzing adaptive behaviour in organizations will be explored in the conclusion to this chapter.

We now turn to a brief outline of the conventional descriptive model of change as innovation, rather than adaptation in organizations.

Change as innovation

A change may be described as innovative if it involves some notion of discontinuity with what went before, the idea of a qualitative shift. The more accentuated this is, the more radical the innovation.

It should be noted at the outset that conventional models of innovation (e.g. Hage, 1980; Melio, 1971; Zaltman *et al.*, 1973) rest on a systems view of organizations. It is within this meta-perspective that the processes of innovation have been analyzed in terms of four stages: problem recognition, initiation, implementation and routinization. Hage (1980) provides a useful account of some of the major issues involved, and it is on his overview that the following summary is based.

Problem recognition

The recognition of failure and search for solution has been identified as the first stage in the process of innovative change. The recognition of failure involves the identification of some sort of "performance gap" (Zaltman *et al.*, 1973). Hage (1980) suggests that the frequency of such detection will depend on how easy it is to measure performance criteria, how frequently this is undertaken, and the variety of performance criteria used. When measurement is easy, frequently undertaken and against a variety of criteria, any deviations will be quickly revealed and, in all probability, before performance gaps have grown large. In these circumstances, the innovation rate is likely to be high, but each innovation incremental rather than radical. The process may be viewed as one of successful adaptation just as much as innovation.

But when the opposite situation prevails—when performance measurement is difficult (e.g. the quality of education, rather than its cost), infrequent—often a corollary—and when few measures are employed, then the detection of a performance gap is likely to be delayed. As a result the gap is likely to grow large prior to its eventual detection. Hage (1980) suggests that the size of this gap also depends on the severity of the standards employed and the length of the time span used in measurement. If decision-makers' standards are high, and they tend towards optimizing rather than satisficing solutions, then performance gaps may be perceived to be large enough to justify moderately radical innovation. Furthermore, a long-time-span of planning may heighten this awareness. Overall, though, extremely radical innovation is most likely to occur when an undetected performance gap has grown so large that its detection has taken the form of a crisis and the gap is then seen to exist in many areas of previously unmonitored performance (Knight, 1967). Such a situation may jolt an organization from its accustomed application of "single loop" learning to the radical readjustment involved in "double loop" learning

(Argyris and Schön, 1978). According to this model, then, the organization most likely to embark on a *radical* innovation, paradoxically, is one that has difficulty in measuring output, infrequent measurement, low standards and short-time spans. (This parallels stage 1 of Greiner's description of the stages of a successful change.)

Initiation

This stage in the process of innovatory change has been identified as involving the search for and acquisition of relevant resources, whether money, personnel or technology (Hage, 1980). "Organizational slack" or un-committed resources available to decision-makers for managing new activities, is an important concept in explaining success or failure in initiating a change programme (see, for example, Berg, 1979; March and Simon, 1958; Pfeffer, 1981, pp.103–6). For, first, there is the need for uncommited finance in order. to acquire new personnel and technology. It is difficult to initiate change programmes which require taking resources from existing groups or activities already being conducted, as, at the outset, a ready-made opposition will be created. Secondly, the need for new personnel, as Hage (1980) points out, is likely to stem from two sources. If a radical innovation is dictated by the failure of the existing decision-making coalition, a new set of decision-makers, possibly from outside the organization, may be preferred (this parallels stage 2 of Greiner's description of the stages of a successful change). If the planned innovation is even moderately radical the organization may lack personnel with the appropriate experience and change-oriented values. Thirdly, the new personnel may have to develop new technologies in order to achieve the objectives of the innovation.

However, as Hage (1980) points out, although the statement that "the more radical the innovation, the greater the need for new personnel, funds and technologies", may appear tautological, its implication for the process of change is important. That is, that for an innovation to get off the ground, the process of seeking new funds, personnel and technologies must be undertaken.

Implementation

This stage is generally marked by the emergence of tensions, resistance and conflict.

It has been suggested that the extent of conflict that will emerge during the implementation process will be influenced by the amount of behaviour change, and the amount of change in both power and status demanded of existing personnel and positions in the organization (Hage, 1980). New personnel, in new occupations, specialists in new technologies, and with different values from existing organizational members, are likely to demand changes in the latters' role behaviour, in implementing the change programmes. For example, the introduction of rehabilitation services in prisons puts pressure on existing prison officers to redefine the custodial nature of their role; the introduction of a computer changes the role of an invoicing clerk and the supervisor (see McCleery, 1957; Mumford, 1972; Mumford and Banks, 1967). The innovators often have unrealistically high expectations of the changes they seek to introduce, which may become translated into unrealistic demands for behaviour change upon the part of others in the organization. The resistance and conflict engendered may then be exacerbated by the communication blocks arising from different ways of viewing problems and the new jargon of the new technologies.

The resulting role conflict is likely to go hand in hand with conflicts over power and status. As Hage (1980) points out, new personnel and occupations have to be slotted into an organization chart and, if the change is to succeed, be allowed some discretion over resources. This inevitably raises questions of relative power and status positions. Because new personnel require some autonomy to develop the innovation, this is likely to place them directly in conflict with existing lines of supervision. The feedback of conflict on the job autonomy of the innovators, may result in a reduction of their freedom to manoeuvre, which as Hage (1980) points out may either reduce the radicalness of the innovation, or, if the innovators refuse to compromise, further heighten the conflict.

In presenting such a model of the implementation stage of innovation, the question of why individuals and groups resist change must arise. Hage (1980) summarizing a range of commentators (e.g. Caplow, 1964; Homans, 1961; Mann and Williams, 1960; Toffler, 1970; Zaltman et al., 1973) suggests three explanations. First, existing power holders may resist change because of their "vested interest" in the existing order. This is likely to be particularly marked when the gaps in privileges, power and prestige between them and the lower participants in the organizations are marked—in other words in organizations that are highly centralized, stratified and lacking egalitarian values.

Secondly, change may be resisted because people have a limited capacity for absorbing change. This is likely to be evident in those who have lacked the opportunity to learn how to cope with change—that is, people who, in the past, have been engaged on routine work, rarely changing jobs or encountering any new ideas, experiences, or even colleagues. In other words, they are those who are "occupationally role integrated" (Gowler and Legge, 1972). But evidence would suggest that, even those who, through the regular experience of innovation, have developed a tolerance of change, find it difficult to accept an acceleration in the rate to which they have become accustomed.

Thirdly, there is the cost-benefit theory, which essentially is an exchange theory approach. It suggests that individuals calculate the balance of costs and benefits to themselves, and to the organization, in deciding whether to accept or resist change. Hence the key issue is what determines the weights attached by individuals and groups to particular costs and benefits—when do organizational members resist innovations that benefit the organization (however defined), and when do they accept innovations that have costs for them? Hage (1980) presents several hypotheses, partly based on the predictions of the "vested interest" and "capacity for change" theories. When organizations are highly centralized the dominant coalition will weigh the costs of the loss of power heavily. When organizational members have had little experience of change, they will weight the cost of role–behaviour change more highly than those used to change. Members of centralized organizations characterized by a routinized technology or product/service will more readily accept innovations that improve productivity than those that improve product/service quality. In contrast highly decentralized organizations, with a high concentration of professionals and specialists, will be more accepting of innovations in product/service quality, but resist attempts to increase the quantity of work.

At the implementation stage, then, resistance to innovation can invariably be anticipated. Hage (1980), however, identifies one important factor that may inhibit the degree of role, power and status conflict and enhance a willingness to accept radical innovation: consensus about the extent or depth of the crisis facing the organization. If such a consensus exists, the less the dominant coalition will resist radical change because of their vested interests. If they perceive that, short of innovation, they might lose everything, self-interest will dictate acceptance.

Routinization

Resistance to an innovation at the implementation stage may be so great that it never properly gets off the ground. If sufficient co-operation is achieved to experiment with some—probably watered down—version of the change programme, then the question arises as to whether it should be institutionalized. Hage (1980) suggests that such factors as consensus about the performance gap, time span before evaluation, ease of measuring costs and benefits and the cost of the innovation, will all weigh in the decision whether or not to routinize it. It is suggested that routinization is most likely to occur when, given a consensus about the performance gap, decision-makers are prepared to allow a relatively long-time span for experimentation, and before evaluation. The shorter the time span allowed, the more likely negative costs will outweigh positive benefits, as the costs of the conflict in the early stages of implementation will have been incurred, but the potential benefits may not have had time to mature. Ease of measuring costs and benefits is also an important factor. Non-measurability reduces the visibility of benefits, which may reduce the likelihood of an innovation being accepted and then institutionalized. Paradoxically, though, if sunk costs are perceived to be high, it may be hard for management to admit failure. The innovation may then be routinized in anticipation of long-term benefits.

In conclusion Hage (1980) argues that while "organic" organizations (Burns and Stalker, 1961), being more receptive to change, may have a higher rate of innovation, they do not necessarily produce one large radical change, as their style of introducing innovations tends to be participative (this is because the concentration of specialists is high and the power structure decentralized). As a result a potentially radical programme is watered down in negotiating its acceptance. In a mechanistic organization, paradoxically, the potential for radical change is high. This is because delayed identification of a performance gap may lead to a crisis so severe that there is consensus about its existence, while the centralized structure is likely to be more accommodative of unilateral action.

Having outlined some descriptive models of how change occurs, before considering their implications for evaluation design, I now turn to the third aspect of descriptive models of change. That is, how outcomes are actually assessed and the practical limitations of the normative prescriptions about the measurement of effectiveness.

Assessing effectiveness — in practice

How is the effectiveness of organizational change programmes actually assessed, and what are the problems frequently encountered? Generally speaking a formal evaluation often founders through different interest groups' inability to agree on evaluation criteria or on the functions an evaluation should serve. As these issues will be discussed extensively in later chapters, I will not anticipate in any detail the arguments developed there. Suffice to say at this point that the normative prescriptions about measuring effectiveness in terms of goal achievement, system resource acquisition, or participant-satisfaction all encounter practical and conceptual obstacles in implementation.

For example, while assessing a programme's effectiveness in terms of its goal achievement is often claimed to occur, I believe this to represent an aspiration, a shared value and rhetoric about what should take place rather than a "factual" reality (in objectivist terms). This is because it is a reification to attribute goals to a change programme—only the *people* involved with the programme have goals and the programme may, (or may not) represent an instrument or a series of activities through which they seek to achieve them. A list of the "official goals" of the programme is, first and foremost, an artifact of those drawing up the list. As Perrow (1961) in relation to organizational goals, and Weiss and Rein (1970) in relation to social change programmes, have pointed out, official goals are generally too vaguely defined to serve as standards of evaluation and are too divergent from actual operating objectives to be taken as anything more than a rhetoric that can encompass many different interests. "Freedom from want" or "service to the customer" is sufficiently lofty to evade challenge and sufficiently embracing to conceal the goal and prioritization conflicts that will inevitably emerge once anyone seeks to operationalize it.

If the "operative" goals of the programme (i.e. those actually pursued) are to be taken as evaluative criteria, they first have to be identified. This may not prove easy, as each participant may hold changing and potentially conflicting goals (e.g. a production manager may seek volume increases, quality improvement and cost reduction and pursue these goals differentially at different points in time). Even if such goals can be identified and prioritized for each individual, there is the problem that *different* individuals may hold different and conflicting goals, and hence that of prioritizing *between* goal sets. Is a programme a success if it achieves some (or someone's) goals but fails to achieve others? To cope with this difficulty a system of weighting goals according to the effort expended in their pursuit, and then measuring programme effectiveness by the degree to which the weighted goal set is optimized, subject to internal and external constraints, has been suggested (Steers, 1975).

But, it has been argued, this is to assume that the set of programme goals chosen was the "right one". Suppose a programme of planned organizational change achieved its goals (e.g. innovated a radically new product — such as Rolls-Royce RB211 engine), but at the cost of organizational survival? In such a case, the success of a change programme should be assessed in terms of its contribution to some measure of *overall* organizational effectiveness. Measuring organizational effectiveness is a highly problematic area (see, for example, the discussions of Goodman and Pennings, 1977; Keeley, 1978; Mohr, 1982; Steers, 1975), but one measure (besides goal achievement) that has been advocated rests on a "system resource" model (Yuchtman and Seashore, 1967). In this model effectiveness is defined as the organization's "bargaining position, as reflected in the ability of the organization, in either absolute or relative terms, to exploit its environment in the acquisition of scarce resources" (Yuchtman and Seashore, 1967, p.898). For example, the success of a new educational curriculum (a technological change) might be defined and measured in terms of its impact on a school's ability to attract good teachers, pupils and parental support. But this measure is not without problems in practice. Bargaining position cannot be an end in itself, as it is only meaningful if exploited to some other end. Similarly it is difficult to define what constitutes a resource, without reference to some goal to be achieved (Mohr, 1973). Nor is the problem of prioritization avoided, as conflict over resource acquisition strategies may arise.

An alternative approach to assessing a change programme's effectiveness, rests on the assumption that ultimately, it is designed for participants' benefit. Hence a programme's success should be judged by whether it delivers participants sufficient satisfactions to motivate their continued participation (Barnard, 1938). A training programme, for example, might be deemed a success, if participants enjoyed it and recommended it to potential participants, irrespective of whether they learned anything new, or later applied their learning. But while this approach sidesteps problems of identifying and reconciling programme goals, it is still confronted by different participants' potentially conflicting criteria of what constitutes a satisfaction (Keeley, 1978).

Identifying and prioritizing between conflicting goals, system–resource acquisition strategies, and participants' satisfactions is a major practical and conceptual problem in implementing the normative models of assessing change programmes' effectiveness. Prioritizing between such values involves the problem of how to devise common scales for the relative worth of qualitatively different values (e.g. morale and productivity) while bearing in mind the tendency of the combinations to be non-linear (i.e. combinations may be valued positively or negatively beyond predictions possible from their individual utility functions taken separately). Even if this can be tackled— some might say fudged (as through the use of economists' theoretical indifference curves) there is still the issue of how to weight differentially the preferences of different change programme participants (Mohr, 1982).

In the face of these problems it is not surprising that many change programmes are not assessed systematically. Instead the different parties involved make intuitive assessments, each with different evaluation functions in mind and, consequently, with different and highly subjective lists of questions and selection of data. If one of the normative models for assessing effectiveness is employed as the basis for an evaluation design, expectations are often unrealistic as the difficulties involved may not be fully understood or anticipated. Either way, because change programmes, through their allocation of scarce resources, are inevitably political, such evaluation as does take place will scarcely remain untouched by political considerations.

Summary

The descriptive models of change discussed here suggest that a change programme may be a far "messier" and more problematic entity to evaluate than the normative models might suggest. Indeed, if change as "ordinary action" is viewed from one of the subjectivist perspectives, even to talk of "it" as an "entity" is a misnomer. But how those involved—including an evaluator—conceptualizes a change programme will have implications for the choice of evaluation design.

In the following section, the conclusion to this chapter, the implications for evaluation design of the change models outlined here are explored.

Implications for evaluation design

The first is somewhat paradoxical. Whether one views change programmes from a normative or descriptive perspective, it is evident that not only are the concepts of planning and change overlapping in that both label similar sets of behaviour, but that the *whole process of change is an evaluatory act*. All planning models—with the possible exception of the garbage can— involve the notion of an assessment, however unsystematic, of some gap between the present and a desired future state, prior to choosing a strategy, the change programme, to narrow the gap. This evaluation-in-planning is mirrored in the change models "problem recognition" stage (see both Greiner and Hage). The fact that planning involves acts of evaluation is of course recognized by professional evaluators in their discussion of the role of "needs assessment", in planning social change programmes (see for example Anderson and Ball, 1978, pp.17–22). In designing change programmes (or in terms of planning models, "choosing between alternatives") evaluations are made as to the most appropriate strategy to adopt. Resistance to change represents individuals' or groups' negative evaluation of its likely conse- quences for them. Finally, planning and change models, whether normative or descriptive, include the assessment of outcomes as an integral part of planning and change processes, being the step prior to the routinization of change. To speak of the "evaluation of planned change programmes" is much the same as speaking of "the evaluation of acts of evaluation", or to say that planning processes are synonymous with change processes and both constitute evaluation processes.

If, for a moment, the evaluation of planned change programmes is viewed in this light, a potential problem becomes apparent. Can we separate out these various acts of evaluation so that it is meaningful to speak of the formal evaluation of a change programme as an act separate from its planning and implementation? For if one cannot separate change *from* its evaluation, the preconditions for treating change as the subject *of* evaluation must be debatable.

Elsewhere (Gowler and Legge, 1979) I addressed this issue by examining the implications of different planning models for the choice of formative or summative evaluation designs. It may be useful now to look again at these arguments, bearing in mind the implications of models of the change process as well. First, a word about formative and summative designs.

This distinction (Scriven, 1967) is one of the most basic in evaluation design and will be discussed in subsequent chapters. Suffice to say here that formative, or process, designs concentrate on providing regular, systematic feedback to programme designers and implementers [using an array of qualitative and the "softer" quantitative methods] in order that they might modify and develop the programme in an on-going fashion. The survey feedback methods used by action researchers are an example of this. Summative, "impact" or outcome, evaluation, in contrast, is concerned with identifying and assessing the worth of programme outcomes, in the light of initially specified success criteria after the implementation of the change programme is completed. Because it attempts to estimate as precisely as possible the effect, and its magnitude, of the change programme upon specified dependent variables, while controlling for the effect of potentially intervening variables, experimental and quasi-experimental methods are logically preferred.

In one circumstance the planning aspect of the change process cannot be clearly separated from a change programme's formal evaluation. This occurs when the planning is rationalistic, if not completely rational (for example, when a mixed scanning model is followed) and the evaluation design is formative. Then planning and evaluation overlap to such an extent that in practice they are virtually synonymous. In other situations, though, it is practically possible to distinguish formal evaluation designs from the other evaluatory acts involved in the change process. But here the problem may be one of incompatibility between planning and change processes and evaluation designs — or even their mutual exclusivity.

For example, if planning is rationalistic, even to the limited extent of a mixed scanning approach, it will be iterative, and therefore summative designs will prove incompatible, if based on experimental or quasi-experimental methods. For the monitoring and adjustment activities "rationally" advocated would contradict two requirements of experimental methods of outcome evaluation: that the change programme should be held constant throughout implementation and that implementation must run full-cycle. These requirements will also be contradicted if the programme experiences the continual compromises and adjustments in the face of opposition, predicted by the descriptive models of the change process. In the process of implementation a change programme may cease to resemble its original conception (Pressman and Wildavsky, 1973).

Ways around this dilemma have been proposed. Suchman (1970), for example, has suggested that a change programme should be conducted as a four stage developmental process. He differentiates a pilot phase when the change programme evolves on a trial and error basis; a model phase when a defined strategy is run under controlled conditions; a prototype phase when the model programme is subject to realistic operating conditions; and an institutionalized phase when the programme becomes an ongoing part of the organization. It is only during the model phase that the programme must be held stable for experimental evaluation. However this would require co-operation between the different organizational interest groups which may not be forthcoming if resistance to the change is severe and rapidly mobilized.

If, however, planning change resembles the disjointed incrementalism or garbage can models, the feasibility of undertaking a traditionally rigorous outcome evaluation is threatened from another quarter. An experimental or quasi experimental evaluation requires that the change strategy embodies a theory of cause and effect (W strategy should result in X outcomes in Y circumstances for Z reasons) and that strategy, environmental conditions and desired outcomes be clearly specified and measured (such requirements are discussed in detail in Chapter 4). The problem is that these descriptive models of planning and those of the change process would suggest that objectives — the desired outcomes — may be either unclear or inconsistent or simply not agreed by those responsible for the change programme. Similarly, there may be a lack of precise specification of its initial design (quite apart from the fact that any design may be modified during implementation). In these circumstances the evaluator will lack the initial conditions necessary to carry out a valid experiment.

The question then arises, is this specification of initial conditions — including goals, always necessary in an outcome evaluation, or can a softer, non-experimental design by employed? This raises the broader issue of what functions evaluation designs (both outcome and formative) are meant to serve — a question that is dealt with in detail in the next chapter. If we assume for the moment that some evaluation functions can be served by a less rigorous outcome design, then Scriven's (1973) suggestions about "goal-free" evaluation are relevant. This design simply aims to identify as many of the change programme's outcomes as possible, including what, from a goal based approach, might be unintended side effects. The evaluator does not even seek to identify the programme's goals, partly on the grounds that to do so might induce a managerial bias, but instead concentrates on the extent to which identified outcomes fulfil the participants' needs. (An analogy might be with a consumer group's evaluation of a washing machine, which rests on assumptions about consumer requirements rather than producer goals). Of course, the problem with this approach is in the attribution of apparent outcomes unequivocally to the programme alone. Or, in deciding which aspect of the programme has resulted in which outcome, or why. However, depending on the function the evaluation is designed to serve this may prove no major drawback.

Then, again, if the conventional descriptions of disjointed incrementalism and garbage can forms of planning are accepted, along with those of formative evaluation, it can be seen that the *systematic* monitoring and adjustment processes implied in formative evaluation are excluded, by definition, from circumstances in which planning resembles these models. Unless, of course, one is prepared to equate sporadic, *ad hoc* tinkering in response to the unanticipated emergence of unacceptable, if unsystematically validated consequences, with formative evaluation. This would be to deny both the commonly accepted functions and systematic nature of formative evaluation—in fact to change its definition. But, if the definition is so changed, then again, planning and formative evaluation become virtually synonymous.

But, suppose, hypothetically, the ideal conditions existed? The planning of change was rationalistic, programme's goals were agreed and clearly specified along with the theories and assumptions underlying the programme design. The change process conformed to the stages identified in Greiner's model as being the route to successful change. Co-operation was secured to the extent that Suchman's model phase could be run under controlled conditions. In these circumstances, a rigorous summative evaluation design could be implemented. But even if this was the case, such a hypothetical illustration only serves to raise the question—what functions would such an evaluation serve? For it could be argued that to achieve such conditions, necessary for the evaluation's validity, only serves to undermine its external validity. In other words the conditions in which the change programme was designed and implemented would be so far removed from the "messy" conditions identified in the descriptive models of planning and change to render it and its evaluation of little generalizable relevance.

The descriptive models of planning and change would suggest that these are highly political and value-laden processes. Evaluation as part of the change process is subject to these pressures. Choice of evaluation design is likely to be constrained by the information the most powerful participants require and why they require it. Possibly, for example, a "good news" evaluation is called for—which may rule out the advisability of adopting a rigorous summative design. No evaluation design is value free—the questions it asks and the data it selects rests on implicit value assumptions. Therefore, if the nature of the change process appears to eliminate—or encourage—the use of certain designs, the evaluator should be conscious of the value position implicit in his or her choice. It has already been suggested that disjointed incrementalism produces small, piecemeal and adaptive changes, while Hage has pointed to the fact that radical innovation appears to be the exception rather than the rule (from an objectivist standpoint). If, paradoxically, the change process is conservative and protective of the status quo, the evaluator needs to consider to what extent his or her choice of evaluation design is implicitly reinforcing this process. To the extent it does so, it could be argued, the more difficult it is to see even formal evaluation as an activity distinct and separate from other change processes. The whole issue of values in evaluation will be considered further in Chapter 6.

Finally the evaluator's choice of design will, above all, be constrained by his perception of what is "really" happening in the change process. To the extent that he (or she) views reality from an objectivist standpoint, he is likely to see the behaviours he observes in terms of some systems model—such as is explicit in Hage's description of the process of innovation. If this is his or her position an evaluation design that adheres to positivistic assumptions is consistent with his view of the world—up to a point. For it should be noted that although organizational change is conventionally viewed from an open systems perspective, the methods that dominate in positivistic approaches—use of controlled experiments and attitude questionnaires—are based upon a closed system assumption. That is, that the environment generated by the investigation has no important impact upon the subject under study (Burrell and Morgan, 1979, p.60). The contradiction of conceptualizing change in open systems terms, then researching its "true nature" by closed system designs is rarely confronted by positivistically oriented evaluators. However, if the evaluator sees change from an action frame of reference or a (limited) interactionist one, an interpretive design is logically called for. In so far as evaluation is part of the change process, the evaluator cannot view with consistency the processes and actions he observes from one ontological standpoint, and then apply a design that rests on assumptions drawn from another. The implications of this assertion are further discussed in Chapters 4 and 5.

So, choice of evaluation design will in part be constrained by the nature of the changes processes involved, or rather the models of the processes held by the participants—including of course the evaluator. Yet, as suggested in these conclusions, the choice of design (and possibly of evaluator!) should also be influenced by what functions the different parties to the change seek from it, if it is to generate "useful" information. I now turn to the question of evaluation functions in Chapter 3.

Notes

(1) At first sight it may appear somewhat paradoxical that the "radical change" paradigms are likely to be rejected by management and evaluators as practical approaches to the analysis of organizational change. This may be clarified by outlining what they involve when applied to organizational analysis. "Anti-organization theory" (radical change/subjectivist paradigm) is just that (Burrell and Morgan, 1979). It comprises a form of humanism based on the assumption that existing social arrangements, particularly large scale organization as an expression of capitalism, alienate man from his true consciousness, and is concerned with how man can liberate

himself. The implication is a rejection of large scale organization and "embracing" an alternative life style. As such it appears unhelpful in analyzing change programmes planned within and executed by and to, members of large organizations. The posture is too rejecting of the concept of organization.

A different criticism can be levelled at "radical organization theory" (radical change/objectivist paradigm). This perspective sees contemporary society as characterized by deep-seated conflicts which, through political and economic crises, generate radical social change. Whereas "anti-organization theory" focuses on man's consciousness, "radical organization theory" concentrates on existing structural relationships in society from a Marxist perspective. Its implications for analyzing organizational change programmes are that these must be viewed as expressions of the society of which the organizations are a product. As products of a capitalist society they can only reflect management's definition of problems and hence are protective of the status quo. The role of a change-agent or evaluator in an organization who accepts this perspective should be one of the "mole", "seeking to carry out action research which has discontinuous revolutionary change as its objective" (Burrell and Morgan, 1979, p.366). While I would not deny that this perspective in analyzing organizational and social change programmes would provide the change agent and evaluator alike with new insights into their actions and, for the evaluators, the possibility of highlighting the inherently conservative nature of many change programmes, the political (with a small and large "p"!) adviseability of using such analysis is questionable. The change-agent or evaluation researcher who sought to implement or evaluate organizational change within a capitalist society from such a perspective would be sacked or starved of resources. The very real impediments to an evaluation researcher acting as a truly radical critic of the programmes he evaluates are fully discussed in Chapter 6.

Chapter 3

The Functions of Evaluation Research

In Chapter 1 it was suggested that the crisis in the utilization of evaluation findings reflected a deeper problem — that of what functions evaluation research can and should serve. Consequently, in this chapter, the answer to a range of questions about the functions of evaluation research is sought. In particular, I seek:

(1) To identify the different interest groups, or stakeholders in an evaluation.

(2) To identify and classify the different functions which evaluation research can fulfil for these different groups.

(3) To identify what evaluation design requirements the selection of a particular evaluation function imposes on the evaluation.

(4) To suggest which functions, with their related design requirements, are likely to prove mutually incompatible, either in theory or in practice.

The stakeholders in an evaluation study

Programmes of planned change generally involve actors in at least four different roles. There are those responsible for funding the programme, those who design it, those who implement it and those who are at its receiving end. In addition, if the change programme is to be formally evaluated, there are the evaluators and those funding the evaluation. These roles may be occupied by completely different individuals, or there may be, and often is, some overlap, as for example, when the designers are also responsible for the evaluation or the implementation. Furthermore, when "social" change programmes are evaluated, given the enhanced political and public dimension, the "stakeholding audiences" (Stake, 1975) many become both more differentiated and more inclusively defined. Thus Rossi *et al.* (1979, pp.293–295) divides these roles into nine (for example, distinguishing between policy-makers and programme staff) while Cronbach *et al.*(1980, pp.100–103) include the whole "policy shaping community", of policy and operating officials; "constituents" (direct and indirect clients) and illuminators (reporters and academics who "reflect on public affairs and offer interpretations"). Guba and Lincoln (1981, pp.306–309) provide an alternative approach, useful in public service and industrial organizations alike, suggesting that stakeholding audiences may be identified by asking a series of questions about who are involved in producing and using the change programme, who are likely to experience its benefits and whom its costs.

The different roles involved may be illustrated by a well publicized industrial change programme. In Shell U.K. Ltd, a multinational oil company, in the mid-1960s a change programme was introduced that sought to tackle manpower problems such as unfavourable (managerially defined) workers' attitudes and inefficient restrictive practices, as part of a general drive towards greater efficiency and better financial performance in response to more challenging market conditions (beginnings of O.P.E.C. cartel, the nationalization of oil companies by oil producing countries, price wars in U.K., industrial relations innovations on the part of a major competitor). These problems had been exacerbated by (but had also partly led to) an earlier programme of redundancies unprecedented in the company's history. The change programme involved the adoption of a "new (participative) philosophy of management" that was to be implemented through four channels: through demonstration job design projects, through the design of a new refinery, through managers acting as change agents in their departments (i.e. managing their departments by the principles of the philosophy) and through the introduction of joint working parties of management and worker representatives (to explore possible new working arrangements prior to negotiating productivity deals) (Hill, 1971).

This change project involved many different groups. It was *funded* by the Shell U.K. Ltd, head office, who set up an Employee Relations Planning Unit, "to produce long-term plans for dealing with the problems at shop-floor level" (Hill, 1971, p.24). The E.R.P. co-opted consultants from the Tavistock Institute to assist them in formulating these plans, and later to *design* the change initiatives through which the new philosophy they had jointly evolved was to be implemented. Both the E.R.P. and the consultants were involved in *implementation*, as were managers, of various levels of authority, at the different refineries. The "clients" of the change initiatives, given the participative philosophy, were both the ultimate producers and consumers of the exercise. It was *evaluated* in 1967 by the E.R.P. and the Tavistock Institute consultants, an evaluation funded by the company, and subsequently—ten years later, by two independent university researchers.

The point to be made here is that *not only did each of the participants— or role incumbents—in the change process have a vested interest in the evaluation, but, given their different structural perspectives deriving from their different roles, they had different requirements of it too.*

A range of structural or organizational factors can be identified that are likely to differentiate the participants in a change programme and, in turn, their relationship to and requirements of its evaluation.

(1) Participants may belong to different organizations, with different objectives and cultures (cf. Shell U.K. Ltd, profit-making, production and commercially oriented, possessing a relatively bureaucratic culture, with the Tavistock Institute, non-profit-making, service and academically oriented, possessing a relatively organic culture).

(2) Participants, while belonging to the same organization, may be differentiated horizontally, by the department or function they work in, vertically by their level in the hierarchy, and geographically, by the location of the unit in which they work.

(Although the majority of the participants in Shell's change programme worked for Shell U.K. Ltd, they were differentiated by function or department (cf. personnel specialists with line managers), by position in the hierarchy (cf. Head Office Board members, with senior plant management, with shop floor operatives), and geographically (some participants worked at Head Office, some at Stanlow Refinery, some at Teesport)).

(3) Participants may be working for the same organization during a change programme, but with different degrees of attachment to that organization. (Compare at Shell, its full-time employees with the co-opted, part-time paid consultants. In many social change programmes unpaid volunteers, accepting directions and control from the organization, may be added too).

(4) Participants' roles in relation to the change programme specifically (apart from their on-going roles in the organization) are likely to differ, for example, in terms of (a) function, (b) intensity of involvement (whether full-time or part-time, duration of involvement), (c) status (level of influence in relation to decisions affecting the programme), (d) whether initiating or passive, (e) whether chosen or imposed.

(5) Participants' involvement in the change programme is likely to differ in terms of how its perceived success or failure is likely to influence their on-going roles and prospects in their employing organization.

How these factors are likely to influence participants' evaluation requirements will be considered later in this chapter. But first we must identify both the overt (manifest) and covert (latent) functions that evaluation can serve.

The overt functions of evaluation

Decision-making

Most commentators agree that the major overt function of evaluation research is to provide information for decision-making. Weiss' (1972c) comment that:

> The basic rationale for evaluation is that it provides information for action. Its primary justification is that it contributes to the rationalization of decision-making.

is so frequently echoed by such a wide range of other writers (e.g. Angrist, 1975; Campbell *et al.* 1970; Caro, 1971; Cooper and Mangham, 1971; Edwards *et al.*, 1975; Hamblin, 1974; Nicholas, 1979; Stufflebeam, 1968; Suchman, 1967; Warr *et al.*, 1970) that it is almost a cliché. But in what ways can evaluation research facilitate decision-making and what types of decision are involved? Each of these questions will be considered in turn.

Role of evaluation research in facilitating decision-making

In what ways can evaluation research facilitate decision-making? The answer lies partly in what we understand by evaluation research and partly in what we understand by decision-making.

Traditionally evaluation research, within the positivistic paradigm, as discussed in Chapter 1, is concerned with the measurement of the impact of a change programme upon specified dependent variables. Did the change have a positive or negative impact, or no effect at all? As such, it provides hard data about the consequences of decision choices, and thus *can reduce uncertainty about the relationship between means and ends in decision situations.* For example, suppose decision-makers wished to achieve a mutually agreed objective (higher productivity) and, having defined how this objective was to be operationalized, had the choice of several change strategies aimed at increasing productivity in the terms agreed. One might involve changing a control system (e.g. introducing an incentive payment system in place of time rates) another, changing methods of working (e.g. job design), both designed to increase levels of machine utilization. Suppose, too, that the decision-makers were uncertain about the likely outcomes of the strategies but had no pre-existing preferences between strategies. Evaluation research, for example, by evaluating pilot projects conducted as quasi-experiments, might assist their decision-making by providing information about the impact of the strategies (positive, negative, no effect) on levels of machine utilization. This would provide information from which they could *learn* about the cause-effect relationships they wished to manipulate and so exercise *control* over behaviours for which they had responsibility.

The assumption here is that "hard facts" are necessarily useful to the decision-maker. But this is to make further assumptions about the nature of the decision-making process—namely that it is, or should be, a rational process as suggested by the example. If rationality may be defined as denoting thought and action which are consciously in accord with the rules of logic and empirical knowledge, where objectives are coherent, mutually consistent and achieved by the most appropriate means (Mitchell, 1979, p.154).

just how rational is decision-making in practice? To what extent is decision-making in organizations really characterized by goal consistency, attention to empirical data about the nature of means–ends relationships logically identified as relevant to goal achievement?

As already discussed in Chapter 2, most commentators would agree that the risky decision-making that is embodied in the planning and implementation of change programmes if often far from rational, and almost inevitably so. Indeed it has been suggested by Brunsson (1982) that a certain amount of irrationality in decision-making is necessary to secure sufficient motivation and commitment on the part of participants to get major strategic decisions translated into action. As Brunsson (1982, pp.34–37) points out, evaluating all possible alternatives, or even as many as possible, however "rational", evokes uncertainty, which reduces motivation and commitment. If people do not know which alternative will eventually be chosen, they have to build up motivations for and commitments to several alternatives at the same time, and this diffuses that supporting any single alternative. Considering just two alternatives, including one that is already known to have no chance of being chosen, however "irrational", does not have these negative effects, and may even enhance motivation and commitment. Considering an "unacceptable alternative" can by comparison highlight the virtues of the "acceptable" one, while commitment can be generated through criticisms of the unacceptable alternative just as much as through endorsement of the acceptable one.

Similarly, consideration of all the relevant consequences that all possible alternatives might have, however "rational", can also evoke much uncertainty, as inconsistent information produces confusions and doubt, and stimulates conflict among decision-makers (Hoffman, 1968). Also, it is difficult to weigh positive and negative consequences together (Slovic, 1966). To avoid this uncertainty, Brunsson suggests, decision-makers tend to search for consequences in only one direction—for the initial opinion about an alternative. This is consistent with some of the information biases that will be discussed below: people tend to anchor their judgements in the first cues they perceive (Tversky and Kahneman, 1974). Searching for the positive consequences of an acceptable alternative and suppressing the negative ones, not only enables decision-makers to avoid uncertainty—active search for arguments in favour of an alternative helps to generate enthusiasm and commitment for it.

Brunsson further suggests that the prescription of the rational model of decision-making, that alternatives and their consequences should be evaluated in the light of objectives, is a dangerous strategy from the action point of view. It contains the risk that decision-makers will formulate inconsistent objectives and have difficulty in assessing alternatives. For producing action, a better strategy, and one consistent with the "disjointed incrementalism" (Lindblom, 1959) and the garbage can (Cohen *et al.*, 1976) models of planning and decision-making, is to start from the consequences and invent objectives afterwards. "The objectives are arguments, not criteria for choice; they are instruments for motivation and commitment, not for investigation" (Brunsson, 1982, p.35). Similarly the actual decision is not so much a choice which follows from "rational" analysis, but an expression of commitment to carrying out an action.

Brunsson's conclusion, that it is not surprising that managers make decisions irrationally because this may, in fact, constitute an "action rationality", is consistent with what we know about their behaviour at work—that managers are essentially doers, not thinkers. From Mintzberg's (1973) and Stewart's (1967, 1976) research, involving many different types of organization and levels of management, several characteristic behaviours emerge. First, managers spend most of their day in conversation with people—on average 75–85% of their day. Secondly, most of their time is spent in unscheduled and *ad hoc* interaction—indeed, irrespective of level in the hierarchy, only about 35% of their day is spent in scheduled meetings. A third characteristic is the short duration of most managerial activities. For example, Sproull (1977, 1978) noted that education programme managers changed the focus of their attention once every six or seven minutes, while Mintzberg (1973) observed that chief executive officers seemed to complete more than half their activities in less than nine minutes. Finally, many of their interactions are initiated by other people. Sproull's (1977) education programme managers initiated only about 50% of their conversations, while Mintzberg's (1973) chief executive officers initiated only about 30% of their contacts.

Elaborating these findings, Sproull and Larkey (1979, pp.93–94) make several further and, from the point of view of rationalistic decision-making, alarming observations about managerial communication. They suggest that it tends to be local; casual, at least with respect to subordinates and peers; personalized, and specific and anecdotal. It also tends to be idiosyncratic (i.e. managers develop "sources" on which they feel they can depend for reliable information on a wide range of topics) and *not* highly redundant (i.e. if they are seeking information they tend to seek only until they find the first person with that information—there is very little double-checking; similarly if information is being sent, one person is told directly and relied on to "spread the word round").

As Sproull and Larkey (1979, p.92) comment on these findings:

> Research on managerial time allocation provides a picture strikingly at odds with the picture of the careful analytic decision-maker of the idealized, normative models. The manager emerges as a constantly busy person, turning and turned from problem to problem throughout the day, with no time to think, gather accurate information, or weigh alternative courses of action, and barely time to make superficial responses to complicated problems.

They go on to suggest (1979, pp.94–98) that evidence from cognitive and information processing psychology lends further support to this picture of decision-making as, at best, highly bounded in its rationality. Simon (1957) has suggested that constructing simplified representations of complicated decision situations or problems, in order to render them "manageable" is a universal human characteristic. Several mechanisms have been proposed as to how we do this; by looking for explainable constructs, often using simple inaccurate theories in a cultural context and then ignoring or reinterpreting data that do not seem to fit (Nisbett and Wilson, 1977); by using global assessments of a person, or situation, as a substitute for considered and independent judgement about their separate attributes as in the "halo effect" and stereotyping; by simply rejecting "too much" information that would complicate a decision (Cohen and Weiss, 1977; Jacoby *et al.*, 1976; Russo *et al.*, 1975).

Once decision-makers have constructed a simplified representation of a problem situation, they then have to assign probabilities of occurrence to events relevant to that situation. The processes by which people evaluate the probability of uncertain events would also suggest that the normative models of decision-making have little basis in reality. For the heuristics identified as commonly used "all have the property that they often lead to inferences that would be classed as erroneous by statistical decision theorists" (Sproull and Larkey, 1979, p.96). In using the "representativeness heuristic" (Kahneman and Tversky, 1972; Tversky and Kahneman, 1971) it is suggested that individuals both tend to overestimate the representativeness of small samples (the "law of small numbers") or overgeneralize from early results and underestimate the power of large samples. "In erring either way people appear to be fond of simple causal explanations that can be created and held somewhat independently of data" (Sproull and Larkey, 1979, p.96). A similar error occurs when individuals fail to allow for regression effects (Campbell, 1969; Kahneman and Tversky, 1973).

Tversky and Kahneman (1973, 1974) have identified two other heuristics that lead statistically and practically speaking to information processing errors. In resorting to the "availability heuristic" individuals assess the probability of events by the ease with which relevant instances of the events (e.g. death by tornadoes, snake bites, botulism, plane crash) can be imagined—irrespective of their actual likelihood (Slovic *et al.*, 1976). Secondly, using the "anchoring and adjustment" heuristic individuals make errors in over or under weighing new information, such as that produced by an evaluation. "If there is a natural starting point for judgment, such as widely shared preconceptions about a program, new data may adjust that starting point, but the effect is likely to be less than it should be" (Sproull and Larkey, 1979, p.97).

Sproull and Larkey (1979, p.97) identify further findings of cognitive psychologists that cast doubt on the assumption that managerial decision-making corresponds to the rational normative models. For example, it would appear that "people rely on decision procedures which are easily explainable and justifiable to others and themselves" (Tversky, 1972) and, that "consumers decision processes are effected more by adjectival than by numerical information" (Johnson, 1978) (so much then for the quantitative emphasis of "good" evaluation research!). Furthermore, "decision-making behaviour is strongly influenced by the amounts of available information, information formats, and internal standards (and scripts) held by decision-makers" (Abelson, 1976; Johnson and Russo, 1978; Payne, 1976; Tversky, 1969) and "the greater the amount and complexity of available information, the cruder (simpler) the heuristics that decision-makers will employ" (Payne, 1976). Above all there is abundant evidence that people hear what they want or are trained to hear, and seek information consistent with their own views and disregard conflicting evidence (Anderson and Jacobsen, 1965; Bruner and Postman, 1949; Dearborn and Simon, 1958; Wason, 1960; Webster, 1964). What then are the implications of all this for the status of evaluation research?

The point to be made here is that *the contribution which the "factual information" produced by evaluation research can make to the reduction of uncertainty will differ, depending on how rational the decision-making process is.* The more rational it is, the more facts are likely to be required (to enable a choice between a range, if not the whole range of alternatives) and the greater likelihood that the facts will be allowed to "speak for themselves". This is because a rational process implies some agreement over the ends to be sought and no pre-existing value preference about means—other than that they should be the most appropriate to achieving the ends, criteria for "appropriateness" having also been agreed upon. In such circumstances the uncertainty confronting the decision-makers is likely to relate to whether the chosen course of action—the means—does in fact satisfy their criteria for appropriateness. Thus information about impact to a large extent can "speak for itself" because the questions it addresses and frames of reference in which it is to be interpreted are agreed. But if the decision-making process fails to confront a lack of agreement over ends — as when in "muddling through" a course of action may be chosen that to each decision-maker represents the means to a different end — it is impossible to find a common frame of reference through which to collect data about and judge the appropriateness of means to ends. The uncertainties in the means–ends relationship are not only likely to be different for the parties to the decision (because each might have a different end in mind), but the researcher may have problems in identifying these different information requirements because some of the ends are unlikely to be made explicit. In these circumstances the information produced by an impact study is likely to be examined by the different parties to the decision from different perspectives informed by different value preferences about means and ends. When this occurs the value of the "facts" provided by an evaluation study depends less upon their empirical validity and more on the decision-makers' perceptions and interpretations of them in the light of their different preferences. If the "facts" do not correspond with these preferences, what we know about human information processing would suggest that it is likely that decision-makers will either not "hear" them or "hear" only what they want to hear. Thus the less rational the decision-making process, the less the facts will "speak for themselves" and the more individuals will "speak for the facts". The empirical validity of the facts is then less a decisive input into future decision-making, than the decision-making process itself a validator of the status that can be accorded to the data produced by the evaluation study (Weiss, 1972a, p.4).

The question this raises is whether evaluation research's traditional emphasis on the usefulness and importance of "true information" and "hard facts" about programme impact is either appropriate or cost-effective if the decision-making process which such data are meant to inform lays few claims to rationality. For if it is not rational it is quite probable that the decision-makers will disbelieve or denigrate the "facts" they do not like and treat as "facts" only that information which accords with their preferences. Certainly the evidence we have about the utilization of research would tend to support this contention.

The implications which this state of affairs might have for evaluation methodology are developed in subsequent chapters.

Types of decision

As "social" change researchers Anderson and Ball (1978), following Scriven (1974), point out, evaluation research can contribute to three types of decision about change programmes:

(1) Decisions about programme installation;

(2) Decisions about programme continuation, expansion/contraction, and certification;

(3) Decisions about programme modifications.

Greiner (1967) and Hage (1980) make similar comments about change programmes in industrial organizations, as do the action researchers (e.g. Clark, 1972). Decisions (1) are essentially part of the planning of change. As this has already been discussed in some detail, I will not linger over the information requirements involved. Suffice to say, these are the decisions which in theory focus on assessment of the need for the programme, evaluation of the adequacy of the conception, estimates of cost and of operational feasibility, and so on. Information, therefore is required to answer such questions as "is this the best alternative to meet the hypothesized performance gap", "does it really exist", "in whose eyes", etc. This is to assume though that the planning process is at least relatively rational and, as already discussed, it may not be so.

Decisions (2) and (3) are generally considered to require different sorts of information, as different questions are involved. In the case of decisions about programme continuation, expansion/contraction, certification, the information required is to answer the question "Was X a success?", "did it achieve its objectives?", "What were its effects?". Such "impact" or *"summative"* information (Scriven, 1967) about programme effectiveness (see Chapter 2) may be examined from either a comparative or absolutist perspective (Anderson and Ball, 1978, pp.28–29). From a comparative perspective, the results will be assessed in comparison with the performance of another group (either subject to the same or an alternative change programme) or with the earlier performance of the same group. For example, in the case of automating a car assembly plant: "are our manning figures now comparable to our competitors, or are they 'better' than the plant figures of X years ago?" From an absolutist perspective, the results will be judged in relation to performance criteria derived from programme objectives. For example, "we sought to make Y percentage of the workforce redundant, have we achieved it?" In assessing programme effectiveness, short-term and long-term effects need to be differentiated and assessed. Questions may also need to be asked about the change programme's possible side effects, quite apart from its success or failure in meeting intended outcomes. For such information about programme "products" to be of real use to the decision-maker, it often needs to be accompanied by contextual information that relates information about programme effects to the broader perspectives of policy-making—for example, information about the continuing need for the programme, its costs, the demand and support it generates. The sort of questions this additional information might seek to answer, depending on the evaluation design, might include:

Has the programme been so successful that it is no longer needed?
Are its results commensurate with its cost?
Can the same effects be achieved at less cost?

Can greater effects be obtained at the same cost?

Decisions about programme modifications require information about programme processes rather than programme products, as the purpose is to improve an on-going programme rather than to pass judgement on the effects of a fully developed one. Such *"formative"* information (Scriven, 1967) (see Chapter 2) may be collected about all aspects of a change programme's operation: its objectives, content, methodology, context, personnel policies and practices (Anderson and Ball, 1978). Decision-makers may require information about a wide range of questions relevant to programme development, such as:

How acceptable are the change programme objectives to all the parties to the change?

Is the content of the programme relevant to its objectives? Which components of the content most adequately serve which objective? Are the components appropriately sequenced?

Given the objectives and content, how should it best be presented? Length of training sessions? Balance between lectures, case studies and exercises?

How are organizational/community politics likely to affect continuing support for the change programme? Are staff relationships co-operative or competitive?

How were programme participants selected? Who leaves and who stays? Why?

(Anderson and Ball, 1978, pp.30–33).

Learning and Control

Implicit in the notion that evaluation can assist decision-making, is the assumption that evaluation can contribute to individual and group learning and facilitate the control of organizational and social change.

Evaluation enables individuals and groups to *learn* about the processes of change and the outcomes of different strategies. In fact, formative evaluation, in particular, is essentially about learning through feedback, how to improve change processes. Summative evaluation also assumes learning — that decision-makers learn from the data about programme effects, about the nature of the alternatives open to them.

The more informed decision-making that should result from this learning, in theory at least, should enable decision-makers to more effectively *control* the change processes they initiate and with them, their environment. The assumption here is that evaluation provides feedback about the products and processes of change programmes, which reduces uncertainty for the decision-maker, and enables him or her to adopt a more controlling, proactive and less *ad hoc* reactive position.

However, this is to see the learning and control functions of evaluation very much from the point of view of those who initiate an evaluation rather than of those who are its subject. In particular those who are responsible for implementing a change programme may view evaluation's control function in a very different light—that the information sought is only indirectly to do with the effective control of change, but directly to do with management control of their own activities and future careers. In this circumstance, although the evaluators may "learn" from an evaluation, it may inhibit the potential learning of the implementers, in two ways. First, they may seek to "play it safe" rather than experiment, in order to avoid the risk of a potential disaster and a negative results report from the evaluator. This may prevent a change programme developing its full potential. Secondly, their defensiveness may be such that either they reject the evaluator's findings in an attempt to reconcile any dissonance these might provoke, or they undermine the evaluation process through deliberate uncooperativeness or on occasions wilful misunderstanding of their data collection role (see, for example, the case quoted by Anderson and Ball, 1978, pp.158–159). In such circumstances, two major functions of evaluation—learning about and control of change processes—may result in behaviours dysfunctional to learning and control. This again illustrates how different parties to an evaluation are not only likely to have different functions for it, but to regard these functions from very different perspectives.

A further illustration of this point may be found in the debate about whether evaluation research can or should hope to contribute to learning of a different sort, that is discipline based knowledge or, as Burgoyne and Cooper put it, the establishment of "enduring truths" (1975, p.54). Many commentators suggest that, at the very least, although applied research and evaluation research share methods, evaluation is always differentiated from applied academic research by its purpose and emphasis.

> The stereotypes are as follows: Research is knowledge-oriented; evaluation is decision-oriented. Research derives from themes and principles; evaluation is atheoretical or, at least, diffuse and eclectic in its sources of inspiration and hypotheses. Research provides generalizable knowledge in the form of new themes and principles without necessarily offering immediate practical pay-off; evaluation provides immediate practical pay-off without necessarily providing generalizable knowledge. (Anderson and Ball, 1978, pp.9–10)

However, as argued in Chapter 1, such a clear-cut distinction between what is specifically labelled as "evaluation research" and much applied and action research into organizational change is too sweeping. Much evaluation research is highly sophisticated both theoretically and methodologically and seeks to contribute to the advancement of academic knowledge and as well as providing an input into policy-making (e.g. Campbell, 1969; Campbell and Erlebacher, 1970; Pressman and Wildavsky, 1973). In contrast, much action research aims at practical improvements in the design of organizational structures and processes as well as adding to our understanding of organizational behaviour (e.g. Bate and Mangham, 1981; Warr *et al.*, 1978). And such a distinction ignores the covert career functions both evaluation and "applied" researchers may wish their studies to serve. Ironically while the "applied", "academic" researchers may be interested in the "practical" applications of their work, in order to secure lucrative part-time consultancy assignments (a characteristic noted among Business School academics for example), evaluation researchers may be interested in enhancing the knowledge generating aspects of their work, in order to secure academic posts. For as Weiss (1972a, p.9; 1973, pp.52–53) has pointed out many evaluation researchers regard evaluation research as "second best" to academic pure or applied research and aspire to return to such work both for its own sake and for the greater security that a tenured academic post offers as compared to the generally short-term evaluation contracts. In these circumstances although the overt learning function of the evaluation may be decision-oriented, the evaluator's covert learning intention may be to achieve discipline based learning about basic processes in order to gain reputation with and secure an entree to an academic peer group. The aspiration may indeed be quite compatible with the decision-oriented function, if policy decisions are involved which call for an experimental or rigorous quasi-experimental evaluation design. The decision-oriented and knowledge-oriented learning functions may come into conflict though if the decisions to which the evaluator is supposed to contribute are more of a tactical nature, and the information required of the evaluator utilizes rather than contributes to discipline based knowledge. If the evaluator then attempts to develop a knowledge-oriented rather than decision study, perhaps by trying to persuade the decision-maker that he or she is asking the wrong questions or by developing personal research "on the side" to the detriment of the time that should be spent on the commissioned evaluation, the resulting study is likely to lack relevance for the decision-maker and fail to be utilized.

When the study design to produce decision-oriented learning is also appropriate to knowledge-oriented learning, then the latter learning function is likely to be overt. If the two are incompatible and the evaluator pursues the latter to the detriment of the former (in terms of study design or resource allocation) then its function of knowledge-oriented learning may remain covert.

The covert functions of evaluation

By "covert" is understood those functions of evaluation which one or more stakeholders in the evaluation consider it inappropriate to admit to publicly or to all the other parties, mainly because it serves their interests to the possible detriment of those of the others. Typical covert functions might include:

(a) Rallying support/opposition to the change programme;

(b) Postponing a decision;

(c) Evading responsibility;

(d) Fulfilling grant requirements (Anderson and Ball, 1978; Weiss, 1972a).

All these add up to the function of maintaining a group or individual interest in the face of actual or potential opposition.

Rallying support/opposition to a change programme

Any change programme requires resources of time, money and people and, as such, particularly if the programme is large or highly innovatory, is likely to develop some sort of new institutional presence. Once that institutional presence has come into existence the individuals involved may become as interested in maintaining it, and with it, their jobs and promotion, as in the initial change programme itself. Thus, for example, although organizational development departments came into being to run programmes that would change organizational climate, once in existence, members sought to develop their range of activities in order to maintain their department's existence. Similarly, once a change programme has an institutional presence, it may attract opposition from other groups, not necessarily hostile to the objectives and processes the change programme embodies, but competing for the same set of resources, and their own institutional survival. A case in point would be supervisory opposition to schemes of job enrichment (Roberts and Wood, 1982). In these circumstances evaluation may be used not to facilitate rational decision-making about a programme's continuation, modification or termination, but in order to generate support for or opposition to the programme's institutional sponsors' demands for further resources.

Evaluation may also serve this rallying function when, quite apart from their own institutional survival, a programme's supporters genuinely believe that the programme deserves further financial support on the strength of its intrinsic merits—or when its detractors genuinely believe that it is at worst misguided or at best less deserving of limited funds than other potential programmes. The "Garrison Case" cited by Alkin *et al.* (1979, pp.157–201) provides a clear illustration of evaluation being used to rally a sceptical community's support for bilingual education and, ultimately, to secure further funding. In contrast Anderson and Ball (1978, pp.154–155) reference a true but anonymous case of an attempt on the part of a conservative school board, under siege from the liberal elements of its predominantly white middle-class constituency, to use evaluation to discredit the small scale experimental busing programme it had been forced to concede, in order to nip in the bud any potential large-scale extension. Furthermore, Klein's (1976, pp.141–178) account of her battles in Esso Petroleum, as a socio-technical systems change agent resisting takeover by organizational development consultants from the Institute of Social Research, Michigan, whom she believed to be misguided, indicates a situation where systematic evaluation research could have played a supportive role.

When evaluation is deliberately used to rally support or opposition to a change programme, an implicit assumption on the part of the evaluation's instigators is that the result will support whichever case they wish to make. When the supporters or detractors of a programme genuinely believe in its virtues or deficiencies, the information provided by an evaluation is sought merely by way of confirmation. Not surprising then is their reaction if the findings are either ambiguous or in the opposite direction to that expected and desired. When the findings are ambiguous the likelihood is that the evaluation sponsors will put pressure on the evaluators to interpret and present them in the desired light (Brickell, 1976; Guba, 1975). This may not necessarily be done cynically. Particularly if the evaluation sponsors are also involved in running the change programme, they may genuinely believe that their intuitive and clinical judgements have identified positive benefits that the evaluators' instruments have failed to detect or have underrated. Such assertions were frequently made in the early 1970s by organizational development consultants who claimed to experience positive changes in organizational climate in spite of minimal changes in scores on attitudinal measures and no measured change in behaviour (Friedlander and Brown, 1974; White and Mitchell, 1976). But, as Weiss (1973, pp.51–52) points out, not only do "practitioners have to believe in what they are doing; evaluators have to doubt" but they may consider their "own clinical judgement as a better guide than aggregate data on crude and oversimplified measures". If the results are unequivocally in the opposite direction to what was expected, however, the evaluation sponsors may simply ignore or even suppress them. Such was the fate of the evaluation results obtained in the minority busing case, cited by Anderson and Ball, referred to earlier, while Feldman and March (1981) cite similar examples of evaluative information ignored or discounted in decisions about governmental support for the development of a commercial supersonic aircraft (Merewitz and Sosnick, 1971), about investment in a new manufacturing facility (Bower, 1970) and about buying and installing packaging equipment in the manufacturing department of a Swedish firm (Hägg, 1977).

Postponing a decision and evading responsibility

These two functions of evaluation have been identified by Weiss (1972a, p.11). Briefly, and to summarize Weiss, evaluation, in order to postpone a decision, can be used in the same way as appointing a committee and awaiting its report. However, as Weiss points out, commissioning an evaluation study can be even more effective, as it is likely to take longer.

Evaluation can also be used by decision-makers who, being pressed to arbitrate and choose between two competing viewpoints, desire a potential scapegoat for their decisions, in case, at a later date, the decisions prove misguided. Also, by effectively handing over the decision-making to the evaluators, decision-makers do not have to openly align themselves to either interest group, thus preserving greater freedom of action by not making enemies, even if sacrificing the support of potential friends. This use of evaluation may superficially resemble its use to provide data to inform rational decision-making. The difference is that the intention in the first case is to improve the quality of the decision-making, in the second the intention is to off-load the decision-making function and establish a potential scapegoat, irrespective of the resulting quality of the decision. The former requires a well-designed evaluation study; with the latter the fact of its existence is more important than the quality of its design.

Fulfilling grant requirements

Some evaluation studies are commissioned purely because the funder of the change programme (whether "Head Office", or a government body) requires them as a condition of the funding. This is particularly prevalent when the change programmes in question involve social change initiatives and when their funding is from public money. On both counts issues of public accountability are involved and, whether justice is done or not, some form of justice must be seen to be done. The problem is that the type of evaluation study most frequently prescribed by funders (particularly government bodies), a summative or impact study, is neither immediately helpful and may be a positive liability to the programme staff who have undertaken the evaluation themselves or cooperated with independent evaluators. An impact study inhibits the programme staff from making such day-to-day modifications that their experience of the programme might suggest are desirable. At the same time, while potentially preventing the staff from doing the "best" job they can, it may be used to judge them as well as the programme's success (or lack of it). In these circumstances, if the evaluation is conducted by the programme staff themselves, it may degenerate into a ritual exercise; if conducted by independent evaluators, the programme staff may either have little incentive to cooperate, or may even find ways of subtly sabotaging the evaluators' research. A good example of just such sabotage is provided by Anderson and Ball (1978, pp.158–159), where a remedial teacher who felt personally under threat, undermined the evaluation by delaying pre-testing until the programme was underway and then, "mistakenly" post-tested only those children who had not already been pre-tested!

The meta function of evaluation

The overt and covert functions evaluation can serve for the parties involved in a change programme are essentially expressions of the *meta-function* all evaluations serve. *That is, to either sustain, or question the status quo.* As this meta-function of evaluation lies at the heart of the accreditation crisis, I do not intend to elaborate upon it here, but to deal with it and its implications for evaluation design in Chapter 6.

Summary

Each of the stakeholders in an evaluation will wish it to serve a number of overt and covert functions. Because change programmes almost inevitably involve changes in the allocation of scarce resources and hence are invariably political, it is likely that the decision-making environment in which they are developed and evaluated will be less than "scientifically" rational and that the covert functions of evaluation, at least to some of the parties involved, will be as important if not more important than the overt ones. As Weiss (1975, p.15) has commented, programme administrators and operators are not necessarily irrational—they just have a "different model of rationality in mind"—a political model that involves considerations of "building long-term support for the programme".

It was suggested at the beginning of this chapter that the different stakeholders in an evaluation may require it to serve different functions, and have different views about the priority of these functions. Having looked in detail at the functions an evaluation may serve, I now suggest that the groups identified earlier tend to have the following types of requirement: (1) Those *funding* a change programme are likely to require information for policy making decisions, such as whether to continue the programme, expand it or extend it to other settings. In so far as this decision-making process approaches at least a bounded rationality, and the decision-makers have a genuine commitment to the change programmes overt objectives and no pre-existing strong preferences or prejudices about means–ends relationships, their requirement is likely to be for hard data about outcomes. "To what extent did the chosen means (the change programme) achieve its objectives". However, if their real objective for the change programme is largely political, to show the unions that management cares about the workforce, to bolster the importance of a particular plant or department, or to placate interest groups that something was being done about an important social issue, then the provision of hard outcome data may be of little importance as the policy decisions will be made on grounds that have little to do with the real as opposed to political impact of the programme. In such circumstances a statistically rigorous summative evaluation might even prove an embarrassment. What is required instead is an evaluation that tells the good news.

(2) Those *designing* the programme are likely to require information that, in particular, tests the theory on which the design is based, that is, the underlying hypotheses about means–end relationships. Their interest is less likely to be in identifying the existence and size of the programme's impact for its own sake (which would be of interest to the policy-maker), than for what it says about the theory on which their design is based. Equally the programme designers may wish to compare the relative impact of different programme strategies. This is a similar position to that of many applied academic researchers in organizational behaviour, who have become involved in action research programmes, designing and assessing the effectiveness of new payment systems (e.g. Bowey, 1982), work systems (e.g. Hackman and Oldham, 1976; Mumford and Henshall, 1979; Wall and Clegg, 1981) and participatory processes (e.g. Warr *et al.* 1978). At the same time however, (in contrast to academic researchers who may only fear further access problems) programme designers who are organizational members may be only too aware that an evaluation that shows little or no impact, may have implications for their career prospects and their department's influence in the organization. In these circumstances there may exist a tension between what programme designers require from an evaluation from their professional standpoint and what they require to maintain their career prospects and departmental influence in the organization. If the programme designers are academics or consultants external to the organization in which the change programme is to take place, other considerations may prevail. The more academic the institution they come from, the more likely they are to be interested in testing the theory on which the design is based, irrespective of results, as rigorous work in this area may also further their academic careers for the contribution to knowledge it provides.

The more commercial the consultancy institution from which the consultants are drawn the more likely they are to resemble policy makers in their desire that the evaluation tells the good news, as to a greater extent than in the case of more "academic" consultants their future existence depends on customer satisfaction, which in turn is likely to depend on "good" results.

However, this is not to imply that design consultants from reputable commercial agencies will be only interested in "good news" evaluations (hopefully, their professionalism will guard against that) merely that, in career terms, they can make less use of an evaluation, however rigorous, that showed that the design of the change programme was not successful than an academically oriented programme designer.

(3) Those *implementing* the programme are likely to require information less on the theory behind its strategies and general approach, than information on tactics. For example, if the strategy towards a particular type of change involves a training programme, implementers may be more interested in such matters as optimal group size, should more emphasis be placed on group discussions, films or lectures, than even on which training philosophy should be tested. Because their involvement is with an ongoing programme rather than with theories and strategies that can be generalized to other programmes, the implementers are likely to want feedback rapidly that will help them do better today rather than have to wait for information that would enable them to act perfectly tomorrow—when the programme is over. Hence, in contrast to the "rational" policy-makers, and the more academically oriented designers, their interest is less likely to centre on long-term issues of ultimate impact and outcomes than on the day-to-day processes and possible modifications to the change programme. As far as their covert evaluation requirements go, implementers may well wish that some account is taken of the difficulties and constraints faced in implementation, whether resulting from a poor initial design of the change programme, or lack of resources or administrative problems outside their control. In their desire for an evaluation not to unfairly scapegoat them, implementers share a common ground with designers. But whereas designers may be anxious that any test of their designs takes account of inadequate implementation, the implementers are anxious that problems in implementation resulting from unrealistic or just plain bad designs should not be laid at their door. Where those designing a change programme are not closely involved in its implementation, the different evaluation interests of the two are likely to be most pronounced—particularly if the designers are external consultants who can walk away from the problems their change programme may create, while implementers may be somewhat less than willing conscripts to the programme (as was the case with *some* of the implementers of the Shell "New Philosophy of Management" programme referred to earlier). However, the use of evaluation to avoid scapegoating illustrates the other side of its function as a control mechanism—evaluation can be both threatening *and* protective depending on where one stands.

(4) The *clients* of a change programme, paradoxically, may be less likely than the other stakeholders involved to have any articulated views about what functions the evaluation should serve for them. Most change programmes,

whether social or organizational, tend to place the client into the role of a passive recipient, or the "subject" of whatever manipulations are to take place. In many cases, the individuals involved, for example, schoolchildren, production workers, have no choice, or no direct say, in whether they wish to be involved. As the least powerful participants in the change programme, the only way they can often make their opinions felt about the programme is by "dropping out" (if participation is voluntary) or refusing to fully co-operate if it is not. As such they may have departed from the programme, whether in body or in spirit, before the evaluation takes place. Furthermore, particularly in the case of social change programmes, the direct clients, for example schoolchildren, disadvantaged families and so on, may not even be fully aware than an evaluation is taking place. They may not relate the tests they are given or the questions they are asked to an evaluation study—indeed they may even be unclear about just what an evaluation study is. Depending on the evaluation design (for example, where observation is an important research tool) it may be considered methodologically necessary to keep at least the direct clients "in the dark" about the fact that an evaluation is taking place at all.

However, apart from the direct clients (those actually participating in the change programme) there exists its indirect clients (e.g. the parents of children involved in a change programme, union officials, the "community" and so on). These clients, along with those direct clients who are aware that an evaluation is taking place and understand the concept, are likely to wish it to be responsive to *their* needs as *they* define them. This may involve demands that they have some say in the criteria selected for judging the value of the programme, and some voice in identifying its unintended consequences. In other words, the clients of a change programme are likely to wish that some of the "facts" for decision-making produced by the evaluation will be their assessment of the success or failure of the programme, judged against their criteria, even if these differ from those chosen by the administrators and policy-makers. This issue of values in evaluation—be they utilitarian or justice-as-fairness (House, 1976; Keeley, 1978; Sjöberg, 1975) will be considered in detail in Chapter 6.

Evaluation functions, evaluation design and the problem of compatibility

In Chapter 1 it was suggested that, at the level of action, evaluation findings are often ignored by one or more parties to a change of programme, because they are perceived to be of "little relevance". That is, of course, little relevance to the particular functions that each of the groups involved wish the evaluation study to serve. But as has been indicated in this chapter, this state of affairs is hardly surprising. Not only may different interest groups differ in the overt functions they wish an evaluation study to serve, but in the covert functions also. The latter case is particularly likely because covert functions, by definition, cannot be openly discussed and made explicit between different groups and individuals. Furthermore, the functions any one group may subscribe to are not necessarily internally consistent. For example, those implementing the programme may want information from which to learn how to improve it, but not at the expense of highlighting their "mistakes" and so jeopardizing future funding and career progression.

In these circumstances the selection of an evaluation design that will produce findings perceived as relevant to all stakeholders in the change programme is well nigh an impossibility. Depending on what function of the evaluation is to serve will depend what is meant by relevant and valid data, which in turn will dictate evaluation research methods. The problem is that some methods, as will be discussed in the next two chapters, are mutually incompatible. To add to this dilemma, is the problem that if the evaluation researcher seeks to overcome this difficulty by basing the research design on the (hopefully) consistent functions sought by one group other thorny issues are raised. On what basis should the group to be served be selected and how should the relevant selection criteria be ordered? If the researcher opts to serve the funders and policy-makers and neglects the interests of the implementers, the information may exist on which to base a decision to continue the programme, but not on how to improve it. Alternatively, if the needs of the implementers are given priority much may be learnt about how to improve the programme, but the policy-makers may feel that no relevant information has been provided to enable them to decide whether to expand or even continue the programme—and the programme may be abandoned by default. These issues are considered further in Chapters 6 and 7.

First, however, in the next two chapters, I explore the question of which research methods are appropriate for producing information to meet the various functions that evaluation may serve, and which of these are likely, either in theory or in practice, to prove mutually incompatible.

Chapter 4

Matching Positivistic Designs and Evaluation Functions

In Chapter 3 it was suggested that not only do the different stakeholders in an evaluation wish it to serve different and potentially incompatible functions, but that these functions call for different and potentially incompatible evaluation designs. In this chapter I examine those which may be served by positivistic designs, while pointing out their practical and theoretical limitations. Also, those evaluation functions which cannot be served by such designs are indicated. But, first, although the subject was briefly touched upon in Chapter 1, it is necessary to clarify precisely what is meant here by "positivistic" designs.

Core characteristics of a positivistic design

Any research design is both derived from and is an expression of the paradigmatic position held by the researcher. A paradigm, as defined by Kuhn (1970) is a set of interrelated assumptions about the social world which provides a philosophical and conceptual framework for the systematic study of that world. These assumptions are ontological (about the nature of reality), epistemological (about the grounds of knowledge, about how people know, what they know and what the limits of that knowledge might be) and methodological (about the methods to be employed to gain knowledge about reality). The methodological assumptions essentially are derived from the epistemological which, in turn, are derived from the ontological assumptions of the researcher. Hence any evaluation design derives basically from a particular (in this case, positivistic) world view held by the evaluator.

Following Burrell and Morgan (1979, p.5) the term "positivistic" is used here to characterize a paradigm "which seek(s) to explain and predict what happens in the social world by searching for regularities, and causal relationships between its constituent elements". Let us take in turn the key words in this definition: *"explain"*, *"predict"*, *"regularities"*, *"casual relationships"*, *"constituent elements"*, and consider briefly their implications.

In a positivistic paradigm, explanation and prediction rest on a hypothetico-deductive epistemology. This consists of deducing a hypothesis(es) according to known rules, from a set of initial premises or theory, which is then tested by (among other things) observation and experiment to ascertain whether the theory has explanatory power. Because the hypothesis is deduced from a theory, the theory *explains* the hypothesis, and assuming the observation or experimental result is consistent with the hypothesis, the theory explains this also. But even if the hypothesis is so supported by observation or experiment, it cannot be assumed that the theory is necessarily true, as the hypothesis might be deduced from alternative theories. If, however, the observation or experiment contradicts the hypothesis, according to rules of logic, one or more of the initial conditions of the theory and or its assertions is false. Hence, if the initial conditions have been validated and the findings are reliable, then the theory, or part of it, must be false. From this logic derives a core characteristic of the hypothetico-deductive approach: the criterion of reproducible falsification for the empirical testing of a theory. As Cohen (1980, p.248) puts it "testability requires the ability to define what would constitute negative evidence for the theory".

From this it follows that a second characteristic of the hypothetico-deductive approach is that it is only concerned with theories that generate testable hypotheses. And this, in itself, makes *prediction* central to the approach. For, to quote Cohen (1980, p.248) again, "if a theory makes no predictions about observations, no evidence can falsify it". For a theory to make predictions, there must be at least one set of initial conditions that can be attached to the theory and, in order to arrive at this, there must be agreed some indicators relevant to the concepts in theory. Furthermore time and place scope conditions need to be made explicit, so that it is not possible to "rationalise a disconfirmed hypothesis as being outside the domain of applicability of the theory" (Cohen, 1980, p.248).

The emphasis on *regularities* and *casual relationships* between the social world's *constituent elements* also stems from a hypothetico-deductive world view. The hypotheses which this perspectives derives from theory tend to be of two sorts, (1) those which focus on the "true" nature of the phenomena under examination, and (2) those which seek to establish connections between them. (That these connections are conceptualized in causal—or functional—terms is implicit both in the "if . . . then" approach of deductive logic and, empirically speaking, in the very notion of "regularities" in the behaviour of phenomena—it is the causal relationships between them that is generally assumed to give rise to the observed regularities.) Examining phenomena in this way, rests on the ontological assumption that the world "out there" has an existence which is independent of the processes through which it is researched (Pollner, 1970, p.38). According to Durkheim this is justifiable because "whenever men come to interact together, they produce an emergent level of reality which is distinct from that of the individuals, and which is external to such individuals and exercises control over their actions". This reality is an objective world of "social facts" which, no less than natural phenomena, may consequently be treated as "things", or, specifiable, observable, measurable variables.

The criticism that social phenomena cannot be treated in this way because the social world is a world constituted by meaning (unlike the natural world which has no intrinsic meaning structure) is neatly sidestepped by treating meaning as an intervening variable. Hence

> Actors' meanings are not ignored . . . rather they are turned into variables themselves such as cultural prescriptions, role expectations, norms, values, interests and so on, which can, themselves, be identified in terms of objective indices. Such variables are given independent status vis à vis the actor, in the sense that he is conceived of as the passive vehicle of their operations . . . By focusing on such stabilised social meanings as intervening variables, rather than upon how the actor operates such meanings, explanation can proceed by way of analysing action as to the product of the mechanical association of variables within an external social world. (Walsh, 1972, p.42)

The essence of a positivistic paradigm, therefore, is that explanation is sought through testing hypotheses derived from predictive theories, the testing taking the form of attempts to establish causal connections between specified "objective" variables. This clearly has several implications for the methodological characteristics of a positivistic design and the evaluation functions it can best serve. The methodological implications of this position are:

(1) A concern with establishing experimental controls in order to eliminate the effect of potentially intervening variables upon hypothesized causal relationships, so that valid causal inferences may be drawn. This concern for controlling for "intervening variables" of course derives directly from the way positivists conceptualize causality, not in terms of the activity of an agent or some generative mechanism but in terms of three conditions: that the variables in question tend to appear together, that the variable hypothesized as causal temporally precedes the other variable, *that their relation is not a result of a common relation to a third variable.*

(2) A concern with specifying initial conditions and time and scope conditions so that the degree of generalizability of any causal influences drawn, may also be established.

(3) A concern with "hard" i.e. quantitative, data about the nature of variables and their relationships. Because social phenomena no less than natural phenomena are considered to have an objective reality, not only can they be measured but, tautologically, their *measurability is a prerequisite of their status as social "facts"*. Furthermore, the establishment of causal relationships is seen to involve measurement, that is, the measurement of the covariation of variables, within a controlled setting, as the existence of a relationship is confirmed by the strength of the covariation.

(4) A concern with specifying the nature of the variables as a prerequisite to their measurement.

In terms of the functions evaluation research may serve, the implications of a positivistic approach are:

(1) That it is, in principle, best suited to assessing the *impact* of a change programme on the individuals or situations the programme seeks to change, because of its aim to produce "hard facts" about cause and effect relationships. As such it may assist decision-makers in reaching strategic decisions concerning the continuation, expansion and/or contraction, of a change programme, *if* the decision-makers wish and are able to make their decisions rationally, on the basis of the "facts" of the situation. As discussed in the previous chapter this may not always be the case: if the decision is a major one with important implications for resource allocation, political factors (with either a large or small "p") are likely to influence the rationality of the process; if the decision is less important, the typical management pattern of time allocation is likely to dictate a "muddling through" decision-making style, in any case.

(2) Because the positivistic paradigm is dominant in "normal" science (Kuhn, 1970) and because it emphasizes objectivity (both in the sense that the researcher stands "outside" the facts, and, by virtue of his methods, assesses them impartially) positivistic designs tend to be regarded by informed laymen as reputable, unbiased and capable of establishing the "true facts" of a situation. As such they are theoretically appropriate when the evaluation is intended to serve a public accountability function — no matter that this function in practice is particularly in demand when large sums of money, and hence, political considerations are involved, which conversely may undermine the potential contribution of hard facts to decision-making! Associated with the public accountability function, is the broader control function, as discussed in the previous chapter.

(3) Again, because of the dominance of the positivistic paradigm in the scientific community, positivistic designs are often selected by the academically oriented evaluator to fulfil career advancement functions. In principle, such designs may assist his/her career by generating "enduring truths" about causal relationships and, failing that, if the results are non-significant,

at least they may be regarded as methodologically sound by potential academic colleagues and prestigious journals, such as *Journal of Applied Psychology* and *Administrative Science Quarterly*.

(4) Quite apart from career advancement functions, positivistic designs may be selected to fulfil learning functions *per se*, as discussed in the previous chapter.

These then are some of the methodological and functional implications of adopting a positivistic paradigm. In *principle*, positivistic designs are appropriate to some of the evaluation functions discussed in Chapter 3. The question is, though, how do these theoretical "matches" work out in practice? Do the constraints of a field setting so undermine the implementation of tenets of positivistic design that the hard facts sought to satisfy decision-making and accountability functions are more apparent than real? To consider these questions it is necessary to look at actual positivistic designs in field settings.

Positivistic designs in field settings

In this section the extent to which the tenets of positivism are capable of being implemented or become compromised out of existence in a field setting are considered. The key issues here are those reflected in the methodological implications of positivism, raised earlier. In other words

(1) Can the effect of potentially intervening variables upon hypothesized causal relationships be eliminated—or at least accounted for—so that valid causal inferences can be drawn? That is, can potential threats to the internal validity of an evaluation design be successfully surmounted? (This is to assume of course that it is first possible to show that a cause is related to a presumed effect, irrespective of whether the relationship may be causal. In other words to establish by correct use of inferential statistics, what Cook *et al.* (1977, pp.107–109) have termed "statistical conclusion" validity.)

(2) Is it possible to attain a reasonable degree of generalizability from an evaluation? That is, can we protect and develop both the construct validity of an evaluation design (the validity with which inferences are made about general constructs on the basis of particular change programmes/manipulations) and its external validity (validity of inferences to, and across, persons, settings and times)?

(3) Can the impediments to using quantitative methods in the specification and measurement of relevant variables and relationships be overcome?

(4) Can the "outsider" role of the "objective" researcher be maintained in a field setting?

I will take each of these issues in turn.

The problem of internal validity — establishing cause
and effect in evaluation

What are the major threats to the internal validity of a positivistic evaluation
design? In their seminal paper, Campbell and Stanley (1963), later echoed
by other researchers (e.g. Riecken and Boruch, 1974) list nine major threats
which may be clustered into several broad categories (Alwin and Sullivan,
1976).

(1) *Selection:* Problems of selection processes resulting in prechange
differences between comparison units of analyses (individuals or groups,
experimental or controls) making it difficult to unequivocally attribute post-
change differences to the change programme.

The problems associated with selection are likely to emerge precisely
because it *is* a change programme that is being evaluated. Because the change
is seen to be "good" in some sense, it is unlikely that those selected to
participate will be a random selection of the population. Either they are likely
to be more "deserving", whether defined in terms of greater perceived "need"
through disadvantage (as in many social programmes) or greater perceived
likelihood of benefitting from the programme through above average abilities
(as in many academic or vocational training programmes) than potential
control groups or the population at large. Or, they may have self-selected
themselves to participate and, hence, at least in motivational terms, be
qualitatively different from non-volunteers. Conversely, the evaluator's
selection among participants may be constrained by expediency. For example,
only those participants that were prepared to be interviewed or tested might
be selected, or only the organizational development programmes in
organizations that were prepared to grant access.

An example of some of these potential selection biases operating is provided
by the Rushton Quality of Work Experiment, a change programme involving
the experimental introduction of autonomous work groups into a coal mine
(Goodman, 1979). The first experimental crews were, in general, volunteers,
but selected from a larger pool on the basis of seniority. The exceptions were
the three mechanics, who were assigned by management, none having
volunteered. The volunteers cited both a higher pay rate and learning
opportunities as their motivation for volunteering. "This would probably
indicate a willingness or openness to change, a possible biasing factor"
(Goodman, 1979, p.143). Goodman's study shows a sophisticated awareness
of potential selection problems, which is not always evident, even in classic
studies of evaluating change programmes. The famous Hawthorne studies,
for example, reveal a relaxed and sometimes misguided approach to selection.
Referring to the selection of operators for the Relay Test room, the researchers
comment "it was desirable that the girls selected should be willing and

co-operative, in order that their reactions to the changing conditions of the test would be normal and genuine". Hence "the method adopted for selecting such a group was to invite two experienced operators who were known to be friendly with each other to participate in the test and ask them to choose the remaining members of the group" (Roethlisberger and Dickson, 1939, p.21).

Related to the selection problem is that of regression artifacts. In other words, when individuals or groups are selected to participate in a change programme upon the basis of their extreme pre-change score on the relevant dependant variable (for example, scores of any aptitude test) any post-change shifts in their scores may simply reflect a regression to the mean rather than any real change effect.

As Cummings *et al.* (1977, p.704), referring to the evaluation of work design experiments, put it: "if a group is chosen because it is composed of, say, people who are most disgruntled, or because it is the newest plant, or because it offers the greatest possibility of success, the findings will be subject to threats from regression". But it is precisely with such groups that the management of the organization are likely to be most interested in experimenting — as in the case of the Volvo experiments at Kalmar, where the newest plant was chosen and the greatest possibility of success envisaged. If this occurs, the evaluator then has a difficult problem of sorting out genuine change effects from the pseudo-effects of statistical artifacts.

A further problem is what Campbell and Stanley (1963) have termed "maturation" and "selection–maturation interaction". Maturation is when the changes observed in the units of analysis may be a function of the passage of time *per se*, irrespective of the change programme. Selection–maturation interaction is when selection biases, of the types discussed above, result in differential rates of such autonomous change.

The Rushton experiment again provides an example of this maturation problem. Prior to the experimental introduction of autonomous working groups, a gradual improvement in previously poor industrial relations was underway. Indeed without the improvement it would have been impossible for the change programme to have been initiated. However, since one criteria for the programme's success was the improvement of the quality of industrial relations, it was necessary to separate out the experimental from the maturation effects. As Goodman (1979, p.121) points out, this presented problems as the control groups were equally influenced by these maturation effects, and analytical procedures to separate out differential effects were inadequate as number of observations (e.g. of walkouts) was small.

(2) *History:* Problems of the occurrence of events, other and unrelated to the change programme, producing rival explanations of the effects which would otherwise be attributed to it.

A typical example here might be the effects of a strike on the monthly output rates of an experimental group in circumstances when the control group and its output rates, were not affected. When the event is clearly identifiable and its effects measurable, the problem is not too difficult to overcome—for example the effects of the 1974 coal strike on the Rushton experiment (Goodman, 1979). The problems occur when the effects of the event are difficult to measure, yet when there is a strong likelihood that they are influencing the scores on the outcome variables of both experimental and control groups differentially, or of one alone.

(3) *Measurement error:* Problems of random and non-random measurement error in the evaluation design.

A typical random measurement error might occur when changes in the measuring instrument, independent of the level of the variable being measured, leads to changes in obtained measurements (for example, a change of interviewer may produce different scores on a post change as compared to a pre-change observation). A typical non-random measurement error, referred to as "testing" may occur when, through a process of sensitization, the scores on a first test or responses to a preliminary interview influence the scores on a second.

(4) *Mortality:* The differential loss of respondents from comparison groups, either due to factors associated with selection processes, or to the change programme itself, or to events after the selection processes unrelated to the change programme.

One problem with any longitudinal study is that respondents may leave the organization or department in which the change programme takes place. For example Lawler *et al.* (1973, p.52) noted that by the time they came to administer their post-change questionnaire (about the effects the redesign of the job of directory assistance operators in a telephone company) "because of turnover, scheduling problems, and because some operators had stopped doing the directory assistance job in order to work on the toll job full-time, only 17 (out of 39) of the operators present for the first administration were present for the second." A consequence of this is that sample size becomes smaller and thus precludes certain types of data analysis. More dangerously, it confounds interpreting the results. Would those subjects who left have changed, or reacted to changes in the same direction as those that remained? An analysis of the characteristics of people who left versus those who stay is one strategy for determining whether mortality *per se* is likely to be a significant contaminator. A further problem is that of differential mortality, when respondents leave the experimental and control groups in different numbers and at different rates. Differential mortality associated with selection processes is a risk particularly prevalent in research designs where the participants in a change programme are volunteers, but the control group is selected by the evaluator, and lacks the volunteers' motivation. It is also prone to arise where participants perceive that different costs or benefits are associated with different roles they might play in the research design—as in the New Jersey Negative Income Tax Experiment, in which attrition from the experiment after the three-year period, ranged from 24·3% in the control condition to 6·5% in the highest pay condition.

In essence these threats to the internal validity of a research design all constitute rival explanations of any observed variations in the dependent variables following the intervention of a change programme, thus potentially denying the genuineness of its effects. How can these problems be overcome?

By use of the Experimental Method?

The die-hard positivist would argue that there is only one way of avoiding these rival explanations and that is by designing a "true" experiment. Essentially an experiment involves the establishing of theory-derived hypotheses about the likely effects of the independent variable—the change programme—upon the dependent variables, and the random assignment of units (individuals, work groups, organizations) to two groups—an "experimental" and a "control" group. While the first step, hypothesis generation, is necessary for causal inferences to be drawn from subsequently observed conditions, it is the second step, *random assignment, which rules out any competing explanations of the observed changes.* For random assignment protects comparability between experimental and control groups by ensuring at the outset that they differ only through the operation of chance factors (which may largely be accounted for through statistical inference). This comparability, in composition (similar mixes of people or other units in both groups), in experiences (experience same time-related processes during the period of observation) and in predisposition (self-selection tendencies same in both groups) eliminates most internal validity threats because these mainly arise from attempting to compare non-comparable groups. Once comparability is assured then observed differences between experimental and control groups, following a change programme, can be reasonably attributed to the change programme (as a result of the first step of hypothesis generation) and not to differences in composition between the groups. The problem is, though, how easy is it to achieve random assignment in a field situation?

Randomization. It is ironic that while social change programmes generally afford fewer practical difficulties in implementing randomization, they afford potential ethical ones, while in the case of organizational change, where the ethical dilemmas may be muted, the practical difficulties are often insurmountable.

Ethical dilemmas, being more of an issue in social experimentation may be dealt with briefly. The argument is that on the assumption that the change programme constitutes some "good", it should not be withheld from a control group who might benefit from it or benefit from it "most" (Borgatta, 1955; Connor, 1980; Ward, 1973). Happily there are ways round this dilemma, as far as evaluating the change goes. If all stakeholding audiences are already convinced that the change programme is so "good" that ethical problems are presented by a denial of it to a control group, in effect an informal evaluation has already taken place, which at least will influence the acceptance of any systematic evaluation and at worst render it a waste of time. Hence an evaluator may escape this dilemma by arguing that in such circumstances evaluation is too late. Alternatively an evaluator may suggest a *comparative* evaluation between change programmes, so that taking two experimental groups each receives one "good" and effectively acts as the other's control (e.g. McDill *et al.*, 1969; Morse and Reimer, 1956), or argue that randomization is a just allocative principle if there are insufficient resources for all who need or want to participate in the change programme to do so. Furthermore the evaluator may suggest that, if in spite of beliefs in the positive benefits of the programme, some negative side effects cannot be ruled out, then randomization is fairer. Also, he or she may argue, if valid unambiguous *evidence* (which, according to the positivist can best be achieved by randomization) can be obtained about the effectiveness of the programme, reinforcing present *beliefs*, then more resources may be allocated and more people ultimately served. However, these are rational arguments and are only likely to prevail to the degree to which decision-making processes are rational. If the decision is seen as political and if consumer groups are considered to have little real understanding of randomization principles, the less likelihood these arguments will prevail, even assuming that the decision-makers want "hard facts" that may threaten cosy beliefs.

In work organizations, randomization is rarely feasible due to management's desire for change programmes to be implemented in relation to "real" intact work groups or departments and unions' objections to "high-handed" and apparently arbitrary allocation of their membership within the firm's internal labour market. Goodman (1979, p.119) comments on the impossibility of even seeking randomization of workers between experimental and control groups in the Rushton Quality of Work experiment. Wall and Clegg (1981), in reference to their own work system design experiments in a confectionery factory make the telling point that it is not even "necessarily desirable" for "randomization cuts across established relationships, attitudes, skill-interdependencies, behaviours and practices that are critical aspects of working life, thus introducing a strong element of artificiality". It is not surprising, then, that it is virtually impossible to identify any programme of organizational change where true random assignment has been attempted for effective evaluation. Even if this was sought there are three major technical problems (quite apart from the practical difficulties already mentioned) that either impede initiating randomization, or undermine its integrity after initial implementation. There may be *no extra units* to serve as controls as the change programme is all embracing; there may be *differential mortality* (when individuals drop out of initially randomized experimental and control groups, possibly at different rates and for different reasons); the *"Hawthorne effect"* may develop. As the first problem is relevant to securing any constructed, non-reflexive control group, and the other two to maintaining the comparability of both randomized and non-randomized experimental and constructed control groups, a brief elaboration may be useful.

No "extra" units to serve as controls may occur if the change programme is designed to embrace all potential participants and can be offered to all without delay (i.e. without affording the evaluator the opportunity to select a control group which may receive the treatment at a significantly later date). This is likely to be a problem in a small organization, or where the change programme is only relevant to a particular group or category of employees (as in some payment system redesign exercises) (Gillespie, 1973).

Differential mortality, and its resulting problems has already been mentioned. However, there is the complicating problem, that in certain circumstances, it may actually constitute an outcome measure in its own right. For example, an organization participating in the "Youth Opportunities Programme", organized by the Manpower Services Commission in Britain, designed to provide work experience and training for unemployed school leavers, has the problem, in evaluating the success of its activities, of how to interpret mortality. If a young person "drops out" is this because she finds the programme "a waste of time" or because the programme has given her sufficient skill and confidence to secure regular employment?

Furthermore, there is the "pseudo-mortality" problem of evaluating the effects of any strategy, if participants in the experimental group remain within the measurement framework but participate differentially in the activities of the programme (for example, if some employees attend all training sessions, but others turn up only occasionally). In this case, if the results of the complete experimental sample are then compared with those of the control group, a conservative bias may be in-built, making the change programme look less effective than otherwise might appear. If, to compensate, supplementary analysis is undertaken, breaking down the experimental group according to some measure of the extent to which sub-sets of individuals really participated in the programme, there is then the problem of defining and measuring degrees of participation, and the inevitability of subjective post-facto assessments and the risk of attendant bias. Of course a practically, if not theoretically, similar problem occurs if the change programme is implemented variably, both quantitatively and qualitatively, by those responsible for its implementation. For example, trainers may differ in how much informal individual contact time, apart from formal group sessions, they allow trainees, and in the quality of that contact time. Possibly the best way of coping with these allied problems is at the implementation rather than the evaluation stage—by trying to ensure uniform treatment delivery via the training of the personnel involved and general monitoring of programme implementation. The latter strategy, though, particularly through the possibility of Hawthorne effects, may raise other problems in maintaining the internal validity of the experiment.

"Hawthorne effects" refer to the phenomenon whereby a positive response results from the fact of the attention participants receive, rather than being due to the effects of the programme *per se*. (Conversely, it has been broadened to include the negative responses on the part of controls, or those receiving less desirable treatments, due to their perceived unfavourable treatment.) Randomization, because it is likely to lead to a "focused inequality" (Cook *et al.*, 1977) between experimental groups and controls, is vulnerable to both these types of Hawthorne effect.

The solutions to these difficulties—easier stated than executed—are usually considered to be minimizing the obtrusiveness of the experiment, generally by isolating experimental from control groups, which may mean using fewer but larger units, for example, departments rather than work groups. However, if this is not practically feasible, bearing in mind the decision-makers need for "hard" data, the best that can be done is to attempt to establish whether these effects seem likely to have occurred and to what extent. This may be done by collecting pre-test time series data on controls, to establish whether the control group deviates sharply from its pre-treatment base-line, by comparing the control group's behaviours to those of comparable groups (not within the experimental frame) or even by collecting post-treatment time series data (on the assumption that if a Hawthorne effect is operating, whether positively or negatively on the control group, it should cease after the experiment has ended and the group's performance should revert to its pre-experimental base-line, other things being equal). It is more difficult to sort out by such means the extent of a positive Hawthorne effect on an experimental group, because of the problems of disentangling this effect from that of the treatment itself (except through possible reversals of the treatment, as in the original Hawthorne experiments, which are likely to be politically or ethically unacceptable to the administrators involved). However, in practice, few policy-makers or programme administrators are likely to worry about ruling out positive Hawthorne effects—particularly if what is sought is a "good news" evaluation proclaiming the programme's success.

Quite apart from these ethical and technical obstacles to implementing and maintaining randomization, there are often administrative blocks, such as cost (given the longitudinal nature of experiments and the mechanics of listing all eligible units) and the decision to evaluate being made only after the change programme has been under way for some time. In these circumstances threats to internal validity cannot be protected by randomization, so other "quasi-experimental designs" and non-experimental designs have to be resorted to. How effective are they in enabling causal inferences to be drawn?

Quasi-experimental attempts to protect internal validity

Quasi-experimental designs, in essence, attempt to protect internal validity (and hence allow the drawing of causal inferences) by achieving, without randomization, as close an equivalence between experimental and control groups as possible. Although theoretically speaking the lack of random assignment makes it dubious to draw causal inferences, in practice the guiding principle behind the design is to allow the evaluator to rule out specified individual threats to internal validity (such as selection or history) and hence to rule out alternative interpretations of any relationships that may be established between independent and dependent variables. In other words, quasi-experimentation is really aimed at allowing an evaluator to make a causal inference that would satisfy a reasonable man (competing explanations having been ruled out). How then (and how successfully) are the various threats to internal validity, discussed earlier, contained by quasi-experimental designs?

All quasi-experimental designs rest on the notion of a control group of some sort, for without a control group it would be impossible to infer that the change programme had caused any observed differences in the criterion variable. Take for example, an attempt in an industrial organization to reduce, say, absenteeism through a programme of job redesign. It is observed that absenteeism drops markedly from its pre-change levels over the period of the change and remains low a year after. But without a control group it is impossible to make causal inferences about this single group, pre-test–post-test change. History might be a factor, for example, rapidly increasing unemployment rates over the period may be influencing absence levels; statistical regression may have operated if the programme was introduced in response to abnormally high absence levels; and drawing general conclusions about the efficacy of job redesign may be impossible if the single experimental group is highly unrepresentative of the general population, or if there are likely to be selection–maturation effects (for example, as male workers get older and marry they tend to go absent less).

Control groups

The question then is what should be the nature of the control group (and in what sort of design should it be nested) in order to protect against these threats? Control groups can be of two basic types: the "constructed" or "non-equivalent" comparison groups on the one hand and the reflexive control group on the other. In the first case a control group may either be constructed by selecting individuals from a larger pool of potential participants or a pre-existing group may be selected that corresponds as closely as possible to the experimental groups on those characteristics which are assumed to have some influence on the social processes involved in the change and ultimately on its outcome. When the control group is constructed individual or aggregate matching can be done (i.e. either individual members of the experimental and control group who closely resemble each other on selected measures can be paired up, or the overall distributions on each matching variables can be made to correspond for the experimental and control groups as a whole). This was the procedure, for example, in constructing control groups in the Rushton experiment (Goodman, 1979) and the experiment in collaborative union-management problem-solving and change implementation conducted by Nurick (1982). But, although "constructed" or "non-equivalent" control groups should be selected on general grounds of similarity, they should not be selected on the basis of similarity of pre-test scores as this may generate regression artifacts (Campbell and Erlebacher, 1970). If either a constructed or non-equivalent comparison group is not practical, the second type of control group—a reflexive control—may be used. In other words, the experimental group, through the use of time series analysis, may serve as its own control group. This may be the most practical alternative in situations where self-selection may be an important determinant of change programme effectiveness, or when the experimental group is highly idiosyncratic in some way, or the change programme is all-embracing (as in some individualistic social change programmes involving universally applied legislation—such as breathalyser or seat-belt laws). Without doubt, it has been the procedure very frequently used in work system design experiments in organizations (Cummings *et al.*, 1977).

Interrupted time series with comparison series design

The strongest quasi-experimental design in terms of ruling out threats to internal validity is the interrupted time series with comparison series design. This design involves a series of measurements at periodic intervals before the change programme commences and continuing measures during the programme and after it ends. The same series of periodic measurements are then taken for a comparable (i.e. non-reflexive) control group. The strength of this design is that, if properly constructed (for example, if a sufficiently long pre- and post-change series of measurements is taken) it is possible to detect whether the measures taken immediately before and after the change programme are a continuation of earlier trends or whether they mark a decisive change. If they do mark a decisive change, and if internal validity threats have been controlled for, it is then possible to infer causal relationships between the change programme and behaviours reflected in outcome measures. How does this design control for threats to internal validity? Take the absenteeism example cited earlier. First, the existence of a comparison group (say within the same factory and labour market, matched for age, length of service, product line, pay level, supervision) rules out the threat of history (both groups will experience the same labour market, product market and control systems influences). If one group does experience an idiosyncratic event (e.g. a strike) its effects are amenable to identification. With a comparison group for which pre-test and post-test measurements have been taken (but without selection of the control group being based on the pre-test scores) selection threats are reduced. The existence of time-series analysis controls for regression artifacts—they can be identified as their existence must be assumed if the readings following an extreme departure from the overall trend revert to the overall trend. Time series analysis, along with a comparison group makes for easier detection of measurement errors, such as errors deriving from changes in record keeping. It also allows for the detection of maturation effects, by examining the ongoing trends.

Much quoted examples of the use of these designs are in relation to work system design changes, measuring performance changes, for example Coch and French (1948), Davis and Werling (1960), Ford (1969), Paul *et al.* (1969) and the Rushton experiments already cited (Goodman, 1979). Other changes to organizational control systems and working practices have been evaluated in this way though—for example, the effects of management by objectives programmes on subordinates' attitudes and performance (Ivancevich, 1974).

Coch and French's (1948) experiment, now of classic status, may illustrate this design. Conducted in a pyjama manufacturing factory, subject to continual work method changes and resistance to such changes, the experiment was designed to evaluate the effects of participation upon productivity and resistance to change. Three experimental and one control group were matched with respect to the efficiency ratings of the groups before transfer, the degree of work method change involved in the transfer, and the amount of "me-feeling" observed in the groups. For a control group of 18 individuals a change in methods was introduced in the usual manner. The work was redesigned by the production department, new payment rates were set, and workers informed of the changes. For three experimental groups, involving a total of 28 workers, the opportunity to participate in making the changes was provided. In one group this involved the participation of elected representatives, in the other two experimental groups, each worker was allowed to participate directly. Daily readings of production levels for each group were taken 11 days before the experiment began and for one month after, for each individual, for 40 days before the changes occurred and 30 days after. The rate of recovery in production levels was found to be proportional to the amount of participation involved. Interestingly the design allowed the identification of contamination effects — one experimental group's production figures for a period of seven days were depressed as they had insufficient material to work on. Turnover and grievance rates among experimental subjects were lower than among control subjects, but as only three workers, all from the control group, left the organization during the experimental period, statistical inferences could not be drawn.

Single interrupted time series design and pre-test–post-test comparison group design

Weaker designs than the interrupted time series with comparison series design are those which in effect constitute only part of that design, i.e. either a single interrupted time series design *without* a constructed or non-equivalent control group (i.e. relying on a reflexive control) or a comparison group design *without* an interrupted time series analysis (i.e. relying on pre-test and post-test measurements alone).

Such designs, demanding less rigorous specification and control, are often more feasible to undertake in an organizational context, where time constraints and the fact that all the potentially comparable employees may have been involved in the change rule out either measurements over a very extended time period, or the opportunity of constructing a meaningful control group. Examples of single interrupted time series designs are Bowey (1982) (effect of payment system change from piecework to day rates in a garment factory, on output and quality), Lawler and Hackman (1969) (impact of employee participation in the development of pay incentives), Rice (1958) (the impact of the introduction of automatic weaving and work system design on productivity in a textile plant) and Nicholson (1976) (effect of management sanctions on absence). Comparison group designs without an interrupted time series analysis are illustrated by various work system design experiments, for example, Bowers and Seashore (1963) (effect on productivity), Cummings and Srivasta (1977) (effect on quality), Van Beek (1964) (effect on quality) and Morse and Reimer (1956) (effect of participation on satisfaction). What threats to internal validity do such designs risk?

In the first case, single interrupted time series designs, the threat of history cannot be ruled out. Even if non-planned unforeseen change agents (historical events, business cycles, secular and developmental trends) can be accounted for qualitatively, it is difficult to estimate the magnitude of their effect, independent of the planned change programme. As the reflexive control group was younger (by definition) than the experimental group, maturation effects have also to be taken into account. Furthermore, a single interrupted time series design without a comparison group cannot demonstrate effects of gradually introduced changes, as small shifts over a long time period can be submerged by trend data. Obviously too, this design is extremely vulnerable if measurement systems are changed during the period of observation.

However, in a relatively stable setting, into which a discontinuous change has been introduced, this design can be most effective. Nicholson's (1976) evaluation of the effects of a sudden clamp-down of management sanctions on the absence behaviour of a female workforce, provides a good example. In the organization he studied, management's awareness of the rising cost of their sick pay scheme, in the face of inflation, led to the introduction of a sequence of verbal, written warnings and, finally dismissal, for persistent absentees. Nicholson hypothesized, on the basis of an articulated theory, that the clampdown would have two effects: a trade-off of uncertified for certified absence and a trade-off of shorter for longer spells. His design involved the collection of absence data for two matched time periods (i.e. covering the same months of two successive years) before and after management action. As a further control, data on medical certification were collected for four six-month time periods (two "before" and two "after"). Interviews were conducted with members of the personnel department to reveal any outside influences that might have influenced absence trends (e.g. influenza epidemics) and unemployment statistics for the area were checked for the entire period, to ascertain whether any changes occurred which might have influenced absence patterns. Finally, the sample consisted of all the female hourly paid workers differentiated by shift and function, but excluding a small group of women who had been with the company for less than the full time period for which absence data were collected (two years). Care was taken in the assessment and use of group and individual absence and autobiographical records, compensating measures being employed. The design was appropriate to the basic stability of the setting, and because care was taken to control for extraneous influences and alternative explanations, his findings (in support of his hypothesis) have good—if not perfect—internal validity.

In the second case, the pre-test–post-test comparison group design, the lack of an interrupted time series makes it difficult to control for selection–maturation threats to internal validity. There is no way of knowing (because there are no trend data) whether the observed effects might be due to the different kinds of people in the different groups maturing at different rates. This is a major problem if this design is used in educational youth training contexts, and particularly if the comparison groups are non-equivalent rather than constructed and matched. If, in an attempt to control for selection–maturation effects, selecting on the basis of pre-test scores is done, there is, as mentioned earlier, a great danger of regression artifacts occurring. Alternatively, if this is avoided by comparing two pre-existing "natural" groups as in many work design changes, there is a high risk of straightforward selection threats to internal validity. Identifying regression artifacts without time series analysis, is in any case, largely guess-work — and regression artifacts may well be present if the change programme is a direct response to an extreme pre-test score on the part of the experimental group.

However, if carefully constructed, bearing these problems in mind, such designs can yield results that have at least a face validity. Take, for example, the experiment conducted by Morse and Reimer (1956) into the effects of participation on a clerical department of a non-unionized industrial organization. Four parallel divisions existed within the department, which, for the purpose of the experiment, were grouped into pairs matched for the degree of participation which existed, the nature of the work, and the existing satisfaction of the personnel. For one pair of divisions participation was increased through the "autonomy program", for the other pair participation was decreased using the "hierarchically controlled program". The changes were introduced through a training scheme for supervisors which continued over a period of six months and was designed to ensure that greater or less participation would occur within the respective pairs of divisions. Measures of perceived participation and of satisfaction with the company, management and the job itself, were taken prior to the experiment and repeated 18 months later. The results were generally supportive of the theses underlying the experiment: greater participation was perceived by the "autonomy program" groups and increases in satisfaction measured, while decreases in both were recorded in the "hierarchically controlled program" groups (see also Wall and Lischeron, 1977).

Several commentators have suggested strategies for strengthening both these designs, in situations where developing a full interrupted time series with comparison series is impractical. For example, in a single interrupted time series design use of non-equivalent variables is a possibility (i.e. the specification of some other dependent variables that should not be affected by the change programme but which would be affected if some plausible alternatives, such as history or maturation, had affected the dependent variables at which the change programme was directed) (Cook et al., 1977). This strategy is not without its problems though: it is often difficult to identify such variables, especially if the initial causal theory is not precisely specified, changes in the outcome variables may effect changes in these variables, and, such an approach is dependent on accepting a null hypothesis — that nothing has happened to the non-equivalent dependent variable — which, particularly from a positivistic standpoint, is logically dubious.

Another strategy, useful when the design cannot use a non-equivalent or constructed comparison control group is the "removed treatment" (Cook et al., 1977). This involves testing the effect of a change programme by comparing measurements of the dependent variables when the change programme is operating, with when it is removed (for example, in an industrial organization industrial performance might be measured before an incentive payment system is introduced, during the time it operates, and after it is withdrawn, the assumption being that if it is effective, performance will rise while the payment system is in operation, but revert to pre-change levels after it is withdrawn). It is argued, for example, by Cook *et al.* (1977) that this strategy can sometimes rule out such threats to internal validity as history (because historical events with effects in opposite directions rarely coincide with the times when a change programme is introduced and then removed), maturation (*if* linear and not cyclical) and testing (as it is not plausible to assume that taking a test increases scores at one time, but causes them to decline after the treatment has been removed). However, again there are problems with this strategy. First, if the removal of the change programme is disliked by the participants (as the removal of an incentive payment system might well be), any change in the opposite direction after the removal of the programme may be due to disappointed expectations—hence giving rise to a construct validity problem. Secondly, if measurement is only taken at three time intervals—prechange, during/immediately after change programme, and some time after the programme has been removed, then if the second reading is deviantly high, it is likely to be interpreted as a change effect even if it isn't (again this is an argument for a time series of readings). Finally, this strategy is only of use if the change programme is expected to have an immediate but permanent effect that logically should wear off when the programme is removed. If effects are expected to persist over time, this design is clearly *not* appropriate, and, if against expectations, effects *do* persist over time, false negative conclusions about programme effects may be drawn.

As Riecken and Boruch (1974, pp.107–108) and Cummings *et al.* (1977, p.703) point out, if, for practical reasons one of these weaker, quasi-experimental designs has to be used, threats to internal validity, to some extent at least, may be held in check by attention to change programme implementation (e.g. keeping measurement systems constant, introducing— and removing—change programmes abruptly, delaying reaction to acute problems—in order to avoid regression artifacts in pre- and post-change measurement).

At the same time, for all quasi-experimental designs, it should be emphasized that much depends on sensitive interpretation of whether the causal relationships hypothesized *are* the most likely explanation of the observed results, even if theoretically causation cannot be proved. For example, as Riecken and Boruch (1974, p.112) point out, some results can be explained away as regression artifacts, but some cannot. If differences are in the opposite direction from that predicted by regression, or in the same direction, but to a larger degree than predicted, then they cannot be explained either at all, or completely, by regression. If the group that scores lowest on the pre-test (but not selected for treatment on this basis, so regression is not involved) turns out to have gained most, this result would negate the usual selection–maturation explanation. For the administrator who wants "hard facts" about the impact (i.e. causal effects) of change programmes, quasi-experiments can produce "facts" but the hardness may be more apparent (i.e. expressed in quantitative terms) than real (i.e. objective). Ultimately quasi-experimentation, because it cannot *unequivocally* rule out all the threats to the internal validity of a causal relationship, rests on *subjective* interpretation, and, as such, is open to some of the value criticisms which positivists are prone to level at evaluators wedded to more explicitly qualitative approaches (such criticisms will be dealt with in Chapters 5 and 6). The question then becomes whether subjectivity may be equated with partiality (or objectivity, for that matter, with impartiality). In other words, crises about the validity of the data elicited by different methods can already be seen to be interlinked with crises about values—a question which will be addressed in detail in Chapter 6.

Non-experimental and correlational designs

Many administrators wanting "hard" data about the "facts" of a change programme's effectiveness confuse numeracy with hardness and assume that correlational analysis, irrespective of the design in which it is embedded, can "prove" causal relationships. This, of course, is a fallacy, as in such analysis, however quantitatively expressed, it is impossible to prove that changes in the dependent variables are really the result of the change programme, and not just reflections of the effects of uncontrolled threats to internal validity (i.e. selection, history, regression artifacts etc.). Many managers' and administrators' difficulty in accepting that correlational analysis cannot prove causality, combined with their frequent desire for quick and cheap evaluations is understandably matched by researchers' willingness to trade methodological rigour to secure some research access to the "real" organizational settings. Both pressures account for the popularity of such designs as single case before and after studies, without comparison group [see, for example, King-Taylor's (1972) evaluations of work system changes effect on productivity and quality and Sadler and Barry's (1970) evaluation of an organizational development programme's effect on attitudes]; or after only, but with a comparison group [for example French *et al.* (1960) experiments on developing participation in a Norwegian factory or Conant and Kilbridge (1965) work system design experiment in an electronics factory, both using attitudinal measures]; or even after only without comparison group [for example, Buchanan and Boddy's (1982) study of the attitudinal effects of word processing on video typists]. None of these designs can demonstrate causality as all are riddled by the failure to control for rival explanations. Can they then serve any evaluation functions at all?

Leaving aside the covert functions in organizational politics, which such designs may serve when used by "trapped" administrators eager for an "eyewash" or "whitewash" evaluations (Campbell, 1969), non-experimental and correlational studies can serve as cheap pilots to ascertain whether it is worthwhile to undertake the expense of a more costly rigorous study. Researchers themselves implicitly make this point, when embarrassed by potential methodological criticisms of their blatantly weak designs, they assert that their research is "only exploratory". As Weiss (1972a, p.74) points out, because the effects of a change programme are likely to be relatively small, and because most threats to internal validity artificially increase the size of the apparent effects, if a non-experimental study suggests little change, then it is unlikely that the change programme had any effect. In other words, if a weak design does not identify any change effects, in spite of its tendency to exaggerate the size of apparent effects, then the expense of a more sophisticated design can be avoided. If some change is identified, Weiss argues, then the change programme may be examined by a more rigorous quasi-experimental design to identify just how much of the change may be attributed to the change programme itself.

As suggested above, a major practical advantage of non-experimental designs as compared to experimental and quasi-experimental designs is that they are quick (especially those which do not rely on any pre-testing, and hence the need to wait for the change programme to have an effect) and cheap. Given the budgeting constraints many managers and administrators work under and their oft expressed need for approximate information now rather than exact information later, when it is not too late to inform the decision-making process, non-experimental correlational designs may be the only feasible strategy open to the evaluator, if the administrators at the same time insist that quantitative data are also required. (If the administrators do not make this a condition, purely qualitative designs, depending upon the question to be answered, may be more appropriate.) In these circumstances, it is often suggested that, wherever practically possible, the evaluator should "patch on" (Campbell and Stanley, 1963; Evans, 1975) specific measurements to rule out any (qualitatively) suspected rival explanations. Obviously, if expert judgement and familiarity with the situation are needed to interpret quasi-experimental designs the same has to be said, but even more emphatically, of non-experimental, correlational designs. Subjective judgement and qualitative "knowing" are increasingly essential when the design itself cannot minimize potential ambiguities in interpreting findings.

Internal validity — in practice

Before turning to the question of external validity, is it possible to make any generalization about just how internally valid is much of the research on the impacts of organizational change?

It should be noted that researchers most prone to adopting the positivistic designs discussed here are either educational evaluators (evaluating schools' "technology") or, in industrial and commercial organizations, those evaluating various forms of "quality of work" and more general organizational development experiments. Both these types of change rest on psychological theories about needs and need hierarchies, as embedded in Hackman and Lawler's (1971) Job Characteristics Model, for instance. Hence social psychologists tend to be involved in designing and evaluating such change programmes and, not unnaturally, often carry with them a preference for the traditional natural science methods of psychologists rather than the non-experimental, often historical methods of a sociological tradition.

If we, therefore, limit our generalizations to part of this group (i.e. mainly social psychologists evaluating work system and organizational development experiments in industrial and commercial organizations) some sobering findings emerge. Cummings *et al.* (1977) have analyzed 58 experiments involving the restructuring of the content and conditions of work in organizations (i.e. experiments in job enrichment, participative management and autonomous group working, often involving changes in payment systems and to organizational structure generally). From the 51 studies in which impact on some aspect of *performance* was measured (for example, productivity, costs and quality), a "rather bleak" picture emerges (Cummings *et al.*, 1977, p.688). Taking together both questionable threats and uncontrolled threats, *no study was found to be entirely free from a possible threat to its internal validity*—threats from measurement instability, mortality and selection interaction being the worst culprits, being present in over 50% of the experiments (mortality in 90%). Furthermore threats from history, instrumentation and regression are possible threats to slightly less than 50% of the studies. Nor are matters improved if one considers only the studies where *attitudinal* impacts were measured. Indeed "the internal validity of the attitudinal findings is weaker than performance findings" (Cummings *et al.*, 1977, p.701). While instability and instrumentation are sources of proportionally fewer threats to the internal validity of attitude findings, testing and selection were threats for more of the attitudinal studies than for the performance experiments—the former because of reactivity and the latter because of absence of pretests needed to determine whether or not comparison groups were different before the experimental treatment. Furthermore, 95% of the studies suffered from threats due to mortality, and 61% due to selection-interaction. Nor is there any reason to suspect that Cummings *et al.* (1977) selection of studies to analyze is anyway atypical of the published research. Later published work—for example Blackler and Brown's (1978a) critical evaluation of Volvo's experiments in work redesign, at Kalmar suggests similar weaknesses in Volvo's own research (Gyllenhammer, 1977) designed to assess the impact of the new work practices.

The problem of external validity — generalizing from an evaluation

When deciding whether to introduce or extend a change programme, administrators need to know not just whether the programme works, but whether it will work in a setting which may be different from the one in which the original change programme was introduced and evaluated. But, as Campbell (1969) and Bracht and Glass (1968) have pointed out, factors which threaten the internal validity of an evaluation can logically threaten the extent of its generalizability. Particularly relevant factors, as itemized by Bernstein *et al.* (1976) are selection effects, measurement effects, confounded treatment effects, situational effects and effects due to differential mortality. Just how these factors can affect the generalizability of an evaluation will be discussed below. (However, as their derivation has already been discussed, it will not be repeated here.)

Selection effects

The problem here is that it is difficult to generalize from groups whose members' responsiveness to the change programme may be unrepresentative of superficially similar populations. For example, it is always dangerous to generalize findings about volunteers to non-volunteers due to the effect of potential motivational differences. Again, generalizing from groups chosen because of their presumed likelihood of demonstrating hypothesized effects (selection by excellence) is dangerous if the results are positive. Generalizing from studies which lack a comparison group is always dangerous—not only may the group differ significantly from apparently similar groups, but the internal validity of the findings is questionable.

The best way to overcome these problems is, of course, by random sampling from a designated universe, which allows the generalization of results to that universe. However, unless the change programme enjoys widespread implementation (as in some social change programmes backed by legislative change) this is unlikely to be feasible. In such circumstances, technically speaking, generalization is not possible. Practically speaking, though, if there is no reason to believe one group differs significantly from another, tentative generalizations may be made. Bernstein *et al.* (1976) argue that in such circumstances confidence in generalization is increased by replication of results, particularly if replication is with different populations.

Measurement effects

Bernstein *et al.* (1976) suggest that six types of measurement problems can affect the generalizability of results, viz. measurement error *per se*; pre-test sensitization; post-test sensitization; interaction between measurement and individual level factors, such as knowledge of a language; lack of "match" between measurement and causal lags and omission of relevant dependent variables. The implications of these problems for external validity are as follows:

If unreliable measuring instruments are used, estimates of relationships are usually attenuated (Lord and Novick, 1968) and, as a result, generalizations will tend to be conservative. Although this is probably preferable to overestimates, it can result in the halting of a change programme because of its assumed ineffectiveness, or inflated cost benefit estimates. If pre-test and post-test sensitization are estimated to exist, then logically the findings, which may be either enhanced or attenuated, can only be generalized to populations which have been similarly tested. Interaction between measurement and individual level variables, for example, using non "culture-free" tests, or using interviews with respondents lacking verbal ability, may lead to underestimates of the effect of the change programme, at least upon a specific sub-group of respondents.

Problems resulting from a mismatch between measurement intervals and causal lags and the omission of relevant dependent variables fall into a rather different category, being essentially problems arising out of the special nature of evaluation research rather than problems that might apply equally to all forms of positivistic research. Bernstein *et al.* (1976, p.118) make the useful distinction between "most research which begins with a dependent variable, or set of dependent variables for which causes are sought" and "much evaluation research (which) begins with an independent variable, and asks what it causes". Given this perspective it is understandable why the above two problems are a particular issue in evaluation research. In both cases, unless the theory from which the causal hypotheses are derived is well developed (and this is unlikely the more radical the change programme), it will be difficult to specify either causal lags or all the relevant dependent variables. If there is a mismatch between measurement and causal lags, again an underestimate of programme effects may be made (Armenakis *et al.*, 1983). If relevant dependent variables are omitted, generalization to other settings, which might have particular interest in the "omitted" variables, is less useful than it might have been. (It should be noted, of course, that both the problem of lag and omission of relevant dependent variables have implications for internal as well as external validity.)

Ways of overcoming these problems really centre on care in selecting reliable and appropriate measurement instruments and especially in the case of the last two problems, care in evaluation design (see Bernstein *et al.*, 1976, pp.114–120).

Confounded treatment effects

When change programmes are carried out in organizations it is often difficult to ensure that the participants are carrying out/receiving a uniform programme across all the units involved. Even when the same formal inputs are supposed to be implemented, how they are implemented can vary from situation to situation, not to mention the informal additions or subtractions which may have taken place unofficially in the light of different experiences on different sites, at different times. This makes it difficult, without close implementation monitoring or analysis of variance, to generalize from one version of a change programme implementation to the likely effectiveness of formally similar programmes even in similar settings. A further problem is multiple treatment effects, that is when the participants in a change programme have participated in several programmes all aimed at achieving the same or similar effects. Thus, in an industrial organization changes aimed at increasing productivity may be implemented simultaneously. For example, job redesign often goes hand in hand with investment in new equipment, changes in supervision, and pay increases or a new payment system. This was not only the case in the Rushton "Quality of Work" experiment, where changes also occurred in the pay system, communication and authority systems, and in training practices, but, of the 58 experiments analyzed by Cummings *et al.* (1977), all but seven studies involved multiple interventions. Similarly, in social change programmes, because most are aimed at the socially and economically disadvantaged, it is often the case that the same individuals may either simultaneously, or sequentially, be participating in more than one programme. For example, Bernstein *et al.* (1976, p.123) suggest that "persons receiving monies from the Negative Income Tax Experiment may also be participating in the Model Cities Programs, Job Training Programs, and the like". In either situation, it is difficult to pin down which change programme (or aspects of a programme) is responsible for any observed changes in the outcome measures. This is particularly a problem if the change programmes are experienced simultaneously, as it is difficult to assess whether their effect is selective, additive or interactional. But the experimental design required to systematically sort out the separate effects of the different changes (several experimental groups, each with different combinations of experimental factors, with matched control groups), as Goodman (1979, p.123) remarks of the Rushton experiment, "would have been difficult (if not impossible) to implement".

Finally, generalizability of inferences may be very limited if interactions between the change programme and special characteristics of the individual participants occur. Two directions of interactional effects may occur, disordinal interaction when a change programme has opposite effects for different sub-groups of participants (e.g. some experimental groups and their controls get worse, while others, and their controls get better, as in Hunt and Hardt's (1969) study of an educational programme for disadvantaged black and white schoolchildren) or ordinal interaction, when the effects are in the same direction, but of different orders of magnitude for different sub-groups (with the consequent implication of differing cost–benefit ratios for the different sub-groups). A way round this problem is simply awareness of the potential interactional effect of common individual variables, (age, sex, skill level, socio-economic status) and the change programme in question. Of course, "obvious" variables can be identified and allowances made, in a fairly mechanistic fashion. However, the more radical the change programme and the less well developed the theory on which it rests, the more problematic this process becomes.

Situational effects

Typical situational effects (which to some extent overlap with the problem of lack of standard programmes across sampling units) are identified by Bernstein *et al.* (1976, pp.126–131) as staff effects (some programme implementers are more charismatic, committed, enthusiastic and generally effective than others), Hawthorne effects (as discussed in the preceding section on internal validity), novelty effects (the newness of the change programme may generate a response that would not occur if it was routinized), history (for example, change programmes may be more effective if implemented during a climate of reform and expansion rather than recession and cut-backs, or vice versa), and geographic setting (for example, note the influence of setting on various therapy/training programmes).

The problem with at least three of these effects (staff, Hawthorne and novelty effects) is that they are most likely to occur in the new experimental programmes that are most prone to evaluation. The problem of novelty effects (along with history and geography) can to a certain extent be coped with by replication (are the effects of a new programme maintained in subsequent implementations? does a programme seem to have different effects, at different points of time and in different physical settings?). However, novelty effects, at least, may well go hand in hand with staff effects (more enthusiastic staff on the first run of a programme) and, hence, any results suggesting a diminishing effect need to be interpreted with this also in mind.

With staffing and Hawthorne effects, the results may not be generalizable to non-experimental or routinized settings. Indeed, a more constructive approach, it is often argued, is to capitalize on such effects by seeking to raise the quality of staffing on the routinized programmes, and to maintain those aspects of an experimental implementation which encourage enhanced effects in non-experimental settings.

Differential mortality effects

The problems here have already been discussed earlier in this chapter and will not be repeated. Suffice it to say that when differential mortality occurs as between experimental and control groups, and when the loss appears to be non-random, external validity, as well as internal validity, is seriously undermined. If the mortality is assumed to be random across both groups, then estimation models may be used to some extent. If the loss is assumed to be non-random all that can be done is to attempt to identify what determines differential attrition, and counteract the effects.

Summary

The nub of the problem of external validity is that not only is it threatened by any threat to internal validity, *but the very controls which are designed to protect internal validity may themselves undermine the generalization of results to other, non-experimental settings, precisely because of the resulting artificiality of the experimental setting.* The theoretical reaction to this difficulty—make all implementations of change programmes as similar to the experimental model as possible—is often just not possible in real life. Another suggestion has been to decide how a change programme would actually be implemented in a typical setting, and to measure effects under these, rather than truly "experimental" conditions (Cook *et al.*, 1977, pp.108–109). The problem with this might be that a common-sense gain in external validity is achieved, but at the expense of internal validity.

External validity — in practice

On the basis of Cummings *et al.* (1977) assessment of 58 work experiments, it would appear that the external validity of such evaluations is as questionable as their internal validity. In particular, regarding both performance and attitudinal findings, generalizability is made questionable by selection threats (for example, heavy reliance on volunteers and "co-operative" units) and situational threats (the artificiality of the experimental setting). Cummings *et al.* (1977) estimate that selection effects threatened 94% and 100%, and situational effects, 90% and 76% of the performance and attitudinal findings respectively. Furthermore, although performance findings, thanks to the use of unobtrusive measures, were virtually free of testing sensitization effects,

57% of attitudinal findings were estimated to be so contaminated. On these grounds the external validity of these studies must be weak. However, the experiments *were* performed over a wide range of populations and settings (e.g. in terms of sex of participant, type of work performed, blue- or white-collar job status, numbers of individuals involved, union membership, countries in which the experiment was conducted), which adds some weight to the generalizability of the findings, *but* within these weighty technical limitations to external validity.

Specification, measurement and the role of the objective, "outsider" evaluator

Measurement

It is not my intention to discuss the statistical procedures which may be employed in experimental and quasi-experimental designs as the subject is highly technical and has been amply covered elsewhere (see, for example, Boruch and Rindskopf, 1977; Cohen, 1969; Cronbach *et al.*, 1972; Cronbach, 1979; Lord and Novick 1968; Nunnally, 1967; Riecken and Boruch, 1974). Rather, at this point, I wish to focus on why two assumptions of positivism— those of objectivity and prediction—direct the evaluator towards quantitative rather than qualitative approaches, and towards emphasizing the importance of reliability, sometimes at the expense of validity, of specification and measurement.

Positivism assumes the phenomena have an objective reality "out there" when more than one observer can agree their specification and measurement. Inter-subjective agreement is more easily achieved by quantitative measurement rather than qualitative assessment, because it enhances reliability (House, 1980). For example, agreement on, say, the sound quality of electronic equipment is likely to be higher if observers can measure its performance through an instrument recording decibel gain than if relying directly on their ears without the assistance of the intervening mechanical "neutral" instrument. Prediction, similarly, asserts the need for measurement and reliability of measures. As stated earlier in this chapter, to predict not only involves the establishment of causal relationships through the measurement of covariance but involves the principle of replication. A measure which produces different results upon replication may indicate that *either* change has taken place *or* that the variation in the measured phenomenon is due to inconsistencies in measurement. Given that the whole purpose of a positivistic evaluation is to measure the impact of a change programme upon the dependent variables, the reliability of measures is, not surprisingly, a *sine qua non* of such an evaluation study.

Thus the outcome of both these assumptions, it has frequently been argued (House, 1980; Patton, 1978), is to elevate the principle of measurement reliability even above that of its validity (that is, the degree to which the instrument succeeds in measuring what it purports to measure). This is particularly prevalent in those evaluation studies where political pressures exist to use standardized tests in the interests of equality as well as for the convenience of comparability (for example, in the evaluation of educational programmes).

The problem though is that while reliability is a necessary it is not a sufficient condition to ensure validity. If validity is sacrificed in the interests of higher reliability, the evaluator may find himself evaluating the success of a change programme on the basis of irrelevant criteria, as the measures are not measuring what they purport to measure.

Briefly, the validity of an instrument can take several forms. Content validity concerns the extent to which a measuring instrument encompasses a reasonable sample of the totality of responses, behaviours or other attributes which characterize the variable of interest. In a training programme in plumbing, the range of activities that compasses the skilled plumber's necessary repertoire might be listed, and the trainee's competence judged on his proficiency over the range of tasks. Construct validity concerns the meaning of the variable under investigation, the extent to which the measuring instruments actually reflect it, and the validity of interpretation of observations. This form of validity is extremely important when trying to measure and interpret conceptually such slippery outcome variables as "well-being" or "stress" (Cook et al., 1981). Criterion validity encompasses concurrent and predictive validity. Concurrent validity concerns the extent to which scores or responses from one measure correlate with a generally accepted and accurate standard (for example, how a "new" I.Q. test correlates with an already well validated one). Predictive validity concerns the extent to which measures can predict responses/behaviours that may occur in the future (for example, an aptitude test would have high predictive validity if it could predict who would do well or poorly at a specific job unfamiliar to the person tested).

Thus, even if the experimental design protects against other threats to the internal validity of an evaluation study, if the content and construct validity of measurement instruments, in particular, is low, any relationship identified between the independent and outcome variables is likely to be misleading. But whereas if reliability is low, the error is random, if validity is low errors are systematic and hence slant the results in a particular direction. Typical sorts of biases which need to be guarded against are observer biases when designing measuring instruments and when using subjective rating scales, participant bias (deliberate distortion, giving responses aimed to please, or unintentional biases, such as the various Hawthorne effects discussed earlier), pre-test sensitization (the effects of taking a test or answering questions upon responses to a second test or questionnaire) and so on (see Riecken and Boruch, 1974, pp.130–136). Ways of overcoming these problems of bias (e.g. "blind" measurement, estimating extent of bias, minimizing participants' awareness of the measurement process, minimizing visibility of the experiment) have been touched upon earlier and are fully discussed in Riecken and Boruch (1974, pp.130–136). The key considerations in avoiding these problems would seem to be care in instrument design and pre-testing, and expertise and experience on the part of the evaluator administering the instrument.

The evaluator as objective "outsider"

Leaving aside for the moment whether, in the wake of Heisenberg's uncertainty principle, it is still an epistemologically tenable position, positivistic designs assume that the role of the evaluation researcher, ideally, is one of objective observation, specification and measurement of the facts, which exist "outside", independent of and unaffected by such activities, except when consciously manipulated in the course of the experimental process. Indeed, the whole object of experimental design and the design of reliable and valid measurement instruments is to distance the researcher's personal idiosyncracies lest they affect the facts he is studying. Not surprising then is the scientists' emphasis on due procedure and careful adherence to methodological canons, along with an ideological corollary, that the scientists should conform to the "distancing" norms of rationalism, universalism and emotional neutrality.

Yet the paradox of positivism is that it implicitly recognizes that advances in understanding cannot be divorced from the personal insights and characteristics of individual scientists. Hence, as Mulkay (1976) points out, the norms of rationalism, universalism and emotional neutrality, in practice, are balanced by an exactly opposite set of formulations—intuition and freeranging imagination, a particularistic respect for senior respected colleagues or "father figures" and commitment to one's research. Paradoxically, the latter two norms in particular can lead to unconscious biasing on the part of the researcher. First, she may not subject to as rigorous a scrutiny the work of a respected senior colleague as that of a junior unknown (certainly a characteristic betrayed by some editors of academic journals!). Secondly, quite apart from such extreme cases as that of Paul Kammerer (Koestler, 1971) where commitment led to the actual faking of results (see also Zuckerman, 1977) the researcher's attachment to a beautiful theory threatened with destruction by ugly facts, may encourage an unconscious bias in data interpretation. Positivism, by recognizing the individual attributes required for seminal research is caught in a cleft stick as these same personal attributes can also involve subjectivity and bias, contradicting the "objective" ideal.

Intellectual commitment to the theory on which a change programme is based, or involvement in its design, is not the only source of unconscious biasing in the interpretation of evaluation research results. Quite apart from that which may stem from the interactions between researcher and the less than passive researched (see our earlier discussion of Hawthorne effects, measurement problems and differential mortality) the evaluator's own assessment of the practical and career implications that his findings may have in the real world of decision-making, may lead to bias of varying degrees of consciousness (Riecken and Boruch 1974, p.131). But the realities of a field setting may place more direct and explicit external pressures on the evaluation researcher to abandon his "objective outsider" role. Brickell (1976) vividly portrays, through a series of case examples, ways in which the parties to various evaluations he conducted brought direct pressure to bear upon how he undertook his evaluation research and presented his findings. To quote from just one of the examples:

> While meeting with area superintendents to explain the study (about the impact of paraprofessionals in schools on pupil learning commissioned not by the area superintendents, but by central administration), one of their spokesmen opened up with something like this:
>
> "Okay, you evaluators. Let's get one thing straight from the start. We have these paraprofessionals here in these schools not only to help kids learn but to link us to the community. That's why we have them. That's why we are going to keep them. We're not looking for a report about test results that will cause any trouble with the board of education downtown. They've got their reasons for giving us the money to hire paraprofessionals; we've got our reasons for taking the money. So no matter what you find out about kids' achievement, we're going to keep our paraprofessionals. Don't make it difficult".
>
> Alerted thus, we made our study. And we were lucky that time. We found that the presence of paraprofessionals did in fact improve pupil achievement. Were we delighted: *We never told anyone, of course, but the experimental groups became our home team and the control groups became visitors from out of town. We sat on the edge of the field throughout the game, voicelessly cheering "Make a significant difference".* (1976, p.2) (added emphasis)

So much for maintaining the role of "objective outsider", even when, as is implied in this quotation, there is a formal adherence to a positivistic design! Brickell goes on to present various examples of quite explicit pressures put upon him by interested parties to limit the data he could gather, shape his questionnaires, influence the designs he employed, guide his interpretations of his data, and even rewrite his reports. As he states, the nub of the problem of maintaining an independent role is

> . . . being conscious of the fact that what I say will be used in the winning and the exercising of power, that my findings are going to be lined up on one side or the other of a contest that somebody else has already set up, and that jobs are on the line—*maybe my own job.* (1976, p.5) (added emphasis)

Private communications with colleagues suggests that those researching changes in industrial organizations may be subject to similar pressures. Questionnaire items may be considered "too sensitive" to be placed before union members, and unpalatable reports may result in a refusal to release the data for publication (on the grounds that it is invalid, unrepresentative, misinterpreted, etc.), and refusal of further access. Brickell concludes by suggesting that the only way to remain completely independent of external political pressures (by adhering to five rules, including *reporting findings in such a way that they have no implications for the project being evaluated*), is in practice impossible. Instead he suggests that the evaluator should attempt to cope with the political influences he experiences by adopting "spongier" rules, such as trying to understand what the client thinks, what he stands to gain or lose from the evaluators, reassuring the client that he can interpret *any* findings so as to give helpful suggestions for improving the change programme; gathering evidence addressed to the real success criteria of the powerful decision-makers; trying to get a supervisory mechanism for the evaluation study that includes a cross-section of all the powerful decision-makers; and, finally, writing the report carefully, mentioning extenuating circumstances for any lack of success of the change programme.

Thus the "objective outsider" role which (theoretically at least) a positivistic evaluation design requires an evaluator to adopt in order to implement the experimental/quasi experimental method and present his findings "correctly" appears at odds with the "responsive-insider" role which in the real world may be necessary in order to achieve some degree of utilization of the evaluation's findings. Indeed, it could be argued that in so attempting to mediate this tension between methodological and utilization requirements the evaluator may encounter a series of "double-binds". If his findings are to be utilized, so the argument goes, they must serve the evaluation functions of the interested parties. The *overt* function that evaluation serves for Brickell's "powerful decision-makers" is to provide information to assist strategic decision-making about change programme continuation/extension/ termination, i.e. "hard" information about its impact upon selected dependent variables. And, as it has been argued, this is best achieved by positivistic designs which require the evaluator to act as "objective-outsider".

But if he acts in this manner, according to Brickell at least, his evaluation findings may be ignored, as the role he has adopted, (and his resultant findings) are insufficiently responsive to the same decision-makers *covert* political evaluation requirements (e.g. rallying support or opposition to the change programme). Thus, simultaneously, the conflicting requirements for utilization, from just one interested party to the change programme, place incompatible role demands on the evaluator.

Summary and conclusions

In this chapter I have discussed the ontological and epistomological characteristics of the positivistic paradigm, viz: "explanation", "prediction", "regularities", "causal relationships" and "constituent elements" (variable analysis) and their consequent methodological corollaries, viz: a concern with internal and external validity, specification and measurement, and the role of the evaluation researcher as "objective-outsider". The resulting design choices, of experiments and quasi experiments, have been discussed, along with some of the problems involved and limiting assumptions. What conclusions can we now draw about the appropriateness of such designs in serving various evaluation functions?

At one level it can be said that such designs are the most appropriate way of assessing the impact of a change programme upon specified dependent variables, as the concern with protecting internal validity does assist the attribution of causation. And, as stated earlier, this information can assist the policy-maker in his decisions on continuing, extending or terminating the programme.

Such information, by adding to the stock of knowledge about fundamental processes, also assists change programme designers—either directly, as when they evaluate their own change programmes (e.g. Wall and Clegg, 1981) or, indirectly when they read the published accounts of previous relevant studies (e.g. Wall and Clegg's use of Hackman and Lawler's 1971 study). In so far as the design focuses upon the assessment of comparable techniques (e.g. individual as compared to group selection interviewing) or different approaches to problem solving (e.g. improving productivity through either job redesign or redesign of the payment system) it may assist programme designers in choosing between alternative design strategies and policy makers in assessing the cost and benefits of alternative strategies.

However, we should be clear as to the nature of this information. It is not so much about the impact of a change programme on dependent variables *per se*, it is about statistical relationships between one set of measures representing a conceptualization/specification of the change programme and another set of measures representing outcome variables. Thus, irrespective of the experimental controls exercised to maintain internal validity, the extent to which the findings can be considered to say anything meaningful about the change programme will depend on how closely the measures used mirror the programme. Furthermore, because such designs demand the specification of outcome variables at the outset, they also require a clear articulation of the theory underlining the programme design, in order that its potential effects can be hypothesized, specified and measured. If the theory is not articulated (or worse still, if a change programme is implemented which lacks any articulated theoretical base) it is difficult if not impossible to systematically identify what the change effects are likely to be. And if "effects" are hypothesized at random, important real effects may be missed as they have been neither specified nor measured.

But the major problem with positivistic designs (assuming one accepts the epistemological assumptions upon which they rest) are the ethical and practical problems of protecting internal and external validity. As discussed throughout this chapter, the ethical problems in obtaining agreement to randomization and the practical problems—particularly that of differential mortality—in maintaining it over the length of time required for the change to have an effect are difficult to surmount. Once quasi-experiments are embarked upon, the imputation of causation must always be questionable—in the final analysis the best the evaluator can say is that the causal imputations made seem the most *likely* explanation. And, as far as external validity goes, there is the difficulty that some of the requirements to protect internal validity, by increasing the artificiality of the implementation, only serve to undermine its external validity—a requirement which may be of particular relevance to the policy maker. If, in fact, the internal and external validity of an evaluation design is weak, it is questionable as to what extent its findings about the impact of a change programme can be said to "really" add to knowledge *per se*, or the knowledge requirements of rational decision-making.

Furthermore, in using positivistic approaches to assess the impact of a change programme, evaluators tend to make one large assumption—that the change programme will actually be implemented according to its design specifications. As Suchman (1969) and Weiss (1972a) have pointed out, if a change programme appears to have no impact on the relevant dependent variables, although this *may* mean that the theory underlining the programme design is wrong, it may equally mean that the programme was inadequately implemented—that its implementation fell short of, or was different from, the design specification, and hence the potential "causal processes" were not activated, and no true test of the programme took place. In other words the lack of change in the dependent variables is only meaningful if it can be assessed that the change programme was implemented according to specification.

Unfortunately, there is plenty of evidence to suggest that this assumption is frequently invalid (see, for example, the cases cited by Patton, 1978; Pressman and Wildavsky, 1973; Provus, 1971; Williams and Elmore, 1976). As discussed in Chapter 2, in coping with resistance to the change and even in adapting to day to day contingencies and unforeseen problems those implementing a change programme can, little by little, depart from the original design, with minimal awareness of the extent to which they have done so. Not surprisingly then is it frequently advocated (Provus, 1971; Williams, 1976) that some form of implementation monitoring should take place, if only to check on the extent, and in what ways, the change programme as implemented has departed from the programme as designed. Various forms of monitoring have been suggested, for example, the monitoring of the quality and quantity of programme inputs ("effort evaluation") and the monitoring of the "internal dynamics and actual operations" of the change programme ("process evaluation") (Patton, 1978). As far as maintaining the validity of a positivistic evaluation design goes, the chief purpose behind this monitoring is to ask whether the change programme is being implemented according to design specifications, and, if it has strayed, to what extent can it deviate from the ideal, and in what ways, while still being consistent with the programme's underlying theory and, hence, capable of testing the hypothesized causal processes.

However, this places a positivistic design in another potential double bind situation. Obviously the evaluator needs to know whether the programme has been implemented in a manner consistent with the programme's theory in order to be able to conduct a meaningful impact evaluation. But the more closely the implementation of the programme is monitored the more artificial its implementation setting becomes (with consequent threats to external validity) and, the more likelihood there is of Hawthorne effects (threatening both external and internal validity). Furthermore, if the implementers perceive this monitoring as reinforcing the control function of the evaluation, the hostility this may engender may also affect the validity of the evaluation.

It is conventional for evaluators wedded to the positivistic paradigm to assert the inherent superiority of the experimental method in evaluation and to lament the "practical obstacles" to effectively using this method (see, for example, Campbell, 1969). The notion seems to be that the experimental method is an ideal, regrettably undermined by the "intransigencies of the research setting" and that the good evaluator should nevertheless proceed with experimentation and "design ways of overcoming the difficulties" — such as by using "patched on" quasi-experimental designs (Campbell, 1969). However, it could just as well be argued that the obstacles to experimentation are the reality (at least, the contextual reality) of implementing change, and that positivistic designs that seek to shield the causal processes of a change programme from buffeting by "practical realities" during implementation, render both the programme and the inferences drawn from its evaluation unreal.

This raises a further point. Positivistic designs place emphasis on quantitative measurement and the expression of phenomena and relationships in statistical terms. But it should be borne in mind that *statistical inferences drawn from an experimental evaluation can only, in theory, be extended to material in an identical frame* (Deming, 1975). If the evaluator wishes to generalize to other situations, strictly speaking he enters the realm of subjective, if expert, judgement on the extent to which the results are applicable outside the confines of the experiment. The experiment is only then a tool to assist his judgement. If this is the case, might not his subjective expert judgement of the programme's effectiveness and generalizability, be better served by other methods of evaluation that embrace the "practical realities" of situations in which change programmes are designed and implemented rather than seek to exclude their effects?

This brings us back to the question of which evaluation functions are not and cannot be best served by positivistic designs. Experimental designs demand that a change programme's theory, design and mode of implementation be clearly specified at the outset. They demand too that the programme (or at least those components about whose impact hypotheses have been formulated) is held constant long enough for the causal processes to be activated and to have an effect. Feedback of results therefore cannot occur till the programme has run its course, and, moreover, the programme must be held constant. But programme administrators and implementers require rapid partial information answering specific questions about programme components and implementation rather than long-term complete information about its general effectiveness as designed, after it has ended. They want this ongoing feedback in order to facilitate the tactical decision-making involved in the day-to-day management of the programme—*so that modifications may be made if the programme appears ineffective or could be made better.* Thus, an experimental design cannot serve these functions. The feedback it gives is *after*, not during implementation. And, by definition, it rules out modifications to the programme while the experiment is in progress. The evaluation designs appropriate to formative evaluation, which can tolerate such modifications and provide rapid and specific feedback, will be discussed in the next chapter.

A further consideration is how well positivistic evaluation designs serve the needs of the recipients. Although it can be argued that in so far as such evaluations facilitate better informed policy-making, they must ultimately serve the interests of *potential* recipients of change programmes, the extent to which they provide information that meets the needs of clients *directly* involved with the programme is highly questionable (Guba and Lincoln, 1981; Stake, 1975). Experimental designs are invariably élitist in operation—the evaluator as outsider judges the programme using methods and measurement often not readily accessible to the general public. The information provided is not only unlikely to answer their questions, it may be incomprehensible to them as well. Whether or not a responsive evaluation, in the manner discussed by Stake (1975) can meet these needs (in theory) or not (in practice) will be discussed in the next chapter. Either way, the selection of an evaluation design to match the functions demanded of it by recipients of change programmes is interwoven with issues of values, and must be considered in that context too.

Finally, how well do positivistic designs serve the covert evaluation functions of those involved with change programmes? In terms of postponing decisions, evading responsibility and fulfilling grant requirements an experimental design can be highly appropriate. The need for longitudinal data virtually guarantees slow feedback and a justification for delaying a decision. Respected "academic" evaluators who will undertake a "rigorous" study make acceptable arbitrators/scapegoats if the decision-maker wishes to evade responsibility. And, undeniably, positivistic designs have often been specified by those funding a change programme and its evaluation. The only problem though is that the more rigorous the design, the less likely it is that the results will be artificially inflated, and the more likely it is that either the impact will be recorded as non-significant or very small. While this may assist postponing decisions ("let's delay the decision further—or get more evidence"), it may inhibit the decision-maker from evading responsibility further. The "results" may be so equivocal that they may place him firmly back at square one with responsibility for mediating the uncertainty itself.

But when it comes to rallying support/opposition to a change programme a positivistic design can be a mixed blessing. On the one hand, as it is based on the academically dominant paradigm and is seen to be "rigorous" (assuming careful, professional design) its results are likely to have an authority which those emerging from apparently less rigorous designs may lack in the eyes of potential supporters/detractors. But, the more "rigorous" the design, either the results are likely to record a small or insignificant change (and, therefore, although authoritative, be non-persuasive) or they may even be unexpected (the "wrong" results). Either way, although a positivistic design may score in terms of authority, if this is authority backing unpersuasive information, it may be a liability rather than an asset. In such circumstances those who rush to rally support or opposition to the programme are likely to find their needs better met by a design which gives the appearance of rigour, but which may provide results of a more flexible nature.

For essentially the same reasons, paradoxically, it is not *always* true that the more rigorous the design, the more likely it is to serve the academic researcher's career aspirations. Non-significant or negative findings fall foul of many journals and books publishers preference for publishing positive results (Lewis and Lewis, 1980). Blackler and Brown (1978a) and Birchall *et al.* (1978) are not alone in reporting the dearth of published accounts of failed or apparently ineffective experiments in job redesign and participation, while several famous organizational researchers (e.g. Herzberg, Fiedler) have made their reputations on positivistic studies of very suspect methodological quality (Miner, 1980).

So where does this leave us? What evaluation functions can positivistic designs serve? To summarize, we may state the following propositions:

(1) Positivistic designs can provide the "truth" about impact relationships, *if* one accepts that this "truth" can be generalized to the real world where such theoretical truths may be difficult to replicate outside experimental conditions.

(2) At one level this "truth" is of relevance to policy-makers. It gives information about what is likely to occur if the real world can be controlled. But if the policy-maker wishes to act on this information (i.e. achieve the theoretical impact) he may find himself involved in broader questions of change, i.e. how can the setting of the replicated change programme itself be changed or controlled, in order that experimental impact can be achieved in a "non-experimental" situation? (But this is, of course, to render the new setting experimental too.)

(3) The above two propositions assume that policy-makers wish to make a rational decision (or at least decisions of a bounded rationality, on the assumption that in conditions of uncertainty, complete rationality is impossible). Because exact data, for their own sake, are only required if rationality is at a premium—otherwise the appearance of rationality would suffice. But as discussed in Chapter 3, this portrayal of the policy-maker is idealized and not in accordance with real life. In practice, the more important the decision the more likely are political rather than rational considerations to prevail—not least at the information-processing stage, leading to unconscious bias, quite apart from subsequent conscious biasing. The more trivial the decision, the less likely the decision-maker is to bother with exact information, irrespective of how rationally he is able to make the decision. *In which case, it may be that the chief importance of a positivistic design to the policy-maker is that its form (rather than the information it generates per se) accords with the rhetoric of accountability and responsibility and for that reason, if no other, fulfils important evaluation functions.*

(4) On the basis of the preceding discussion it is argued that positivistic designs do not fulfil the information requirements of programme implementers, nor those of its clients.

(5) It is also argued that positivistic designs can be successful in fulfilling a range of covert functions for those involved in decision-making about, and studying, change programmes. However, the extent to which they may do so, for reasons already discussed, may be more apparent than real.

On the basis of these propositions, I suggest that the public support for positivistic designs stems more from their ability to meet policy makers covert evaluation functions, and to enhance an idealized picture of policy makers' rationality in decision-making, than from their real contribution to such overt evaluation function as providing hard, exact information about causal relationships and policy impact to facilitate rational decision-making. As Feldman and March (1981, pp.177–178), in a general discussion on information and decision-making (p.182) put it:

> The gathering of information provides a ritualistic assurance that appropriate attitudes about decision-making exist . . . information is not simply a basis for action. It is a representation of competence and a reaffirmation of social virtue . . . information use symbolizes a commitment to rational choice. Displaying the symbol reaffirms the importance of this social value and signals personal and organizational competence.

Hence, I suggest, *positivistic designs prosper largely through acting as a rhetoric for an evaluation ritual whereby the lack of rationality of actual decision-making and the accountability and responsibility demanded of the idealized decision-maker, are reconciled.* As such, their latent function may be more generalized and more important than the overt functions proclaimed by their protagonists.

In concluding this chapter, it should be noted that the assessment of positivistic designs presented here has been from *within* that paradigm. In other words, while the practical limitations in implementing the tenets of positivism have been stressed, no real criticism has been directed at the tenets themselves. But not only have these practical problems proved disillusioning for many evaluators, they have also led to researchers questioning the very paradigmatic position from which they stem. Hence a deeper level of "verification crisis" exists. The nature of this epistemological questioning, its implications for evaluation design and the evaluation functions that may be served by the emergent qualitative designs are considered in the next chapter.

Chapter 5

Matching Interpretive Designs and Evaluation Functions

This chapter concentrates on two questions. First, it examines what was referred to in Chapter 1 as the "crisis in verification" — that is, evaluators' disillusionment, at an *epistemological* as well as a practical level, with approaches based on the positivistic paradigm. Secondly, it considers which evaluation functions are best served by methods which reject the positivistic paradigm and rest on an opposite and competing world view — that is, the interpretive paradigm.

The epistemological attack on positivistic approaches to evaluation design

Leaving aside the practical difficulties in implementing positivistic designs in field settings, increasingly evaluation researchers are questioning the epistemological validity of the positivistic paradigm for uncovering "truths" about human society as opposed to the physical world (Argyris, 1980; Guba and Lincoln, 1981; Parlett and Hamilton, 1972; Patton, 1978; Reason and Rowan, 1981; Smith, 1981). The criticisms take two forms. First, that positivism in practice, contradicts its own theory of testing; secondly, that its conceptualization of the nature of social reality is inappropriate. Let us consider these fundamental, and interrelated, attacks in turn.

The nature of testing

Even those content to remain within a positivistic paradigm, would be forced to admit that testing cannot and, in practice, does not accord with the logic of hypothetico-deductivism. For although *in logic* a hypothesis or scientific law is conclusively falsifiable, *methodologically* speaking, it is always possible to doubt a statement as there may have been some error in the reported observation (Popper, 1959). In an attempt to control for error in observation, of course, measuring devices are used wherever possible, but there then exists the problem of who or what measures the accuracy and reliability of the measuring device, and who or what checks the checking device—and so on. *Falsification, methodologically, would involve an infinite regression in testing.* Furthermore, at some point even the positivist has to take on trust common-sense beliefs about the world about him or her in order to experiment at all. In order to test a particular hypothesis, the plausibility of all the other hypotheses entering the experiment have to be assumed. Hence quantitative testing *has* to depend on qualitative trusting (Campbell, 1974).

Given this methodological difficulty, whereas it would be unfair to say that positivists will deliberately evade refutation, they can argue that as conclusive falsification is not possible at a methodological level it is unreasonable to ask for it. To reject a useful theory on the basis of the evidence of one or two tests would be to show an uncritical attitude to the test, or an overcritical attitude to the theory. If observations contradict a hypothesis, the assumption that it is false is only justifiable if it can also be demonstrated that no set of auxiliary assumptions can save it (Duhem, 1954). A theory can be provisionally accepted if it has a higher informative content than competing theories, i.e. if it can explain and is corroborated by a larger number of observations. In practice, then in "normal" science the emphasis is not on refutation, but on confirmation (Kuhn, 1970). Moreover, this confirmation is self-validating because the data identified as "facts" that "test" the theory (for example, the readings of a galvanometer) are themselves theory-laden, because explicit scientific theories must be trusted in order to interpret them (e.g. meter readings) (Campbell, 1974; Feyerabend, 1975). The trusting of a theory in turn depends on the weight of consensual agreement among the scientific community as to its validity—a validity which, in a tautological manner, is established by means of the very same testing process, the scientific method. In practice it is the community of scientists who decide whether an apparent refutation is "trivial", "non-scientific" or "counts", using criteria of "what is sufficient and necessary (that) is determined by the system of relevancies of the scientific paradigm itself" (Walsh, 1972, pp.24–25). In normal science, then, falsification is not, and cannot be the major focus of everyday activity—rather it is the attempt to find supporting evidence to evaluate the theory, and to use it. But this use of confirmation comes perilously close to relying on an inductivist practice—while rejecting inductivist logic, with its attendant fallacy of reasoning from "some" to "all".

A criticism closely related to the argument that positivistic designs are tautologically tested by "facts" which themselves depend on theories which are similarly tested, is that such designs are self validating by virtue of the assumptions the researcher has to make in the process of his data gathering. Acting as the "objective outsider" the positivist, in researching the *social* world, has to assume that there is a correspondence between the indicators used by his respondents to identify meaningful objects and events and those used by himself, that they share the same language and meanings to embrace observations and experiences, and that the normative rules governing their perceptions and interpretations of their environment match the theoretical and methodological rules governing his perception and interpretation of the same environment of objects (Cicourel, 1964).

This being the case,

> The whole process of testing . . . is a process by which data are fitted into an existing conceptual framework in terms of the system of relevancies which underlies it and is not, as positivists would claim, a process by which that framework is independently tested. (Walsh, 1972, p.27, added emphasis)

Such doubts about testing procedures can be seen to have more serious implications for social than natural scientists, when juxtaposed with the second major criticism of the positivistic paradigm — that its conceptualization of social reality is inappropriate.

The nature of social reality

Natural scientists can largely shrug off these criticisms of positivism's testing procedures, on the grounds that, theoretical quibbles aside, they "work". That is, by their use we have greatly increased our ability to explain, predict and control physical phenomena. But, anti-positivists would argue this is only so because the physical world can be conceptualized as having no intrinsic meaning, in which case "the scientist is free, as observer, to construct paradigms of nature which explain its operations in a manner that is suitable to his cognitive concerns" (Walsh, 1972, p.17). If the physical world *has no intrinsic meaning*, the natural scientist need not concern himself with questions of "ultimate truth" about the world, only with hypotheses of high informative content (the "truths" of Newton can be complemented by those of Einstein). "In which case they need only concern themselves with the adequacy of their explanations to their purposes at hand" (Walsh, 1972, p.25).

But can the social world be similarly viewed? A major criticism of positivism, is that social phenomena *are intrinsically meaningful*, in the sense that the social world "has a particular meaning and relevance structure for the human beings, living, thinking and acting therein" (Schutz, 1964, p.5). If this criticism is accepted, positivism's view of the social world as an empirical entity independent of the observer's recognition and appreciation of it, is called into question, and with it the paradigm's methodological assumptions.

It should be pointed out, though, that in rejecting positivism's view of the world as "a structure, composed of determinate relationships between constituent parts", a range of ontological positions, rather than just one alternative can be identified (Morgan and Smircich, 1980). The most extreme rejection involves the acceptance of a totally nominalist viewpoint: that the social world is no more than a projection of individual consciousness, that "one's mind is one's world". Retreating back towards the "realism" end of the ontological continuum, Morgan and Smircich identify less extreme positions. Reality may be seen as a "social construction", the social world being viewed "as a continuous process, created afresh in each encounter of everyday life as individuals impose themselves (by language, labels, actions and routines) on their world to establish a realm of meaningful definition". It is only when these forms of social construction are shared by individuals that they take on even a degree of objective facticity. Retreating a step further towards realism, reality can be seen in terms of "symbolic discourse", that is as "a pattern of symbolic relationships and meanings sustained through a process of human action and interaction", which contains enough continuity and shared enduring meanings that such meanings may appear to an observer to be rule-like. However, these shared meanings are only sustained by continual reaffirmation in individuals' everyday actions — and through their interaction individuals may equally modify and change them. Coming closer to the "realism" end of the continuum, reality may be seen as a context in which individuals operate, which may mould them but also be moulded by them. Morgan and Smircich identify two pictures of this contextual reality. The first less "realistic" picture of the two, is of the world as a "contextual field of information", "a field of everchanging form and activity based on the transmission of information". "Human beings are engaged in a continual process of interaction and exchange with their context — receiving, interpreting, and acting on the information received, and in so doing creating a new pattern of information that effects changes in the field as a whole". This process of interaction and exchange though is not such as to imply that the "environment" just acts as a "context" for individuals; rather there is no such distinction between figure and ground as reality is viewed holistically. Individuals and their environments evolve together, through learning and mutual adjustment, rather than the adaptation being one way, and "an adequate understanding of the *process* entails grasping the ecological nature of the context as a whole".

The second picture, which comes closest to, if still some poles apart from positivism, is of the world as "an evolving process, concrete in nature, but ever changing in detailed form". The world is seen as an organism, an open system, in which everything interacts with everything else and it is extremely difficult to find determinate causal relationships between constituent processes.

"At best, the world expresses itself in terms of general and contingent relationships between its more stable and clear cut elements". Although this view of reality, like the "contextual field of information" view recognizes its interactive nature, it tends, in contrast, to see more of a distinction between figure and ground, and, in practice to treat adaptation as a largely, but not exclusively, one-way process. The individual tends to be seen as adapting to the organization, the organization to the environment, rather than all evolving together (Morgan and Smircich, 1980, pp.494–496).

Now the importance of these different ontological positions is that they involve different assumptions about human nature and ultimately therefore—as far as the evaluation researcher is concerned and, as indicated in Chapter 2—different assumptions about the nature of and questions to be asked about, change in society. Positivism, in viewing social phenomena as a set of real entities, and the social world as a network of determinant causal relationships between them, as a corollary views individuals as very much determined by and a product of the "real" external environment to which they are exposed. Change programmes can, quite consistently, be viewed as a set of real discontinuous activities with a beginning and end, designed to change those that are subjected to them. In Morgan and Smircich's (1980, p.495) terms, the individuals towards whom a change programme is directed can appropriately be viewed as "responding mechanisms". The whole logic of change programmes, viewed from this perspective, is that "stimuli in their environment (i.e. the change programme) condition them (the subjects of the programme) to respond to events in (hopefully!) predictable and determinate ways" (Morgan and Smircich, 1980, p.495). Positivistic assumptions then are not merely consistent with impact evaluation—they are a necessary condition. For impact evaluation has to assume that determinate causal relationships can be established and that concrete behaviour can be observed and measured to assess impact.

If these ontological assumptions cannot be accepted, the epistemological foundations of impact evaluation crumble. If, for example, the researcher retreats one step from the extreme positivistic view and argues that reality is a concrete *process*, rather than structure, the assumption that determinate causal relationships can be identified has to be abandoned, as reality is seen as a process in which everything interacts with everything else, even if, for the purposes of analysis, the focus is upon the adaptation of one phenomenon to the context in which it is related. Even with this focus, the more closely processes are examined the more likely are chicken and egg relationships to emerge. From this perspective change may be seen as evolutionary and continuous, without beginning or end. This is even more pronounced when reality is seen as a "contextual field of information", as the mutual and interactive evolution of social phenomena renders any search for causation infinitely regressive. Furthermore, both these contextual views of reality assume that individuals do not just react to their environment (including change programmes) but actively seek to influence and exploit it. Such an assumption would argue that even if one could assume determinate causal relationships, impact results would be likely to contain the distortive effects of subjects consciously manipulating the experimental situation.

However, while this view of reality creates problems for impact evaluation, it is quite consistent with the assumptions underlying implementation analysis and formative evaluation. For both emphasize the need to monitor and understand interactive processes in the context in which they occur. And, as far as formative evaluation is concerned, this is in order to influence change processes in an on-going iterative manner. As such, it not only assumes the interactive nature of cause and effect processes, but is, indeed, part of it.

If the evaluation researcher moves a further step towards the nominalist position and views reality as "symbolic discourse", there is a further shift in emphasis in the evaluation question. If reality is embedded in a network of shared meanings, that are either reaffirmed or changed through the interpretation and interactions of individuals, then the evaluation of a change programme is not so much concerned with behaviour changes in individuals (and certainly not with attributing external causes for these changes) but with the meaning that their behaviours have for those that create and participate in the programme. The objective of the evaluation is not the testing of hypotheses specified *a priori*, but to increase understanding of the nature of change through the discovery of new insights into its meaning to those involved. Although, in theory, this perspective can enrich the contextual understanding of the formative evaluator, in practice it can confuse his attempts to select information for decision-making. If he is content to concentrate on "real" behavioural processes and what they mean to him (and to his colleagues), he can present one picture of "what's really happening" as a basis for decision-making. But if he accepts that reality is embedded in shared meanings, he has then to accept that there may be many "real" change programmes to evaluate, each with its own definition of success. If multiple realities exist, which picture should the evaluator present, how should he weigh or compare them (assuming it's even meaningful to do this)? Is it valid to attempt to constitute a composite reality, or would this in itself just represent another picture of reality in competition with the others? The answer is, of course, that if he accepts reality in these terms, the evaluator must be prepared to present a range of different answers to any generalized set of questions. The difficulty he then runs is that his audience may equate him with a one-man adversarial evaluation, in spite of the crucial difference that, logically, no one view of reality is in a position to win, as all are equally valid. I return to this issue later in the chapter.

Finally if the social researcher views reality either as a "social construction" or as a "projection of human imagination" there would be no role for, or meaning to, evaluation research. If it is assumed that the "social world . . . is created afresh in each encounter of everyday life", or even more extremely that "reality is an act of creative imagination and of dubious inter-subjective status" (Morgan and Smircich, 1980, p.494), any statement that can be made at one point in time about "reality" may have no relevance to subsequent time periods, and each individual's reality is unique. If individuals are constantly recreating their realities (even assuming these are shared) the concept of change has little meaning as there is no steady state reality with which to compare. Similarly "planned" as opposed to "unplanned" change has no distinct meaning, as all reality has the same status of conscious construction. If each individual's reality is unique to himself, no one but himself can share and, hence, evaluate it. Even if it were possible for an "outsider" to evaluate it, the very act would be pointless as it would have no relevance to any other individual. In other words, *certain explanations of the world, by implicitly or explicitly contending that there is no objective world to act upon, render evaluation irrelevant, since they rule out the possibility of acting upon the world.*

The implications of these conclusions raise important questions about how far the evaluation researcher can afford to retreat from the positivistic paradigm — assuming he wishes his research to be used to inform official decision-making and action. But before considering this issue further, it is necessary to touch on several subsidiary criticisms of the positivistic paradigm that derive from the fundamental attacks outlined above.

A misplaced concern with internal validity?

As was discussed at length in Chapter 4, the hallmark of a positivistic evaluation design is an overriding concern with controlling for the effect of potentially intervening variables upon hypothesized causal relationships, so that valid causal inferences may be drawn. This concern becomes largely irrelevant once the researcher moves away from viewing social phenomena as having an objective concrete reality. This is because establishing determinate causal inferences in the sense understood by positivists — that real events or phenomena effect real impacts on other events or phenomena — is no longer a relevant research question. Either causation is conceptualized as infinitely regressive (the contextual view), or, it is conceptualized as not "real" at all, existing only as a social construction, by which individuals seek to explain what they observe through the attribution of commonsense rather than "scientific" cause and effect relationships. Rather than using causation as a concept to explain behaviour, an interpretative approach focuses on the individual's intentions and motivations, his beliefs about what behaviour will achieve his goals, and his awareness of the social rules governing this behaviour (Argyle, 1978).

If this approach is taken, the notion of "controlling for intervening variables" becomes nonsensical, as social phenomena are not conceptualized in terms of "variables", while their categorization as being "intervening" is meaningless without the concept of causality. This points to an essential difference between positivistic and interpretive approaches: whereas the former seeks to achieve explanation by methods which are exclusive (excluding the effects of "intervening variables") the latter does so by methods which are inclusive (embracing a "slice of life").

Put somewhat differently, internal validity, in a positivistic design, concerns the degree of isomorphism between the data and phenomena to which they relate. "There is one reality, and information is internally valid if it describes that reality and facilitates its control and manipulation" (Guba and Lincoln, 1981, p.105). But if the assumption is that there are multiple realities, how does one establish the truth value of research findings? However "inaccurate" they may be (in the sense of not according with any respondent's view of reality) they represent one reality, the world as perceived by the researcher. Practically speaking then, the question becomes how can the researcher test whether the multiple realities he presents ring true to those from whom he derived them? The issue of internal validity is one of establishing the findings' credibility with the groups whose realities they are meant to represent rather than establishing any ultimate and universal truth value. The problems this presents and how the evaluation researcher might tackle them are discussed later in the chapter.

A further question remains though. How does the researcher demonstrate the validity of his findings to his colleagues? Would the demonstration that respondents found them convincing necessarily be satisfactory? The problem is that the interpretive evaluation researcher may wish to convince positivistic colleagues to whom issues of reliability of findings are seen as necessary, if not sufficient, condition for their validity. Is it appropriate for the interpretive evaluator to seek to demonstrate the consistency—in some sense—of his findings? Or does this, in itself contradict his paradigmatic position? This issue will also be considered later in this chapter.

The validity of generalization

An aim of evaluation research within the positivistic paradigm is to establish generalizations, that is truth statements that are context free. To this end, as discussed in the previous chapter, great care is taken to protect the external validity of an evaluation design. But once it is admitted that many truth statements are not free from situational constraints, to what extent can one generalize?

When phenomena can be treated as having no intrinsic meaning, and as "responding mechanisms", generalizations can be made about cause and effect relationships. The mediating effects of context only creep in through specific exclusions and caveats, for otherwise it is encompassed by the independent variable. It is quite possible then to derive physical laws that have a general meaning, free from situational constraints, to which there are no exceptions—although as Cronbach (1975) suggests, even these may decay over time. But this is rarely the case with "behavioural laws". This is because specific human behaviours are very much mediated by the context in which they occur. We are unlikely to observe a parent throwing his children out of an upstairs window on a quiet Sunday afternoon, but we may well observe it if the house is on fire, the alternative exits blocked, and neighbours are standing below to catch the children. Any law about parents throwing children out of windows, or about almost any other activity, is likely to be mediated by context—even if the phenomena, including "contextual variables", are treated as real and the researchers' interest is in observed behaviour and attributed causal explanation *per se.*

But context can also be viewed in terms of the meanings these contextual variables, such as "technology", "size of department", "inner-city area" have for individuals. In which case, the context of individual behaviour must be viewed as either unique to himself (an extreme nominalist position), or shared only with those with whom, interactively, he sustains or changes its meaning. The implication of this position is that generalization is at best extremely circumscribed and at worst beside the point. To generalize at all, we either have to assume that our truth statements are context free (which is a difficult assumption in regard to social behaviour), or we have to specify the limits of generalizability, that is, in which contexts will our truth statements hold. If contexts are "real" and can be objectively defined and measured, problems of comparison are technical. If contexts reside only in meanings individuals attribute to them, whether shared or not, such context is unique to those whose meanings construct or affirm it. No two contexts are "really" comparable (though an act of comparison may in itself be a social construction on the part of the researcher) and hence the notion of generalizing from one context to another is mistaken. Furthermore the purpose of generalization, that is to specify the extent to which a determinate causal statement is context free, is rendered irrelevant by the fact that causal statements, given these assumptions, are irrelevant too. Human behaviour is not caused by "things" or "variables" but rather is a product of how people interpret the world.

The implication seems to be that the more one moves towards the nominalist end of the ontological continuum, away from realism, the less it is either possible or relevant to generalize (Gellner, 1973, p.81). It might be suggested that some small degree of generalization is still possible when reality is being viewed, in Morgan and Smircich's (1980) terms, as a "concrete process" or as a "contextual field of information". For characteristic configurations of behaviours may be observed and limited generalizations drawn about the circumstances in which they might be expected to appear. But note how even this degree of generalization smuggles back a positivistic view of reality. By suggesting that the configurations can be placed *into* a context (i.e. the "circumstances in which they appear"), rather than constituting the whole reality in themselves, "concrete structures" are smuggled in. For how else are these "circumstances" to be typified for purposes of comparison, unless as contextual "variables"?

Where does this leave evaluation research designs? Again it would seem that the logic of this position is more consistent with a formative than impact design, where generalization to other settings is not a prime consideration and, indeed, where the emphasis is on gaining a deep understanding of the idiosyncracies and unique characteristics of a particular programme in a particular setting. Moreover, in a formative evaluation there is likely to be sympathy with the view that such a distinction between "programme" and "setting" is artificial as in reality either they may be viewed as interdependent and interactive processes ("concrete processes" view), evolving together ("contextual field of information" view), or as a product of how people interpret the world ("symbolic discourse" view).

As far as impact evaluation designs are concerned, these arguments are, in a sense, irrelevant. If one accepts the ontological assumptions on which the arguments are based then *all* the foundations of impact evaluation crumble, as discussed earlier, so whether or not one can generalize from a design that one has already decided cannot produce valid knowledge is neither here nor there. Alternatively if one accepts the assumptions about the nature of social phenomena on which positivistic designs rest, then these problems with generalization do not arise. The nub of the issue is that if one wishes to generalize from an evaluation design, to fulfil the sorts of policy-making functions discussed in Chapter 3, one has to accept that it *must be positivistic*, with all the design constraints that entails.

I turn now to the fourth criticism of positivism—how valid is the role of the "objective-outsider" in social inquiry?

The validity of the "objective–outsider" role

As suggested in the previous chapter, in principle, positivism assumes that the role of the researcher is one of objective observation, specification and measurement of the "facts", which exist outside, independent of and unaffected by such activities, except when consciously manipulated in the course of the experimental process.

For the non-positivist, though, this role is considered neither desirable nor possible. It is not considered possible precisely because individuals are not intrinsically meaningless objects, but rather enact a meaningful relationship with their world, including the researcher who attempts to enter it. The very existence of a "problem" of reactivity, non-positivists argue, would suggest that positivists' assumptions about the nature of social phenomena are mistaken. Quite apart from epistemological and methodological difficulties in maintaining this role, when it comes to evaluation research, as was discussed in the previous chapter, political considerations and desire for utilization further undermine its practicality.

But even if the objective-outsider role was possible, the non-positivists would argue that, given a more interpretive view of reality, a different role is called for because different data are required. If the researcher wishes to understand the meanings which individuals' actions have for them and others, it is necessary to get close to them and learn to see the world through their eyes. This, of course, cannot be done in a laboratory, or through research techniques which prejudge what questions need to be asked, and thus elicit "contrived" data. Instead the researcher needs to adopt an "insider" role, as participant observer, and through involvement in the everyday flow of his respondents' lives, develop "thick descriptions" (Geertz, 1973) of the subject of his inquiry.

However, the "insider" research role provides both problems and opportunities for the evaluation researcher. The opportunities, once again, would seem to lie within the framework of a formative rather than impact evaluation design. Certainly the "thick descriptions" generated should enable the evaluator to gain an understanding of the processes of change (rather than merely treating it as a black box from which, hopefully, predicted outcomes might emerge) and of what the individuals involved identify as its outcomes and what meanings they have for them. In this sense, such an approach can form part of an impact study—but it is one that is very different from that conventionally implied by the term, where the focus is on "objective" impact as defined and measured by the researcher, not subject impact as identified and experienced by those researched. The "insider" role is, of course, totally inconsistent with a conventional experimental or quasi-experimental impact study, as the role adopted could be expected to result in reactivity on the part of the subjects undermining the internal and external validity of the study—if they were relevant issues.

Positivists would argue, however, that a major difficulty with the "insider" role for the evaluation researcher is the extent to which it can ever be said to be truly objective. Stated like this, this criticism involves a major confusion: that objectivity and neutrality are synonymous and hence a lack of objectivity (i.e. subjectivity) is synonymous with a lack of neutrality (i.e. bias). At a conceptual level, this criticism can be quickly dealt with. As Scriven (1972) has pointed out "objective" and "subjective" can be understood in two contrasting senses.

In its quantitative sense "objective" refers to what a number of people experience, and what is therefore amenable to intersubjective agreement, whereas "subjective" refers to what is experienced by one individual. In this sense the researcher as "insider" produces subjective reports, in so far as they are based on observations that are unique to him and non-replicable. But "objective" and "subjective" can also be understood in a qualitative sense, that is, referring to the quality of the observation regardless of the number of people making it. It is in this sense that "subjective" denotes unreliability and bias, while "objective" denotes reliable, factual and unbiased. As Scriven points out the two senses do not necessarily coincide. An observation can be quantitatively objective but qualitatively subjective— for example there are some cultural biases to which a group is more susceptible than an individual (e.g. racial prejudice or jingoism). Guba and Lincoln (1981, p.125) suggest a good example of this lack of coincidence: "one would be more inclined to accept the reports of one magician standing in the wings during another magician's performance than the reports of a large audience, all of whose members were being systematically deluded".

Accepting this distinction, two questions remain. First, recognizing that, in a quantitative sense, the insider's research data are subjective, does this necessarily mean that they are non-reliable, in the sense that there is no way of confirming them? Secondly, does the insider run a real risk of "going native", of being captured by one interest group, and unconsciously projecting its view of reality as being more generally held, or more true than others?

Both these questions concern the key issue of how valid data may be generated by an interpretive design—an issue that will be dealt with in subsequent sections of this chapter. But before embarking on it, it may be useful now to state what are the core characteristics of interpretive evaluation designs.

Core characteristics of interpretive designs

Obviously the exact nature of an interpretive evaluation design will depend in some degree on the extent to which the evaluator has retreated from positivism's ontological position—whether he views reality in contextual terms for example, or in terms of "symbolic discourse". (We can dismiss the extreme nominalist views as they are really incompatible with any evaluation design.) That said, interpretive designs, compared to positivistic designs, tend to have the following core characteristics:

(1) An emphasis on explanation through developing understanding rather than through predictive testing. As a corollary of (1).

(2) An emphasis on grounded theory (that is, based on and inductively developed from the data) (Glaser and Strauss, 1967) rather than on an *a priori* deductive theory.

(3) An emphasis on exploratory, tentative and discovery-oriented investigation rather than on verification oriented investigation.

(4) An emphasis on an expansionistic, holistic perspective rather than on a reductionist, particularistic one. That is, an interpretive design will seek to investigate a change programme in the "round", and let the insights from each stage in the evaluation act as a stepping stone to further exploration of the programme. In contrast, positivistic designs begin with preformulated hypotheses and seek only the information relevant to them. Design is emergent rather than predetermined.

(5) An emphasis on the actions and taken-for-granted meanings of all participants in a change programme rather than on behavioural changes in its "subjects".

(6) An emphasis on iterative processes and the emergent, rather than on determinate causal processes and outcomes.

(7) An emphasis on the "insider" research perspective, on being close to the data, rather than maintaining an "outsider" perspective and being removed from the data.

(8) An emphasis on naturalistic and uncontrolled observation rather than obtrusive and controlled measurement.

(9) An emphasis on the validity, richness and meaningfulness of data rather than its reliability.

(10) A recognition that generalization may be either impossible or very circumscribed, rather than being the corner-stone of the research.

(11) An emphasis on qualitative rather than quantitative methods.

These characteristics all stem from the interpretive evaluation researcher's basic assumption that social phenomena, unlike natural phenomena, have intrinsic meaning and that, as a result, engaging in variable analysis is inappropriate. As most of these characteristics have been discussed in relation to our criticisms of positivism, I will not discuss them further from an epistomological point of view, except to consider the emphasis on qualitative method.

In the wake of an increasing recognition of the limitations of quantitative quasi experimental approaches it has recently become fashionable for erstwhile arch-positivists to advocate the use of qualitative methods (e.g. Campbell, 1974; Reichardt and Cook, 1979). It is argued that qualitative methods can usefully provide "background" data to assist explanation of statistically weak effects, to aid implementation analysis and so on. Equally, it has been pointed out that interpretive evaluation researchers could well use measurements, such as the sociometric, to provide contextual background to the meanings of the actions they observe. In both cases the implication is that the use of the non-preferred method is supplementary, but enriching to the basic evaluation design.

The problem I see with the assumption that qualitative methods can be usefully tacked onto a basically quantitative design, and vice versa, is that it results in an abstracted empiricism. Following Burrell and Morgan (1979, p.105) abstracted empiricism arises when methods are used which are essentially incongruent with the research's avowed theoretical position and violate its epistemological assumptions, such as when "systems theorists . . . spend their energies measuring 'structures' (and) interactionists . . . utilize static measurements of 'attitudes' and 'role situations'." The example I cited of the interpretive researcher using sociometric measurements would be just such a case, if he saw reality as "symbolic discourse", because he would in fact be treating reality, at the very least, as a "concrete process". When evaluation researchers advocate that "qualitative" or "naturalistic" methods can be used in what is basically a positivistic design there seems to be the implicit assumption that ontological positions can be swapped at will within the one design. Indeed Reichardt and Cook (1979, pp.18–19) virtually admit as much when they state "there is nothing to stop the researcher . . . from mixing and matching the attributes of the two paradigms to achieve that combination which is most appropriate for the research problem and setting at hand . . . evaluation should feel free to change their paradigmatic stance as the need arises".

I would have to express reservations about this position. At one level it is, of course, possible for a positivistically inclined evaluation researcher to use a technique, such as participant observation, which is generally regarded as "qualitative", for example, to document the number and length of interactions within a setting. This would be entirely compatible with his paradigmatic stance. For in doing so he would essentially be measuring concrete behaviour and in practice converting a method associated with generating qualitative data into a quantitative method. (The same could apply to his use of content analysis, video recordings and other "qualitative" techniques.) But the whole point of using "qualitative" techniques, particularly if the intention is to supplement a quantitative design, is presumably to gather "rich" qualitative data about participants' meanings and motives, not further measures of their behaviour. Yet, if he does so, the researcher is admitting the existence of individual realities. And, as Guba and Lincoln (1981, p.77) put it

Can one assume both singular reality and multiple realities at the same time? How can one believe in insularity between the investigator and the object of his investigation while also allowing for their mutual interaction? How can one work simultaneously toward the development of nomethic and idiographic science?

Thus we conclude, however reluctantly, that with respect to the basic assumptions that differentiate scientific from naturalistic modes, hard choice must be made . . . (added emphasis) . . .

I would have much sympathy with this statement, but to take its assumptions to their practical conclusion, it does place limitations on the evaluator's choice of method. For, to avoid the charge of abstracted empiricism, or of holding simultaneously two incompatible ontological positions, he must convert whatever method he uses to match his paradigmatic position. In which case what nominally appear to be qualitative techniques are converted into quantitative ones, as illustrated earlier, and vice versa (though it is difficult to see how the latter can be done, without a shift in ontological position, unless it is assumed that there exists high levels of consensus on the meaning of repeating behaviours as, for example, in a game of football). If this position is held, it limits the extent to which evaluators can triangulate method, as those used must be epistemologically compatible (e.g. participant observation and unstructured interviewing used to generate qualitative data).

This point has been discussed at some length, because, with disillusionment in the practicality of quasi-experimental methods, some evaluators might be tempted to think that all may be resolved by plugging the gaps with qualitative methods, yet still proclaiming a positivistic stance. The confusions inherent in this position are generally not made explicit and just assumed away in spite of their implications for the utility and meaningfulness of the data thus collected.

There would seem to be two ways round this problem. Either the evaluator can dismiss the above reservations as epistemological quibbles and use both qualitative and quantitative methods within the one evaluation design. Or the evaluation team itself might contain members of different paradigmatic stances, who can achieve a form of triangulation by testing whether the results of their respective evaluations appear consistent with each other. To what extent this is feasible will be considered at the end of this chapter.

We can now return to some of the questions raised earlier in this chapter, viz.

(1) How does the evaluator cope with the problems of identifying and evaluating multiple realities (and then presenting them as an input to decision-making)?

(2) How can he or she establish their credibility and consistency?

(3) Is there any sense in which he or she can generalize them?

(4) How can he or she maintain his or her role as "insider" without going native?

In a sense these questions mirror those asked in the previous chapter about maintaining internal and external validity in positivistic designs and the role of the researcher as objective outsider.

Identifying multiple realities and establishing credibility and consistency of findings

In a positivistic evaluation the nature of the design, that is the prior ordering of techniques and measurements, is all important. An interpretive design, in contrast, cannot be devised prior to the evaluation — it is emergent (and holistic). In these circumstances it is not possible to point to particular interpretive *designs* (as one can with a "true" experiment, or pre- and post-test comparison series) known to yield findings of varying degrees of validity, as from each evaluation setting a different pattern of investigation is likely to emerge. While similar *strategies* and *techniques* may be used, how they are put together into a "design" will emerge in an on-going fashion in response to how the change programme and the evaluator's understanding of its key issues and questions develop. Furthermore, as discussed earlier, because the evaluator recognizes that there are multiple realities to be uncovered, establishing "truth" in any absolute sense is not the issue. Rather it is developing models of reality which "ring true" to those whose views of reality they are supposed to represent. Hence the question we are left with is not what interpretive designs are likely to yield valid data, but what strategies and techniques may be used to generate models of reality credible to those from whom they are derived?

Strategies and techniques to establish multiple realities

Both positivistic and interpretive evaluators have first to focus their study. But whereas the positivist is likely to do this by deriving hypotheses directly from his theoretical knowledge of salient issues, or working with those presented to him by the sponsors of the study, the interpretive evaluator derives his from immersion in the change programme itself. Whereas the positivist will seek to test his hypotheses through data collected from pre-specified random or representative experimental and control samples, of a pre-specified population, the interpretive evaluator will seek to derive hypotheses from information supplied by a purposive or theoretical sample (Glaser and Strauss, 1967) from which he can optimize learning. This sample, in its entirety cannot be specified in advance, as it can only emerge as the data collected from early respondents suggest hypotheses to be tested and, hence, further data to be collected. The use of a "ripple technique" in selecting respondents is more relevant than drawing up a sample as such, although an initial selection of gatekeepers' representing different parties to the change programme can be made. But even this will go hand in hand with the decision about what initial information will generate worthwhile, if tentative, hypotheses.

Guba and Lincoln (1981) suggest that an interpretive evaluator should focus on several types of information. First, information that will constitute a "thick description" of the change programme: that is, information about the nature of the programme (e.g. its goals, target groups, agents, schedule of activities, costs) its organizational, community and cultural setting and its "conditions". It is also suggested that this information should be collected with an eye to the differences (and why) between the programme as initially intended and as actually implemented and, if implemented in different sites, variations as between sites. In effect, this is the information relevant to implementation analysis. From an ontological point of view it is information particularly relevant to an evaluator who takes a "contextual field of information" or "concrete processes" view of reality (i.e. a view of reality as a context in which individuals operate, which may mould them but also be moulded by them).

The other types of information the interpretive evaluator should focus on, according to Guba and Lincoln (1981) is that which will illuminate the different participants' "concerns" about the programme, the "issues" it provokes, and the values that lie behind both. A "concern" is defined as any matter of interest to one or more participants about which they feel threatened, or think will lead to undesirable consequences, or that they want substantiated or refuted. An "issue", in contrast, is any statement or proposition that allows for the presentation of different points of view and reflects the fact that different participants in the change programme experience and understand its reality in different ways. Guba and Lincoln (1981, pp.320–323) suggest that participants' values can be inferred from the concerns and issues they identify. It is this information that is the core of the study to the evaluator who views reality in terms of "symbolic discourse".

The mechanics of a strategy whereby key concerns, issues and values can be identified, classified and generate hypotheses is fully discussed in Guba and Lincoln (1981). The strategy is essentially the "discovery of grounded theory" approach of Glaser and Strauss (1967). In other words it involves an iterative recycling process of categorizing data via content analyses, characterizing the emerging categories and assessing the resulting category set. In categorizing data the aim is to maximize the internal homogeneity of items in that category and the external heterogeneity among categories. In assessing the category set attention is paid to categories that appear called for by the logic of the set but which have not so far emerged and to categories which seem incomplete and require "fleshing out". The techniques of "extending" (beginning with known items and building on them), "bridging" (beginning with several known but apparently disconnected items, and attempting to identify relationships and connections between them) and of "surfacing" (proposing new information that logically ought to be found in the field and then verifying its existence) are useful here. Closure, that is, when to stop collecting information, emerges when either there is no one left to interview, processes to describe or documents to analyse; or when successive examination of sources yields an increasing redundancy of information without useful reinforcement or when the categories "feel" integrated (that is when there appear clear and stable patterns and regularities in the data) or when over-extension is suspected (that is, when the area of investigation seems far removed from the issue or concern that prompted it) (Guba and Lincoln, 1981, pp.100–101). This process of data classification goes hand in hand with generating tentative hypotheses based on perceived connections between items within categories and between the categories themselves, the testing of these ideas through further exploration and generation of data, the development of firmer and new hypotheses and so on.

The fieldwork techniques through which these data are generated have their roots in ethnography, ethnomethodology and ethnogenic analysis (to take the anthropological, sociological and social psychological approaches respectively), relying heavily on unstructured interviewing, participant and non-participant observation, use of documents and unobtrusive measures. (For general discussions about and examples of the use of these "qualitative" techniques see Special Issue of *Administrative Science Quarterly*, Vol 24, December 1979; Special Issue of *Journal of Management Studies*, Vol 20, July 1983; Cook and Reichardt, 1979; Guba and Lincoln, 1981, esp. Chapters 7, 8, 10, 11; Van Maanen *et al.*, 1982.) References to the use of such techniques, for example, in action research and other organizational development exercises are not uncommon (e.g. Klein, 1976; Warmington *et al.*, 1977). What is more uncommon are systematic accounts of the use of such techniques within an explicitly interpretive framework, as much action research, as already mentioned in Chapter 2, rests on a systems rather than a symbolic interactionism framework (e.g. Rice, 1958, 1963; Warmington *et al.*, 1977). Fully-fledged interpretive studies have been chiefly concerned with recreating the day-to-day "taken for granted" worlds of organizational participants, rather than assessing changes in those worlds [see for example, Fairhurst's (1983) account of the accomplishment of nursing work on geriatric wards or Spradley and Mann's (1975) of the cocktail waitress, or Van Maanen's (1982) of the American police sergeant].

However examples do exist of attempts to use an avowedly interpretive approach in evaluating both the introduction of participation and work systems design in organizations (see, for example, Bate and Mangham, 1981; Blackler and Brown, 1980, 1983; Brown and Kaplan, 1981; Carnall, 1982) and of new technologies (Wilkinson, 1983). Particularly interesting are studies where the researchers, over a period of time, frankly admit to their disillusionment with the conventional action research approaches with which they initiated their work and gradually develop an interpretive approach. Bate and Mangham's (1981) blow-by-blow accounts of their attempts to introduce participation at "Alpen" is a refreshing case in point. In contrast, though, some researchers assert the interpretive nature of their studies while using methods seemingly at odds with the implied ontological position (see, for example, Carnall's (1982) use of an experimental design in assessing the effects of job design changes in electro-mechanical assembly in a precision instruments factory, and his use of structured questionnaires in his study of an organizational development programme in a Norwegian engineering company, while maintaining "the interpretive nature of our approach" (1982, p.123). As with positivistic research, methodological rigour tends to be compromised in a field-setting, where time and access constraints may limit the researcher. Wilkinson (1983, p.103) for example, found that, contrary to his wishes, management rarely allowed him to *observe* meetings between workers and management or among managers on decisions about new technology, and he had to rely on second-hand accounts. These caveats aside, though, these studies are illustrative of the issues of credibility, generalization, and role of the insider considered below.

Establishing credibility of findings

Establishing credibility of findings involves two tasks: how to produce findings that stand the best chance of being found credible by participants and how to test their credibility with the groups whose reality they are supposed to represent (Guba and Lincoln, 1981, p.105).

Leaving aside for a moment the problems of data distortion that may derive from the evaluator adopting an "insider" role, producing findings that are likely to be found credible is largely a matter of triangulation. That is exposing an idea, or piece of data, or an assertion by one informant to data drawn from other sources or generated by other methods, for purposes of confirmation or disconfirmation. Detailed discussion and illustration of how triangulation of sources and methods may be employed can be found in Denzin (1970), Gowler and Legge (1982), Jick (1979) and Webb *et al.* (1966). Thus the evaluator may triangulate sources by comparing two participants' accounts of a set of events (see Brown and Kaplan, 1981; Wilkinson, 1983). He may triangulate methods by comparing this interview data with the official documentation recording these events, with his own longitudinal observations of them (see Birchall *et al.*, 1978). An interesting use of triangulation may be found in Marsh *et al.* (1978) ethogenic analysis of football hooliganism where participants accounts of what they understood to be the meanings of the behaviours they enacted or observed were compared with the researchers' observations of what went on, and video recordings of these events. The assumption here is that because "the very same social knowledge and skill is involved in the genesis of action and of accounts, by recording and analyzing each separately, we have two mutually supporting and reciprocally checking ways of discovering the underlying system of social knowledge and belief" (i.e. the supporter's/hooligan's reality) (March *et al.*, 1978, p.21). Indeed, where the event in question is encapsulated in time and space (a training session; a committee meeting; activities on a hospital ward) and if a video recording can be made without the participants' knowledge (and, of course, there are ethical problems here) different participants' "accounts" of the events shown can be highly revealing.

It is often suggested that quantitative and qualitative methods should be triangulated, so that data generated by participant observation and un-structured interviewing can illuminate quantitative measures, and quantitative measures confirm qualitative impressions. Good examples of researchers attempting to triangulate methods and data in this fashion are provided by Warr *et al.* (1978) and Smith *et al.* (1976). In the first case—an exercise in developing a participatory organizational climate in a steel works—the researchers collected data by means of "before" and "after" questionnaire surveys, "problem record forms" (recording what problems were raised in each participatory group and what was done about them), "meeting assessment forms" (on which employee members of the group would anonymously record their own views about its conduct and success), quite apart from employing both observation of meetings and structured and unstructured interviewing. Smith *et al.* (1976), in their evaluation of Outward Bound, triangulated data on participants' experiences obtained through participant observation with psychometric measurement of their "self-esteem", "self-assertion", "self-awareness" and "acceptance by others". However, as discussed previously, using quantitative and qualitative techniques in tandem can involve problems of abstracted empiricism and covert ontological shifts. The way round this, as Denzin recommends, is to have a triangulation of *investigators*, in other words, to employ a multi-perspective team of evaluators with different ontological positions, using techniques compatible with their own position, producing a set of triangulated *studies*. Indeed, in the Outward Bound study, the quantitative and qualitative data were presented as (and derived from) two discrete but related studies, both comprising an equal part of the evaluation project. This can, of course, present its own set of problems, as in cases when the reality presented by the interpretive study appears to contradict that drawn from the positivistic study, but, as illustrated by Trend's (1979) account of the AAE experiment (a housing allowance programme) the effort to reconcile the studies may well generate further hypotheses and insights.

If efforts are made to corroborate data and interpretations, the models of reality which the evaluator can present to those from whom he or she has derived them stand a good chance of "ringing true". Whether they do so, or not, can only be found out by asking sources whether they believe them. In other words "member checks"—feeding findings (i.e. "factual" data, classifications and hypotheses) back to their sources—is an important technique in testing their credibility. This technique was used extensively by Blackler and Brown (1980, 1983) in their evaluation of Shell's "New Philosophy of Management" programme, and by Bate and Mangham (1981) in their introduction and evaluation of participation in a pharmaceuticals company. Indeed this feedback of findings (if with rather different intentions) is a central technique of much action research—"the survey feedback" featuring in many such exercises (e.g. Beer, 1976). When the evaluation researcher feeds back findings that are intended to be purely descriptive of a group's perceptions, attitudes and concerns, of how its members think and feel, there are likely to be few problems. Participants are likely to be only too willing to correct his or her understanding of what they said happened, the opinions they hold and so on. The problems are likely to occur when the researcher adds an interpretation of what can be inferred from these data in terms of the group's current interests and motivations. Members of the group may be genuinely not fully conscious of their motivations, or if conscious, not see it in their best interests to admit to them. However, the evaluator may turn this constraint into an opportunity by using the reaction to test the existence of interests and values already inferred ("If they have X interest, I would expect them to deny my interpretation"). Indeed this resembles the use of the "strong inference" method as discussed by Platt (1964). A similar difficulty may occur if the evaluator seeks corroboration of information derived from one set of participants by explicitly asking another group if they think it valid (rather than just asking the second group for their own account of the events to which the information refers, and testing corroboration by comparison). The corroborating group may have political reasons to deny the validity of the information if the groups are in competition with each other for scarce resources or otherwise in conflict. Furthermore the evaluator is faced with the limitations inherent in any act of communication and information processing: individuals tend to hear what they want to hear and in the light of what is salient to their immediate interests (see Chapter 3).

To cope with these sorts of problems Guba and Lincoln (1981) and Stake (1975) suggest various strategies. First member checks, as a general rule, are best done continuously and informally, without the informant being aware that information is being checked. This, it is suggested, can be done by presenting informants with hypothetical situations — or trouble cases (to take an anthropological technique), and asking them to respond. Similarly with checking out emerging hypotheses or interpretations of data, little and often seems advisable, partly because it prevents an informant being overloaded with new possibly unacceptable ideas all at once, and partly because the informality of the checking is likely to promote greater frankness than would occur in a formal meeting where members might feel obliged to present "the official line". Bate and Mangham (1981) give evidence of the success of this strategy. Greater frankness is also more likely if discussion takes place with individuals by themselves rather than in a group context, where an individual, with an idiosyncratic view, may be unwilling to speak out.

This is not to say, though, that there is no place for more formalized group feedback sessions. First, these are necessary when the evaluator wishes to check information and interpretation relevant to group level phenomena — for example, an interest group's justification of its opposition to various aspects of a change programme. Testing a model of a group's view of reality must be done at the group level, if the group, collectively, is to "own" the model of their reality as presented to them by the evaluator. The assumption here, of course, is that the group has characteristics over and above the sum of its individual parts, and hence checking group models of reality with individuals *qua* individuals would be just another example of abstracted empiricism. Secondly, group level member checks are useful when two or more groups emphatically deny the validity of the information, both factual and interpretive, presented by the other(s). Guba and Lincoln (1981) suggest that in these circumstances it is appropriate to bring the groups together and encourage them to argue out their different models of reality in such a way as to highlight and clarify their differences, and the nature of their investment in the particular pictures of reality they hold.

One problem that has been discussed at some length by Guba and Lincoln (1981) is that of "misinformation" as they put it. What should researchers do if they suspect their informants are providing "false" information? Guba and Lincoln (1981, p.318) draw the distinction between "unintended" false information presented by the informant about himself ("self-deception"), others ("misconception") and institutions ("myth") and the parallel "intended" false information ("lie", "cover-up", "front"). They suggest that while unintended misinformation can frequently be exposed by triangulation techniques, intended misinformation may require that the informant is subjected to adversarial investigative techniques, such as those developed by investigative journalists (e.g. the key interview) and the legal profession (e.g. cross-examination) (Guba, 1981; Guba and Lincoln, 1981; Owens and Owen, 1981), in order to "get at the truth".

I consider that, although this position is compatible with a basically positivistic outlook, it misunderstands that of an interpretive evaluation researcher. An interpretive researcher would admit that unintended misinformation can exist about *behaviour*, for example, on what day a meeting took place and who attended, how many participants voted for or against a motion, the words they were heard to speak. These are matters that can be observed, recorded and measured. But unintended or intended misinformation about action (the meaning of behaviour) is another matter as what constitutes its nature must always be open to interpretation and hence there is no one "truth" about it. If the question is less one of any absolute truth value of the information presented but rather the motivation that lies behind its presentation in that form (as Guba and Lincoln seem to infer if not state explicitly), then the distinction between unintended and intended seems to break down. For in both cases it is equally relevant to ask what function the information—or view of reality it represents—serves for the person presenting it. Guba and Lincoln (1981, p.318) admit that unintended misinformation about self "usually occurs because of the subject's lack of insight into his own dynamics or because of the need to maintain an integrated personality", while that about institutions "usually arises because of a need to maintain institutional integrity and a sense of personal well-being". It would seem though that intended misinformation serves equally self-protective and enhancing functions, and the difference in kind between intended and unintended misinformation about action at least is more a matter of how conscious or unconscious the informant is that he is presenting a picture of reality that is self-serving. In these circumstances although the techniques of cross-examination and key interviewing may be useful to sharpen up the individuals' awareness that the pictures of reality they are presenting serves specific functions for them and that they conflict with those (probably equally self-serving) of other individuals and groups, their conventionally avowed function of establishing "the truth" or "the facts" is incompatible with the interpretive position.

Finally, Guba and Lincoln (1981, p.316) suggest that "indirect" member checks can be used to further test the credibility of classifications and interpretations. That is, an informant can be asked to nominate an individual whose perspective about the change programme, he or she thinks, is similar to their own. The "parallel sample" can then assess the evaluator's emerging interpretations without any "contamination" from previous interviews. In this way a check can also be made of the extent to which supposed shared realities are really shared, and in what aspects they are idiosyncratic. (This use of a parallel sample also serves to flesh out and refine emergent classifications and hypotheses.)

Establishing consistency

For reasons discussed earlier, interpretive research strategies and techniques, while consistent with the functions served by formative evaluations, are not consistent with summative evaluations and generalizations (both in the conventionally understood sense). Hence issues of data reliability and replication in other settings are not really relevant. However, credibility of findings, when it comes to their utilization (see Chapter 7) may involve establishing their credibility not just with direct participants but with wider audiences ("the public"; other evaluators and "experts") who are potential critics and or competitors for resources, and who may believe that the *sine qua non* of a "proper" scientific study is replicability. Credibility with these groups may be enhanced if interpretive evaluators, having logically ruled out replication in other settings, can demonstrate that their findings would be consistently repeated if the evaluation was replicated with the same groups in the same setting.

Guba and Lincoln (1981, pp.121–124) suggest three strategies for persuading outsider observers that findings are consistent. The first two, triangulation of methods and triangulation of evaluators are the corroborative techniques used to establish validity, the assumption here being that, to the extent that reality is shared, validity and consistency will go hand in hand. (And if there are no shared realities, as discussed earlier, evaluation becomes a pointless activity anyway.) Guba and Lincoln suggest that triangulation of evaluators may be achieved by the use of "step-wise replication" techniques. This involves, in its simplest form, dividing data sources (informants, observational situations, documents) and researchers into two random halves and letting each conduct an independent study. This "random assignment" assumes, of course, that evaluators hold roughly the same ontological position, or it might result in internal team conflicts, or the danger that two different teams, representing different ontological positions and triangulating quantitative and qualitative methods, might produce two apparently different sets of findings that can only be reconciled through synthesis (see Trend's 1979 study). Furthermore, the degree of independence of the two teams has to be finely judged. The more independent the teams, the more persuasive if their findings are mutually consistent. But the more independent the teams are, the more they will have sacrificed the opportunities to learn from each others' data and interpretations, and the categories and hypotheses each derive will be grounded in only part of the available data.

A way round this, as Guba and Lincoln suggest, is to have consistency cross-checks at the conclusion of specific steps in the research process (for example, when each team has arrived at an initial set of categories, to check then; when these are fleshed out and refined, a further check—and so on)—but otherwise to remain independent.

The third strategy to establish consistency is what Guba and Lincoln (1981, pp.122–124) term the "audit". The basic idea here is that the researchers should submit the data collection and analysis procedures developed in the study to independent review by competent outsiders. In order that this may be done the evaluators must maintain documentation of their "decision trail"—(what decisions they took, the data upon which they were based, how they were collected, the reasoning that lay behind them, and so on). On the basis of these data the auditor would be asked to judge whether the procedures used were "good practice" in the light of the evaluation's epistemological and, ultimately, functional standpoint, and whether they were properly carried out. If the auditor judges that these conditions have been met, he or she is asserting that one can have confidence in the evaluation findings to the extent that it has been carried out in a methodologically competent manner, and that the decision steps and conclusions reached by the evaluation team are reasonable, given their epistemological perspective.

While this procedure is technically valid, if the purpose of establishing consistency is to enhance the credibility of findings, results may be disappointing. The problem lies in the choice of auditor. If his judgement is to enhance credibility, he must be seen as independent. If, however, he is a known expert in and sympathetic to interpretive evaluations, his impartiality may be questioned by precisely those positivistically inclined colleagues for whom the exercise is being undertaken in the first place. If, however, a positivistically inclined evaluator is selected, or some disinterested public figure, who is not a professional evaluator, their lack of expertise in, and/or sympathy with the methods of an interpretive evaluation may lead to misunderstandings and biased judgement. On the one hand charges of professional collusion and on the other of professional prejudice may undermine the credibility of the judgemental process. However, at the very least, the audit does generate a documentation of the decision trail that can be thrown open for discussion with wider audiences, if the credibility of the findings is questioned. Rather than the audit "speaking for itself" the evaluation team may, in turn, have to speak to the audit—but at least they come better prepared. (The acts of persuasion involved in presenting findings will be further discussed in Chapter 7 on utilization.)

Generalizing from an interpretive design

As discussed earlier in this chapter, an interpretive evaluation, if it is consistent with the implications of non-positivistic ontological positions, cannot offer generalizations. Does this mean then that interpretive designs eliminate the possibility of generalization altogether?

It has been suggested that while interpretive studies cannot generalize, they can *be* generalized by their audiences (Guba and Lincoln, 1981; House, 1980). In other words, while the evaluator cannot generalize the picture(s) of reality he has developed to other settings, audiences to whom they ring true (and hence who share the meanings they embody) are, in fact, generalizing the evaluator's findings to their own experience. Thus I would maintain that in an "interpretive" design, it is only the *audiences* not the researcher, that can generalize the findings and only to the extent that they share the meanings embodied in the pictures of reality the evaluator has developed.

The evaluator as insider

In interpretive evaluations the researchers aim to construct pictures of reality "from the inside", to provide accurate descriptions of participants' actions, experience and understandings of the change programme. In order to do this, they need to establish (rather than inhibit) an interactive relationship with their respondents based on the rapport that results from empathizing with them. But empathy, so it is often argued, can give rise to two problems. First, if the evaluator "overempathizes" with one set of respondents, he or she may give undue weight to its view of reality in comparison to others (Wax, 1971, pp.139–142). Secondly, the evaluator may become so immersed in the fieldwork situation that she may be oblivious to patterns which underlie seemingly idiosyncratic accounts — a problem of not seeing the wood for the trees. How can the interpretive evaluator avoid these potential sources of bias?

First, it should be noted that, in practice, an *evaluation* researcher's role *per se* offers a protection not available to the "pure" researcher. For, at the end of the day, he or she will have to present a report that is credible to the audiences it will serve — that contains views of reality credible to the groups whose views they are meant to represent but capable of being justified to groups who may disagree with them on either "factual" or value grounds. This in itself is a protection against unconscious over-empathizing with one group at the expense of others. Secondly, and pragmatically, if it does occur, given their liberal tendencies, evaluators are more likely to over-empathize with the less rather than more powerful participants in the change programme — clients at the expense of implementers, implementers at the expense of policy makers and so on (e.g. Bate and Mangham, 1981;

Wax, 1971). In which case at least this bias is likely to be counteracted by pressures from the powerful decision-makers, such as those described by Brickell (1976) and discussed above. In other words bias induced by over-empathizing with the least powerful may be cancelled out by the biases induced by conforming to the external pressures imposed by the most powerful.

In terms of fieldwork method there are several ways of protecting against the dangers of overempathizing. First, there is the use of multiple observers, possibly it split teams, as discussed earlier. Secondly, the more time that is spent on the site, the less likely the evaluator is to continue in his selective perceptions and over-simplifications (Wax, 1971, p.142). Thirdly, evaluators should seek to be aware of their potential biases and of how these may interfere with what they see and hear. To this end, it may be useful to record observations and interview data as verbatim as possible with a separate note of reactions and interpretations (Wax, 1971, p.142). (This will form part of the "decision trail" data available to the evaluation auditor).

The second problem — of becoming so immersed in the fieldwork situation that analytical edge is lost — is an insidious danger as immersion is a necessary condition to establishing a deep understanding of the change programme, and the evaluation researchers may be less on their guard about maintaining analytical, than about maintaining emotional detachment. But they may be assisted in maintaining this detachment precisely because their roles as evaluator will distance them, to some extent, from their respondents. Unlike pure researchers, evaluation researchers will not be tempted to pass as "one of them" in an effort to learn groups' shared meanings, because their role is known. (This is not to deny that "knowing" may break down with clients of the change programme, who may only formally "know" what is going on, or, in some situations, where high levels of rapport have been established, evaluator and informant may both "forget" the role.) But however careful the evaluator is, immersion is likely to lead to the accumulation of a "tacit knowledge" that will need to be surfaced, if it is to be used constructively rather than act as a blindfold to underlying patterns. A useful technique is to develop a system of regular debriefings, in which the evaluator himself adopts the role of informant and subjects himself to being interviewed by another member of the evaluation team (Spradley and Mann, 1975).

Summary and conclusions

This chapter has concentrated on two issues: the attack upon and loss of confidence in positivistic methods, and the emergence of an alternative approach to evaluation design, based on an interpretive position.

To consider the attack upon positivistic designs first. Even if they could be implemented according to the canons of scientific rigour (and we have already thrown doubts on that score in the previous chapter), it can be argued that the ontological assumptions of positivism render any methods based on that paradigm completely inappropriate for establishing "truths" about purposeful social action. Positivistic methods may be able to establish the "truth" about relationships between behaviours, but, it is argued, they cannot reveal truths about the meanings of those behaviours. Unfortunately, it is the meaningfulness of human behaviour that makes it human and social. It can be argued too that the difficulties in implementing positivistic methods (for example, the differential mortality "problem") are actually reflections of the inappropriateness of positivism's ontological position in regard to the nature of human reality. Indeed, from an interpretive standpoint, the paradigm itself represents meanings shared by those who view the world with a common set of assumptions about the nature of reality and the right way to go about testing it. The importance of the behaviours enacted by researchers lies in their meaning—but ironically this meaning cannot be explored by the methods advocated by positivists for testing reality—only by those advocated by interpretive researchers (for example, in-depth interviewing of its practitioners).

If this critique is accepted, it raises further questions about the functions which a positivistic design can serve. In the previous chapter, in which the ontological and epistemological foundations of positivism were not questioned, it was assumed that scientific method could theoretically produce the sort of "true" information about the impact of change programmes required by policy makers, even if there were practical tensions between the requirements for achieving external and internal validity, and between the information decision-makers wanted in theory and in practice. So it can, if the interest is in purely physiological (as in social change programmes directed at the health of the population) or behavioural responses, and if such responses are amenable to direct observation and measurement, rather than elicited through structured questionnaire instruments. But if we assume that policy-makers are interested in action rather than in behaviour as such, and if we accept the criticisms of positivism's ontology, then the major overt function of positivistic designs—providing true information about individuals' experience and reactions to change programme—is largely denied. Similarly negated is the function of increasing the stock of knowledge about human reality, for if that knowledge rests on false assumptions, by definition, it cannot be "true". It is only true to the extent to which the assumptions can be accepted.

This critique, however, does not undermine the extent to which positivistic designs can fulfil covert and latent functions (e.g. rallying support or opposition, evading responsibility, postponing decisions). For here the key issue is not whether the design can produce "the truth", but whether it can *appear* to produce it. It is the meaning that can be attributed to the status of the design that is important. And, as discussed previously, if opinion leaders are prepared to testify to its respectability (and, by implication, to the validity of the "facts" produced) this is good enough. That positivistic designs may be persuasive although, contrary to appearances and reputation, unable to capture the truth of social *action*, only reinforces the earlier argument that their primary function is rhetorical.

What then of interpretive designs? If the chief merit of such designs is to enhance an audience's understanding of the processes and experience of change, can this assist decision-making, learning and the more mundane and covert functions of evaluation discussed in Chapter 3? The conventional reply would go something like this:

> Interpretive designs are of little use to policy-makers as they require impact, cause and effect information which such designs do not seek to provide. Moreover, policy-makers require generalizations which, as conventionally understood, cannot be achieved by interpretive designs as their ontological stance rules out generalization. Interpretive designs can however provide information relevant to a formative evaluation, where programme designers and implementers wish to enhance their understanding of the processes of change and of how their programme is experienced by those coming into contact with it. Interpretive designs, being outside the dominant paradigm, are less useful in serving those covert functions (including the evaluator's own career advancement) where respectability of a design's appearance is all important. Interpretive designs, because they can succeed in increasing our understanding of change, fulfil learning functions . . . and so on.

While going along with some of these statements I would wish to enter some qualifications and point to some paradoxes.

First, while it is correct to assert that interpretive designs cannot furnish the type of information logically and in theory required by the policy-maker (generalizable information about impact) this is not to say that such a study might not influence policy. This is because, as already argued, decision-making and information processing are not completely rational activities, particularly when the decisions to be made are complex and not fully understood. The policy-maker is likely to be very much influenced by the "climate of opinion" in which decisions have to be made, and this in turn is likely to be moulded by precisely the sort of rich "slice of life" data likely to emerge from an interpretive evaluation. It is well attested that vivid experiential information (e.g. individual or journalistic accounts) dominates abstract information (e.g. summaries, statistical information) in many opinion-forming situations (Borgida and Nisbett, 1977; Cronbach *et al.*, 1980, p.188).

Furthermore, although an interpretive evaluation study logically has to eschew generalization, there is nothing to stop the policy-makers personally from generalizing the results to the extent to which they "ring true" to their own experience and that of others with whom they discuss the report. (This is only possible, of course, if those discussing the report share common definitions of situations, and other meanings.) The generalizations they make, in the event, may prove to be mistaken — but in practice they run the same danger if they extend the generalizations of a quasi-experimental evaluation beyond the initial conditions specified in the study. Indeed it could be argued that all action-oriented generalization is ultimately judgemental as correctly speaking "statistical inference ends with the frame and the environmental conditions under which the frame was studied" (Deming, 1975, p.57).

Thus, once more, if we distinguish between the information policy-makers require in theory and what they are likely to use in practice, the inadequacy of that resulting from non-positivistic designs is less apparent. This is particularly true of designs adopting a "concrete process" view of reality, where if the notion of determinate causal relationships has to be abandoned, at least a focus of the adaptation of one phenomenon to the context in which it is related is maintained. It is an easy step to abandon the "chicken and egg" logic of this position and drift back to the ontology of positivism through arguing that X type of change programme "seems to work" in Y type of context, and hence X "causes" the changes observed in the participants in Y.

If we look at the covert functions policy-makers may wish to be served by an evaluation study, in particular rallying support to a course of action they intend to undertake for political reasons (or opposition to a course of action they do not wish to undertake for political reasons), interpretive designs can fulfil such functions to the extent that the data presented are persuasive. The question is, of course, persuasive to whom? An interpretive design may lack "rigour" in the eyes of professional evaluators wedded to the positivistic paradigm and hence its data may be unpersuasive to them [see Blackler and Brown's (1983) evidence of positivists' attack on their (1980) study]. In contrast, it may be highly persuasive to a lay audience who can share in the vivid accounts it presents, and which, unversed in the niceties of experimental method and accompanying statistics, may be suspicious of a quantitative study as merely an attempt to "blind us with science". However, depending on situation, particularly if potentially unpopular decisions have to be made, policy-makers may prefer that the evaluation report persuades a lay majority rather than an expert minority. If the riskiness of the decision is high, though, there are advantages in commissioning a study that is likely to be persuasive to experts (assuming the results point in the "right" direction) who may be scapegoated if the course of action chosen on the basis of the evaluation report is later proved to be a mistake.

However, the issue of evaluation as persuasion (House, 1980) raises the whole question of the "crisis in utilization" and, as such, will be dealt with further in Chapter 7.

An interpretive design can indeed provide just the sort of information required by programme designers, prior to "firming up" a design, and by implementers precisely because it comprises a flexible strategy rather than a rigid design. Feedback can be provided quickly and individuals' reactions to different aspects of the programme can be explored in depth. The data collection and analysis techniques discussed earlier should also allow the evaluator to identify which perceptions and experiences are shared by many parties to the programme, those which are specific to any one group, and those which are totally idiosyncratic and appear unique to one individual.

A practical problem may emerge though. Precisely because interpretive designs encourage rather than inhibit rapid and regular feedback, there may be some danger that the evaluator's tentative hypotheses and emergent pictures of the multiple realities experienced by all those involved with the programme may be treated as more fixed and definite than they are by the programme staff. If this occurs, they may react prematurely to feedback — for example there may be a loss of confidence in one aspect of the change strategy due to vociferous negative reactions on the part of one interest group (particularly if its perceived to be powerful) at the expense of the views of the silent — or as yet unheard — majority. Awareness of this danger though goes half way to combatting it.

An interpretive design's ability to fulfil programme staff's covert evaluation functions (generating support for "their" programme, avoiding the risk of unfair scapegoating, assisting career advancement) is in some respects better, and in some worse, than a positivistic design's. The ability of any design to fulfil these covert functions depends on whether it can produce the desired results (not necessarily the "truth") and present them persuasively. In terms of producing "desired" results, it could be argued that an interpretive design, by identifying multiple realities, gives more leeway in the presentation of findings, than a design which presents unyielding sets of statistics that purport to represent the one true state of affairs. (This is assuming of course that the evaluator draws the line at deliberately massaging statistics in response to pressure from interested parties.) An interpretive design, by presenting different groups' perceptions of the change programme and process, inhibits scapegoating. If a full and multi-faceted account of the programme's rationale, design and implementation is presented then programme designers may be less afraid that failures resulting from poor implementation will be laid at their door, and programme implementers less afraid of being held responsible for problems of implementation resulting from unrealistic or just plain bad designs.

Where an interpretive design is less successful, though, is in its ability to convince the "experts" if the findings run contrary to their expectations and interests. Whether the findings of any evaluation are found persuasive, as discussed earlier, will partly depend on the methodological and stylistic preferences of the various audiences to whom the evaluation is addressed — which are likely to prove most sensitive when the findings are unwelcome. But because positivistic designs still represent the dominant paradigm (Blackler and Brown, 1983) it is easier for a conventional "expert" audience to reject unlooked-for findings emerging from an interpretive design, on the grounds of its failure to adhere to the canons of scientific rigour, than those emerging from a supposedly "rigorous" positivistic design. And, as already mentioned, to demonstrate the consistency of an interpretive study to such an audience might prove very difficult. In practice, though, as far as the programme staff's career advancement goes, this credibility issue may prove less of a problem than in theory, assuming those who commission the evaluation supported the inception of the programme. If an interpretive design suggests positive results, the powers that be will probably be pleased to accept them at face value, and resist detractors on political grounds. If negative results emerge from an interpretive design, programme staff will have included their own interpretations and justifications. From the programme staff's point of view, the real danger is if the evaluation is initiated by a group or individual not involved in and hostile to the inception and continuation of the programme. It is in these circumstances that positive findings are likely to be questioned (and with it the programme staff's success) on the grounds of the non-credibility of the evaluation design. However, as a hostile group would probably question the findings irrespective of the evaluation design, possibly not a great deal is lost.

Turning to the clients of a change programme, in theory an interpretive evaluation fulfils a major democratic function by surfacing the plurality of interests and potential choices involved, including those of the direct clients who are generally among the least powerful participants in the change programme. In practice, though, even if evaluation researchers wish to be responsive to the information requirements of all sections of their potential audiences, in a world of scarce resources choices have to be made about whose information needs are to take precedence, if all cannot be served equally. This is clearly an area where the evaluators' desires to see their findings utilized and their values about how the multiple realities they uncover should be presented may come into conflict. Their findings may stand a better chance of being seriously considered if they are directed at questions of concern to those in decision-making roles, often *their* direct clients — which may be different from the questions which concern the clients of the programme itself. In doing so, evaluators may unconsciously find themselves implying that decision-makers' models of reality are somehow "better" or more valid than those of the individuals for whom they are making the decisions. Once the existence of multiple realities is admitted and any group can assert the validity of its own, then it is likely that the reality of the group with the most powerful voice will be heard above all those others. Although an interpretive evaluation may give the appearance of being more democratic than a positivistic one, paradoxically, then, the reverse may be the case. For, assuming that they are not deliberately distorted in presentation, one set of "facts" emerges from a positivistic evaluation, which while open to interpretation, cannot be simply denied. If the "facts" are uncomfortable to the powers-that-be and supportive of the interests of the less powerful, they may do more to challenge the status quo because they can be presented as "the" truth rather than just as one version of it. Even the powerful have to explain this truth rather than just substitute their own model of reality. "Facts" can be inescapable and refuse to lie down. If this is so, *does an interpretive evaluation then act as a rhetoric for an evaluation ritual whereby the appearance of democracy and non-élitism serves to disguise the greater room for manoeuvre accorded to powerful decision-makers*? This issue will be discussed further in the next chapter on the crisis of accreditation/values in evaluation.

Finally the issue on which group's reality should be given precedence, or how a balanced picture should be presented, raises more than issues of values. Indeed, it introduces an epistemological issue that strikes at the heart of the practical relevance to evaluation of any truly interpretive research. Leaving aside the "contextual" views of reality, once the researcher is committed to a "symbolic discourse" view of it, as has been pointed out, he or she is likely to find different and possibly conflicting images of the change programme and how it is experienced. If each, in a sense, is true, how do evaluators select between them to present a balanced input for decision-making—or do they present the different pictures as raw information to the decision-makers and leave them to make of it what they will? The logic of this ontological position would demand that if a researcher presents his or her own balanced picture of what is seen to be the truth, it becomes yet a further picture of reality, the status of which is only "better" than the others if, paradoxically, the essentially positivistic value position is adopted, that theories (i.e. pictures of realities) of higher informative content take precedence over those of lower informative content. Yet, if this is accepted, the evaluator's epistemological stance is undermined as the implicit assumption, in comparing the truth value of different models of reality, is that there exists some ultimate truth (i.e. something "real!") against which they can be compared. *Such an assumption is virtually a full retreat back to a positivistic ontology, and, if its epistemological implications are accepted, a retreat back to positivistic evaluation methods and designs.*

If, on the other hand, the evaluator presents multiple models of reality, all of equal status, and leaves it to the decision-makers to select what they want, this difficulty, far from being removed, is merely postponed. At some point the decision-makers themselves will have to construct some "balanced" picture of reality (thereby falling into the same trap as the evaluator) or failing that, select one perspective of reality and treat it as "the" truth. If they take the latter course, in practice, they are also acting in a manner inconsistent with the epistemological position of the evaluation by implying that the model they have selected is "better", in terms of truth-value than the other perspectives available to them. If, on the other hand, they construct a balanced model or select one particular model of reality on the grounds that it will best serve their own covert evaluation functions, *irrespective of any ultimate truth-value it may possess*, then no epistemological inconsistency is involved (and the same goes for the evaluator). Furthermore, if the evaluator leaves it to the decision-makers to select between pictures of reality that he or she presents, it is unlikely that they will find such an evaluation report either useful or persuasive, as it will be almost totally non-directive. Again the utilization problem is raised.

So the ultimate paradox in evaluation design would appear to be as follows:

> *Decision-makers in theory want true information. In so far as they want it about human action rather than just behaviour, an interpretive design would appear to generate "truer" information than a positivistic one, as it recognizes that reality is not singular. But the information generated by an interpretive design is difficult to fashion into an input for decision-making unless it is treated according to positivistic assumptions. These assumptions deny the view that reality is multiplex, and hence deny the major ontological justification of an interpretive stance. If, on the other hand, a positivistic design is adopted, this information processing problem does not arise, but its truthfulness as a representation of action may be called into question.*

Is there a way round this dilemma? Does it really matter in practical terms? Are there other approaches to evaluation design that avoid this problem? These questions are best considered by changing the direction of this discussion. To date it has been assumed that an appropriate evaluation design is one that can provide information that will satisfy the various functions any evaluation overtly or covertly seeks to serve. Many, if not all, of these functions require "true" information. But in concentrating on the inquiry aspect of evaluation *research* I have implicitly defined "truth" in terms of the degree of isomorphism between study data and reality (whether singular or multiplex). But truth can just as well be looked at in moral and aesthetic terms. Indeed the very word *evaluation* would suggest this—if evaluation is about anything, it is about establishing the ultimate truth about a change programme—its goodness and worth. It is to this meta function of evaluation, the identification and attribution of value in change programmes, and the issues that surround it, that I now turn.

Chapter 6

Values in Evaluation

The discussion so far has concentrated on how different evaluation designs can identify the "truth" or different "truths" about a change programme—what "its" impact is, how "it" is variously experienced, whether "it" can be said to exist in singular form at all. But these are questions that any social researcher might ask. While recognizing that paradigmatic choices and hence, values, are *implicitly* embedded in all research designs, what differentiates an *evaluation* researcher is that he asks such descriptive questions within an *explicitly* normative and often comparative framework. The purpose of asking "what is" is a preliminary to attributing its value or worth. Is the change programme, its impact and its experience good? Has it "improved" the situation? Has it been more or less effective than alternative change programmes might have been? In decision-making it is the attribution of value that is all important.

In Chapter 1 it was suggested that a "crisis in accreditation" or values exists in evaluation research. In other words, while many researchers' personal values are liberal and reformist, designs demanded by their sponsors, and those which they themselves may recognize as facilitating the utilization of their findings, have an in-built conservative bias. Reason and Rowan (1981, p.xv) express this concern most vehemently, when they assert

> ... old paradigm research continually gets co-opted by those who want to prop up those who run the existing system. It studies those at the bottom while holding up its hands for money to those at the top. Thus in fact it serves to keep those at the bottom right there, and those at the top there.

If this is so then the evaluation of change programmes would appear to present another paradox: while the initiation of a change programme suggests a recognition that something is wanting, or, at least, could be improved in the status quo, at a deeper level, its evaluation may be protective of that same status quo.

However, before I delve deeper into this issue some preliminary questions need to be considered. First, what is meant by "value", and does our very definition of this concept have any implications for evaluation design? Secondly, does the adoption of a particular value position have implications for the choice of evaluation design and vice versa?

Defining value

Many interesting issues are involved in defining this concept — whether it is intrinsic or attributed (Lamont, 1955; Mumford, 1981), what its elements comprise (Kluckhohn *et al.*, 1951), whether there is a distinction between "merit" (context-free value) or "worth" (context determined) (Guba and Lincoln, 1981). Suffice to say here that taking these discussions together, the following definition of and propositions about value would seem to emerge:

(1) Values derive from and are embedded in communities of people who share experience and attributed meanings.

(2) Values are ideas about what "should be" to produce the kinds of consequences an individual or group desires. As such, serving to direct action, they underlie the design and implementation of a change programme just as much as its evaluation.

(3) An entity, such as a change programme, has value if those attributing value to it believe it has produced desirable consequences.

What are the implications of these propositions for evaluation design? First, if people attribute value, rather than it being intrinsic to an entity, the only value that can be found in a change programme is what people feel it should have and then consciously look for. This will obviously influence the questions asked and data sought to the extent that the choice of descriptive questions will be guided by normative concerns. To ask, for example, "did the programme achieve its goals" (a descriptive question) implies that the goals constitute the programme's success criteria and that the value of whatever else happened as a result of the programme is irrelevant unless it can be judged in terms of these goals (a normative concern). In other words, the value position underlying an evaluation is not an appendage or sequential to the descriptive study — it is an integral part and may rule out (or in) certain research designs.

Secondly, values, being views about what constitute "desirable consequences" are likely to vary in content or priority from group to group depending on the extent to which their experience and meanings differ. Whose values then should be embodied in the evaluation criteria, if incompatible values or radically different priorities emerge? If a set of values explictly underlies the programme design, does this imply that the evaluator's success criteria have already been selected—by the powerful decision-makers rather than other parties (implementers, clients) to the change programme? Indeed, research into change programmes in industrial organizations would suggest this is often so. For example, when a change programme—such as that reported by Nicholson (1976)—is designed to "reduce absenteeism" and is evaluated in these terms, the evaluation carries the implication that absenteeism is a "problem", which it is desirable to alleviate. This may be so for management with output targets to meet within a budget, but to the employee absenteeism may be recognized as a legitimate way to reconcile work demands and family obligations and to alleviate stress at work (Edwards and Scullion, 1982). Similarly the invariable choice, in evaluating work system design programmes, of such dependent variables as cost, productivity, quality and labour turnover (Cummings et al., 1977) reflect managerial concerns rather than those of the employees' experiencing the new work system (Blackler and Brown, 1975, 1978a). Even the unreflecting use by well intentioned researchers of such concepts as "self actualization" and "participative leadership" can reflect essentially managerial values, if this goes hand-in-hand with advocacy of changing bureaucratic organizational forms that inhibit the satisfaction of higher order needs. For as Blackler and Brown (1978b, p.341) put it, such bureaucracies may actually enable employees "legitimately to reserve the extent of their commitment to their employing organizations". Should researchers, then, seek to impose their own values in judging a change programme irrespective of the values of other stakeholders? Or, bearing in mind the utilization crisis, should they (as, it would appear, they often do) accept the values of their direct clients—the evaluation sponsors—in framing evaluation questions?

Thirdly, what is the relationship between the evaluation functions sought by the parties to the change—including the evaluator himself—and values that may be embodied in the evaluation design? To answer each of these questions the value positions which may be adopted by those involved in programmes of change must first be considered.

Selecting evaluative criteria

Change programmes are designed to have a range of outcomes or consequences. Evaluative criteria are the standards by which these consequences are judged to be desirable or undesirable. When they are operationalized in ways that facilitate measurement, their magnitude can be assessed, allowing comparison with other change programmes. How are these evaluative criteria determined; what influences their selection?

What people "want" out of a change programme will depend on the roles they occupy in relation to the programme and their general socio-cultural background. What they "count" as desirable consequences will also influence and be influenced by overt and covert functions they wish the evaluation to serve. For example, if one set of participants in a change programme anticipates that it will result in several negative consequences for them, even if other consequences are desirable for another group, it may press for the adoption of evaluation criteria that will serve the function of arousing opposition to the programme. Thus union members who perceive that an investment programme will result in redundancies and deskilling as well as in higher productivity, may press that the evaluation criterion of job retention and the development of "computer aided craftsmen" should stand alongside that of higher productivity in judging the worth of the programme (Wilkinson, 1983). This raises three issues. First, how easy is it to identify what all the parties to a change programme consider to be desirable or undesirable consequences? Secondly, if these can be identified, do desires (want–satisfaction) always constitute appropriate evaluation criteria? Thirdly, if what one group considers a desirable consequence is viewed neutrally or negatively by other groups, or if a range of desirable and undesirable consequences are anticipated, how is the overall worth of a change programme to be judged?

Identifying wants and interests

The evaluation research method adopted can either hinder or facilitate the identification of what different parties to a change programme might consider to be desirable consequences. While the interpretive approach (e.g. Wilkinson, 1983) would make this an integral part of the evaluation research, as an important part of gaining an understanding of participants' views of reality, a positivistic approach would be constrained by the predetermined nature of the evaluation design and by fear of biasing responses. Positivistic designs, in fact, present a potential double bind. If the evaluator feels unable to question respondents about the evaluative criteria they would select, before he has secured measures against the evaluative standards he has already embedded in the research design, the latter are implicitly being accorded priority. If, on the other hand, the evaluator is prepared to discuss evaluation criteria with his respondents, possibly using a version of multi-attribute-utility measurement (cf. Edwards *et al.*, 1975) in theory he is risking their contamination, and, consequently, measurement error in relation to the criteria he selected. The positivists' way round this might be to discuss evaluative criteria with a matched sample who played no further part in the research, but if the programme embraces all potential participants, this may be administratively impossible.

An alternative approach that they might adopt would be to infer participants' values in relation to the change programme in question from the preferences they publicly express in other choice situations. For example, the values of union members might be inferred from the issues they raise through grievance procedure, or those of parents about education in the concerns expressed at P.T.A. meetings. The problem with this approach though is that the values of the more articulate, committed and involved members of any group are likely to be overrepresented at the expense of silent majorities. Furthermore, the representatives of the more powerful interest groups tend to have greater access to public arenas than the less powerful. Many issues never gain a public hearing anyway because, challenging the values of the powerful decision-makers, they are suppressed (Bachrach and Baratz, 1962). This difficulty surfaces in an evaluation when the sponsors impose a set of evaluative criteria upon the evaluator, consistent with their own preferences, while explicitly excluding the addition of other criteria from consideration in their decision-making, if not from the evaluator's research design (House, 1980, p.179).

But even if the evaluator does succeed in surfacing the preferences of the least powerful participants in the change programme, and entering them into the decision process, a further difficulty awaits him. What if the least powerful assert preferences that seem irrational or based on a misunderstanding of their "real" interests? Bate and Mangham (1981, pp.193–194), for example, describe vividly the "false consciousness" of the majority of the workforce at "Alpen" and how this influenced reactions to their attempts to introduce participation. Should these preferences be accepted at face value, or treated as the product of false consciousness and a reflection of the power structure? And if the evaluator suspects that stated preferences are not in the participants' "real" interests, how is he or she to define and identify what their real interests might be? House (1980) in discussing this problem suggests that evaluators work with Lukes' (1974) definition, that their "real" interests are what people would want and prefer if they were able to make choices under conditions of informed autonomy. But lacking these conditions, in practice the evaluator has to make judgements of what *he thinks* they would prefer if they did have a free and informed choice. This may be a short step from inferring what he thinks they *should* prefer, if he allows his own preferences to come into play.

Whether the evaluator takes a liberal position, and accepts individuals, stated preferences at face value, or an idealistic one, and chooses criteria that embody their "real" interests, in the light of his or her values, it will have implications for the evaluation design selected—and vice versa. If liberal, logically a researcher should be drawn to interpretive designs as the best means of identifying the preferences of all parties to the change programme. But a problem arises if different parties' preferences appear to conflict or are incompatible. For if the ontological position consistent with interpretive designs is accepted, that each of the shared realities uncovered is equally valid, there is no inherent reason to select one set of preferences to serve as evaluative criteria to the exclusion of any of the others. The change programme may simultaneously be judged a success in terms of one group's criteria and a failure in terms of another group's. The problem with such relativism is that it does little to assist decision-making or the evaluator's credibility. If he or she does take such an approach ["report the conflicts and be done" as House (1976 p.82) puts it] what is likely to happen is that the change programme's most powerful decision makers will derive their own evaluative criteria, either by giving priority to one group's preferences, in the light of the functions they wish the evaluation to serve (a "good news" evaluation would derive *post facto* evaluative criteria from those preferences which had been satisfied, and ignore those which had not), or by imposing their personal preferences, their "ideals". If, to forestall this prospect the evaluator feels compelled to define a coherent set of evaluative criteria, by selecting and prioritizing between preferences, the drift is towards an idealist position, if by doing so there is the implication that some desirable consequences are better than others.

The position of the idealist, who views some preferences as being "better" than others, is consistent with positivistic approaches to evaluation. The preferred "desirable consequences" can be explicitly specified in the design of the change programme and outcome measures can be derived from them. Thus, in an industrial organization, if "greater productivity" is considered a more desirable outcome than "job creation", this may direct the design of the change programme (productivity to increase via investment rather than by improving the work-rate of each existing worker) and choice of outcome measures (costs per unit of output). The assumption that some desirable consequences can be identified as being "better" than others suggests that they can be compared in terms of some ultimate standard of good, about which there is agreement. This too is consistent with a positivistic world view because it assumes intersubjectivity about the value of outcomes.

Identifying the "right"

As argued earlier, the notion of evaluation is inseparable from that of scarce resources and their allocation. It is in informing allocative decisions that evaluation research fulfils one of its major functions. Hence values in evaluation are not solely about identifying consequences as desirable in the sense of being "good" (want or interest satisfying) but also in terms of how the good is distributed (the "right"). Traditionally evaluation research has rested on utilitarian ethics which define the right in terms of the maximization of the good. The good, defined separately and prior to the right, is the satisfaction of desires, which must be conflated into one surrogate index of satisfaction, so that a net balance of satisfaction (the "right") summed over all individuals can be calculated. This approach, emphasizing the maximization of net satisfaction rather than its distribution, is inherently conservative, as will be discussed below.

An alternative approach to the issue of distribution is that taken by Rawls (1971). Refusing to conflate a plurality of desires into one system, and arguing that the right is prior to the good, he propounds the following principle:

> All social values — liberty and opportunity, income and wealth, and the bases of self-respect — are to be distributed equally unless an unequal distribution of any, or all, of these values is to everyone's advantage. (Rawls, 1971, p.62)

Furthermore social and economic inequalities are to be arranged so that they are to the benefit of the least advantaged, consistent with the above ("just savings") principle. Now, although such notions have been attacked from the standpoint of welfare economics and public policy considerations (e.g. Hayek, 1976; Nozick, 1974) it is on the basis of Rawls' ideas that Keeley (1978) has developed the "minimization of regret" approach to evaluation of organizational effectiveness, and Carnall (1982), an "exchange theory" approach to evaluating organizational change. [Furthermore, House (1980) has analysed the implications of Rawls' conception of justice for selecting evaluation criteria for social change programmes and as a criterion for how the evaluation itself might be conducted.]

To consider briefly Keeley's (1978) and Carnall's (1982) approaches. Keeley argues that organizational effectiveness may be evaluated in terms of whether or not, and to what extent, different organizational stakeholders (managers, employees, shareholders, consumers etc.) regret the consequences of their own interaction within an organization. On this basis he suggests that organizations, change programmes and their evaluation should involve the following steps: (1) identification of organizational stakeholders; (2) determination of the percentage of participants in each stakeholder group who regret the consequences of their organizational participation; and (3) minimization of this percentage for the stakeholder group where the percentage is highest. Carnall (1982), while sympathetic to this approach, points out that Keeley's operationalization of this procedure leaves important questions unanswered, such as "why" and "how" participants regret the consequences of their interaction, and hence what strategies should be adopted to minimize their regret.

His own approach attempts to cope with these difficulties (Carnall, 1982). It rests on the assumption that organizations may be conceived of as complex networks of reciprocal economic and social exchanges between different interest groups, whose power, interests and aspirations are influenced by market position and by "custom and practice". Evaluating a change thus involves mapping its impact upon these exchange relationships, impact being conceptualized in terms of each group's perceptions of its "fairness" relative to other groups' experience in the light of existing allocation norms and compared with the past ("custom and practice"). When a change is perceived as "unfair" by one interest group, in that it detrimentally disrupts an exchange relationship with another group, then, according to Carnall, the "normative order" in the organization is threatened. In such circumstances the maintenance of exchange relationships must be problematic, although the behavioural outcomes which emerge will be influenced by the tactical positions of the interest groups involved. Carnall argues that, in essence, this approach provides a framework by which an evaluation researcher can comparatively describe and understand the impact of change on a range of organizations, while pointing up future problems they may confront. It enables the researcher to assess further organizational effectiveness (however defined) if the assumption is accepted that no organization can be effective (however defined) if its normative order is found to be undermined, following change, rather than maintained or reconstructed (Carnall, 1982, p.115). In illustration of his approach Carnall comparatively evaluates a range of change programmes within industrial organizations (for example, an organizational development programme in a Norwegian engineering factory, the development of group working in a biscuit factory, job design changes in a precision instruments factory).

Leaving aside criticisms about concept definition, overlapping categories and abstracted empiricism, which may be levelled at Carnall's model, it is debatable the extent to which this framework is really based on Keeley's and Rawls' ideas about social justice, in spite of claims to the contrary (Carnall, 1982, p.13). Ultimately in its emphasis on the maintenance of normative order as *the* evaluative criterion (and on the need to maximize it?) Carnall's approach appears to retreat towards a dilute form of utilitarianism.

Evaluation criteria and evaluation design

As already suggested, selecting evaluative criteria is not an act divorced from the design of an evaluation study. This is clear if the value assumptions embedded in positivistic and interpretive approaches to evaluation design are now considered.

The fact that in positivistic designs success criteria must be selected before the study commences in order to be contained in outcome measures, makes it highly likely that the values of the sponsors and powerful decision-makers will figure prominently. As already mentioned, concerns about measurement error and belief that the researcher's role should be one of the objective outsider make it improbable that the evaluator will canvas the attitudes of those whose behaviours he or she wishes to measure about the criteria that should lay behind that measurement. Therefore those "outside" the change programme—policy-makers, evaluation sponsors, programme designers, rather than implementers or recipients/clients are likely to have the real say in what are to count as the "desirable consequences" of the programme. The values of implementing and client groups—what they actually consider to be desirable outcomes—may not be considered at all. Most likely though they will be represented by criteria reflecting what the sponsor of the evaluation, or the evaluator personally, considers to be "in their best interests", which may have little connection with their actual wants. At worst, the criteria selected in the "best interests" of these groups may be merely reflections of the self-interested wants of powerful vested interests. At best they will smack of paternalism. By inhibiting direct access to the values of "subject" groups, the methodological concerns of positivism effectively constrain the researcher's selection of evaluative criteria.

As far as values about what is right are concerned, positivistic approaches and utilitarianism seem to go hand in hand. Positivism assumes that reality is singular and therefore has no problems in conflating a range of desires into one surrogate index of satisfaction so that a net balance can be calculated. The only question is the degree of isomorphism between the measure and the phenomenon, which can be taken care of by attention to construct and content validity in measurement instruments.

At a practical level too utilitarianism is compatible with the overt decision-making functions that sponsors and policy-makers seek from an evaluation study. Policy makers, the funders of change programmes, wish to be able to generalize from evaluation studies. Not only does a positivistic design allow this epistemologically speaking, but, harnessed with utilitarianism, comparative evaluation is facilitated as the multifarious want–satisfactions embodied in different programmes in different contexts are represented by a common surrogate measure. The use of a common surrogate measure also provides a rhetoric of fair play to gloss accountability functions. Individuals responsible for different change programmes will all be evaluated against a common "objective" measure of success, eliminating favouritism and bias. (The fact that using objective umbrella measures, such as educational test scores, rates of recidivism or financial return comparatively can be patently unfair without a necessarily more subjective assessment of the different contexts in which they are applied does not necessarily undermine their rhetorical value, as protestors are immediately put on the defensive of having to argue against "hard facts".) Furthermore the bodies responsible for funding change programmes are assisted in making judgements about the best return on their investment by success being expressed in cost-benefit terms.

What then of interpretive designs? In my view, these rest on assumptions which are incompatible with utilitarianism and less easily accommodated to paternalism. Because these designs assume reality does not reside in objective "facts" that can be measured, but in the shared meanings that individuals derive from and attribute to their common experience, it cannot be singular. It is not possible to conflate what are multiple realities into one all-embracing singular reality—which is what a single measure of utility attempts to do—as, by definition, such a concept is meaningless. Clearly the very concept of a "net balance of satisfaction" is inappropriate, as it assumes that different realities can be compared and equated in terms of one superordinate reality, when by definition, in interpretive approaches, no "one" reality exists, and of the many realities that may be identified by the evaluator, none has a logical precedence over any of the others. Furthermore the usefulness of utilitarianism in facilitating the comparative evaluation of overtly similar change programmes is irrelevant, if interpretive designs logically cannot generalize their findings.

As already mentioned, the liberal position (that each interested party's expressed preferences about a change programme's outcomes should be taken at face value and accorded equal status as evaluative criteria) is consistent with the assumptions embodied in interpretive designs. An interpretive design facilitates the identification of these preferences, quite apart from justifying the relativism that is likely to result from their use as evaluative criteria. Generally speaking, for the researcher to act paternalistically/idealistically, that is to assert that one group's preferences (values) are better than another's, would contradict the assumptions of such a design, unless he or she made it explicit that this was just a personal model of reality, and of equal status to the others identified. A similar difficulty would be encountered if the evaluator sought to distinguish between a single group's preferences about a change programme's outcomes (their expressed values) and what was in their "real" interests as he or she perceived them. The "real" interests would only consist of the evaluator's picture of reality, which could not be judged as more "real" than the "false" preferences identified, as the logic of the interpretive position does not admit any ultimate reality. Indeed, if the measure of the "truth" of what a researcher uncovers, including the truth of a group's values, is its credibility with the group whose reality it is meant to represent, the preferences its members express arising from their attributed "false consciousness" may still be a more valid representation of the group's reality than the researcher's judgement of its members' "real interests". Thus the evaluator wedded to an interpretive design can act in a paternalistic manner by asserting that certain evaluative criteria represent a group's "real interests" to a greater extent than their expressed preferences, but he or she cannot present these as representing any more than his or her own model of reality, as there is no ultimate model against which to judge its validity as compared to that "false" model embodied in their preferences.

What then of the compatibility of Rawlsian ideas of justice-as-fairness to these different approaches to evaluation design? The difficulty here is perhaps less one of logical compatibility with the designs themselves as with the functions sought by them. For example, a positivistic design, epistemologically speaking, would have no problems with the idealistic *form* Rawls' position takes (that some values, such as "basic liberties" should take precedence over others), as the prior selection of success criteria is perfectly compatible with the view that some values are superior to others. The problem, in contrast, would probably lie with the radical *content* of the values—in particular with the acknowledgement that social and economic inequalities can only be justified if they are to the benefit of the least advantaged. As long as positivistic evaluations (quite apart from knowledge functions *per se*) seek chiefly to inform the "big" allocative decisions, which, inevitably are made in a politically charged atmosphere, such radical principles are likely to be considered unrealistic as evaluation criteria. Ironically, too, Rawls allows a way out for decision-makers who might consider his distributive criteria unfeasible in a world where politics is the art of the possible. That is, by allowing the "just savings" principle—that inequalities may be condoned if they contribute to everyone's advantage—Rawls leaves decision-makers with a criterion that in practice, if not in theory, may ape utilitarianism.

As far as interpretive designs go, having identified multiple, possibly conflicting, values that may stand as evaluative criteria, Rawls' principles may assist the evaluator in selecting between them where conflict exists. This is because it would enable him or her to maintain the position that—leaving aside basic liberties and primary goods—all wants can be treated as having the same status, subject to rules of distribution. Of course, in practice this would be according a value about what is right a higher status than other values, which would not be consistent with the interpretive position, if held as an absolute rather than just a personal view of reality. However, by choosing to be guided by Rawls, the evaluator would be able to make choices between potential evaluation criteria and avoid sitting on the fence and presenting apparently conflicting answers to the question of whether the change programme was good or bad. The question would still remain whether the criteria would appear sensible to the evaluation sponsors. Certainly if the evaluator refused to judge between the many potential pictures of reality that could be presented, on the grounds that all were equally true and all value positions by which they could be judged were also equally valid, if he or she left the decision-makers without direction, then it is unlikely that they would select on the basis of the Rawlsian position, because of its radicalism.

Indeed, the evaluation functions that can be most clearly fulfilled by adopting Rawlsian criteria are the covert "political" ones of rallying opposition or support to a programme. In the hands of a radical group conducting its own, possibly unofficial, evaluation of a change programme, be they shop-stewards or social reformers, Rawlsian criteria might be used to highlight how little the programme had achieved in terms of redressing social inequalities in the distribution of social and economic goods. And, while it is difficult to imagine managers or administrators deliberately choosing to use Rawlsian criteria to evaluate a programme, paradoxically, reference to such criteria might well be made as part of a counterattack against the radicals: by illustrating how "impractical" its radical critics were, by showing the high costs to the advantaged (e.g. male craft workers) if Rawlsian criteria were strictly applied (i.e. to female unskilled workers). They might also seek to demonstrate that there are few change situations in which the "just savings" principle cannot be argued to apply. Imagine how an industrial management might use such an argument — that inequalities can be condoned if they can contribute to everyone's advantage — to justify a programme of capital investment that involved redundancies (greater ensuing productivity will enable the payment of large redundancy sums, so the redundant will not suffer, also, in time lead to job creation through expansion, etc.). For those with vested interests in the status quo the "just savings" principle, wrapped up in the rhetoric of the unitary frame of reference (Fox, 1966) is a life-saver. As stated earlier, in practice if not in theory, it can be translated by sleight of hand into a neo-utilitarianism.

This discussion of Rawls' evaluative criteria brings us back to the paradox posed at the beginning of the chapter — that while many evaluators personally hold liberal and reformist values, evaluation contains a conservative bias, that while the initiation of a change programme suggests criticism of the status quo, evaluation may protect it. Let us now consider this "accreditation crisis" in the light of the preceding background discussion, and some suggested "solutions".

Evaluation and conservatism

Is evaluation research conservatively biased? If so, is this bias inevitable or an unconscious side effect of some evaluation designs? With one or two qualifications, which will be discussed later, I believe that it is inevitable and that research designs are a reflection of pre-existing bias rather than its cause.

Why is this? First, almost by definition, evaluation research is the "handmaiden of gradualism", seeking to improve the existing system rather than to overthrow it. To quote Cronbach et al. (1980, p.157):

Evaluation is undertaken so that society [or the organization] will improve its services or their costs will become less burdensome. This is the stance of a friendly critic, not of a person who sees the system as beyond repair. If convinced that a program is rigid and unresponsive to evidence, [the evaluator] is wasting his time in evaluating; only aggressive political action is likely to alter it. If concerned that the system as a whole is unresponsive, he must either become a radical or accept impotence.

The stance of the "friendly critic" was exactly the role Bate and Mangham (1981) considered that they held on embarking on an action research exercise aimed at introducing participation into a multi-national pharmaceuticals company:

> We held clearly to the value of evolutionary rather than revolutionary approaches to change . . . wishing to accelerate "development", willing to tinker with the socio-economic system or have it tinkered with but not wishing radical changes. (Bate and Mangham, 1981, p.13)

This inherent conservatism in evaluation is well illustrated by considering the use of programme goals as evaluative criteria, as proposed in most normative models of change. During the early and mid-seventies, it was conventional wisdom, particularly among positivistic evaluation researchers, that programme goals should serve as evaluative criteria, in the sense that the evaluation study should seek to establish if stated goals were achieved, the test of a "good" change programme being the extent to which it did actually achieve its goals (Gordon and Morse, 1975; Weiss, 1972a). But the use of programme goals as evaluative criteria involves various conservative biases. First, there is the question of *why* the emphasis on goals and goal achievement. As Sjöberg (1975) points out, this emphasis implies a concern for efficiency, which involves notions of rationality, and which in turn find expression in an adherence to the bureaucratic model of organization. But the bureaucratic model in turn rests on principles of hierarchy and accountability both of which are conservative. The principle of hierarchy means that the programme goals are likely to be selected by those with position power, that is those who already have a vested interest in the status quo and its preservation. For example, the indicators developed by Lazarsfeld and Thielens (1958) for ranking American colleges and universities reflected criteria associated with high-status institutions (e.g. research and publications) not low-status ones (e.g. low failure rates on undergraduate courses) (Sjöberg, 1975, p.31).

The principle of accountability has a similarly conservative effect as it encourages change agents to opt for courses of action which can be easily justified. This involves looking for precedents and hence at the tried and trusted rather than the truly experimental. It also encourages change agents not to be "overly ambitious", not to "bite off more than they can chew", which is a further pressure towards conservatism. Conservatism and the principle of accountability, moreover, are likely to be mutually reinforcing. Conservatism demands that any innovatory change programme must prove itself as effective as the existing system. To demonstrate this it must be judged by the traditional indicators, by which the existing system is evaluated. But these indicators may be inappropriate and therefore "through a kind of self-fulfilling prophecy, innovative efforts do not succeed" (Sjöberg, 1975, p.41), reinforcing the belief in the superiority of the existing order. Using short-term productivity measures as a criterion for judging the success of participatory schemes in industry provides a case in point.

Overall then, the "why" of using programme goals has implications for "whose" goals and "what" goals. And, as suggested earlier, the managerial efficiency goals relating to cost and productivity permeate research into change programmes.

Furthermore, a concern with goal achievement (and the goals of the powerful) has tended to go hand in hand with using positivistic evaluation designs, as this concern implies a commitment to a hypothetico-deductive logic (Gordon and Morse, 1975, pp.339–340). But positivistic designs themselves tend to have an in-built conservative bias, for the following reasons.

First, if research designs are experimental, and researchers limit their study to the effects of the experimental variables alone, this conveys the message that other contextual variables are either unimportant or unchangeable. "Most evaluations—by accepting a program emphasis on services—tend to ignore the social and institutional structures within which the problems of the target groups are generated and sustained" (Weiss, 1975, p.20). Evaluation of training schemes (for example, the British Youth Opportunities Programme) for the young unemployed has been criticized for this emphasis. This ameliorative and therefore essentially conservative posture is underlined when one considers such designs' obsession with measures of change in individuals, rather than in systems. As Deutscher (1976) suggests, this defines situations as those in which individuals need to be "developed" or helped to adjust better to their environment, rather than the environment being adjusted by societal reform to better meet the needs of the individual. If individual measures—often already biased against the socially disadvantaged—are used to convince those at the bottom of the hierarchy that they deserve to be where they are, this is a further and insidious way of adapting the individual to the status quo, rather than calling existing structures into question (Bowles and Gintis, 1972–1973).

Secondly, the tighter the experimental controls the more likely it is that the change programme will show very small or no effects (Aaron, 1978; Rivlin, 1974; Rossi, 1972). Or results, if not negative, are likely to differ from site to site. Either way this encourages the reaction that expanding the change programme, at least at present, is not worthwhile—why throw good money after bad, or why not delay spending further money until confusing results become clearer. Such evaluations can have a severe braking effect on the wider dissemination of a change programme, which is already likely to be far from radical for reasons already given (Van de Vall, 1975).

Thirdly, as discussed earlier, positivistic designs tend to be associated with the distributive principles of utilitarianism, which is a conservative philosophy.

For reasons discussed earlier in this chapter, *in theory* interpretive designs have the *potential* to be less conservative than positivistic ones. As Blackler and Brown (1978b, p.347) comment "adoption of this [interpretive] anti-positivistic perspective implies that the way in which we conceive of organizations or people is our choice, and in turn that by our choices, we either create new forms or sustain existing ones". In practice, though, I doubt if this holds—indeed, as discussed in Chapter 5, they may be more open to manipulation by powerful interest groups than positivistic designs. Once the existence of multiple realities, including values, is admitted and any group can assert the validity of its own, then it is likely that the reality of the group with the most powerful voice will be heard above all those others. It is because the meta-function of evaluation is conservative that evaluation sponsors favour inherently conservative evaluation designs rather than their choice of design unwittingly pushing them into a more conservative posture than would be consciously desired.

A contrary argument has been advanced by Coleman *et al.* (1979). They suggest that when evaluation research results reveal defects in a change programme, and particularly when the results are seen as "scientific", the product of a tightly controlled positivistic design, they legitimate opposition to the programme. In doing so, evaluation strengthens pluralism and helps distribute power. While this may be true in theory, I consider that it only holds in practice if the criticisms are condoned by the policy-makers, or if the evaluation is sponsored by an independent radical group. For if the policy-makers have sponsored the evaluation, when presented with unpalatable findings, they retain the initiative in controlling their distribution or influencing their interpretation. Particularly if the evaluators are administratively or financially dependent on the change programme administrators (Anderson and Ball, 1978)—in other words are "internal" evaluators—their chances of disseminating negative findings (or in extreme cases, their willingness even to report them) are remote indeed (Salasin, 1980).

The emergence of ethical codes

What then is the situation of the reformist researcher confronted by the inherent conservatism of evaluation research? It could be argued that it is precisely the conservative bias in efforts to bring about change (for evaluation is part of the change process) that push some individuals into radicalism (i.e. the system should be overthrown rather than reformed). It is difficult to see what involvement true radicals could have in evaluation *research*, where a concern of all methodologies is the elimination of bias. Involvement in formative evaluation would be incompatible with their position, given its overt purpose would be to improve a change programme sanctioned by some part of the establishment. With a summative evaluation it might be a different matter if the radical evaluator's intention was to rally opposition to an "establishment programme", perhaps on the part of its recipients. But this would involve the adoption of an evaluation design that would not seek to be objective, or present a range of different realities—but rather identify solely the negative aspects of the programme. A form of one-sided adversarial evaluation would seem to be indicated, the findings of which would be aimed at the public in general, rather than at programme staff and the relevant policy-makers. Both these latter groups might claim, with some justification, that the findings were biased and therefore of little use in rational decision-making (political decision-making in the hands of opposition groups might be another matter!). However, it is difficult to see how a genuine and identified radical could gain access to conduct evaluation research into organizationally based change programmes, or sponsorship, unless from a consumer group with a vested political interest. Indeed even if the latter form of sponsorship is available, its very nature, combined with problems of achieving access to all involved groups, would probably result in a study resembling investigative journalism rather than evaluation research.

The position of evaluators with liberal reformist views may be less problematic in theory but involve more value conflict in practice. Being reformist rather than radical they are likely to accept the situation that evaluation research is the "handmaiden of gradualism" and, in this sense, conservative. Where value conflict may develop though is in treading the thin line between accepting gradualism and succumbing to co-optation. Accepting gradualism evaluators are committed to the principle that change is best brought about working with and through rather than confronting the existing power structure. This position nudges them towards defining their principal audience as those who have the power to "get things done", who *can* change the design or implementation of a change programme, who can have it extended or terminated, in the light of their findings. But if evaluation researchers seek to serve the information needs of powerful decision-makers in order that their findings are directly utilized, they run the danger of having to design the evaluation in the light of what decision-makers consider to be the key issues, variables and outcomes, which may reflect a vested interest in the status quo. In order to influence the change process evaluators may find that they have implicitly accepted the establishment's view of what form planned change should take and what should constitute a "successful" change.

Role relationships in the evaluation enterprise

It is this dilemma that appears to underlie researchers increasing concern about what should constitute appropriate loyalties to and role relationships with participants in change programmes they evaluate (e.g. Anderson and Ball, 1978; Argyris, 1980; Baron and Baron, 1980; Bate and Mangham, 1981; Reason and Rowan, 1981; Sieber, 1980).

Although this concern has been most insistently and explicitly raised by researchers evaluating American social change programmes—for reasons which will be indicated below—they are not alone. Applied and action researchers, particularly those socialized in an organizational development tradition, have expressed very similar anxieties. For example, those involved in organizational development interventions, frequently recognize the potential conflict between their own humanistic and democratic values and the authoritarian, efficiency-oriented values of the managerial clientele they generally serve (e.g. Friedlander and Brown, 1974; Tichy, 1974), between their espoused value of serving "the whole system", and the practical reality of senior management's sponsorship and ultimately co-optation of their intervention (e.g. Argyris, 1970; Bowen, 1977; Walton and Warwick, 1973). Bate and Mangham (1981, Chapter 10), in discussing their attempts to introduce participation in a large multinational pharmaceuticals company, speak frankly of their own experience, growing radicalism and value conflicts in establishing appropriate relationships with change programme participants:

> . . . Initially, we had high-minded notions about multi-client systems . . . such views have been tempered by experience . . . True to the maxim 'Don't bite the hand of the feeder', we clearly colluded with senior managers . . . and continue to collude with them . . . However, as the story of our journey shows we began to work less and less for them alone . . . over time, our sympathies have moved to the lower levels of the Alpen hierarchy . . . (p.208) . . . Not only have we discovered that we must train the disadvantaged to recognize their disadvantage and fight for redress, we have recognized much more fundamentally that we must fight for our perspective and exploit our advantage to the full . . . No longer the seven stone weaklings with sand in our eyes, we have begun to thumb our noses at authority, begun to flout the control that, earlier, we have been happy to place upon ourselves like all good Alpen employees (pp.194–5) . . . Although politically more astute, we are

less cautious than before. *We do not depend on Alpen for our salaries or research, and could put up with (or rationalize) the ignominy of ultimate rejection by them.* (p.208, added emphasis)

Their last comment is significant. Dependency on the powerful stakeholders in a change programme lies at the heart of many of the role relationship dilemmas identified by those involved in change oriented research/consultancy (e.g. goal conflict over "cooling out" and stabilization, misuse of information, issues about informed consent, coercion and manipulation) (Bowen, 1977; Walton and Warwick, 1973).

The key dependency relationships, where pressure might be exerted, appear to be with change programme designers, implementers, and the sponsors of the researcher (Anderson and Ball, 1978; Cronbach *et al.*, 1980; Fineman, 1981). To consider the relationships with programme designers and implementers first. Anderson and Ball (1978, Chapter 7), referring specifically to social change programme evaluation research, provide a useful framework for analyzing such relationships, which can be more generally applied. They point out that dependency has two major aspects, administrative and financial. On these dimensions evaluation researchers can be either dependent, independent or related to those in charge of the programme. For example, evaluators are administratively dependent on the programme director when they have to formally report to him or her and financially dependent if the programme director controls the funds for the evaluation. In contrast, they are administratively independent when they report to an external authority (e.g. an unrelated governmental or professional body) and financially independent if the evaluation funds come from a source which has no other connection with the change programme. "Relatedness" occurs when both the evaluator and those in charge of the change programme report to the same administrative authority (e.g. the managing director of a company or the Regional Officer in a hospital authority) or when funds for both the programme and its evaluation come from the same organization.

In theory nine permutations of dependency relationships are possible although in practice, as Anderson and Ball point out, financial and administrative relationships tend to be roughly consonant — or highly unstable. Should researchers always seek to be as independent as possible from the programme they are evaluating? Quite apart from the fact that complete independence is impossible, if only due to the obligations incurred in gaining organizational access to the programme — Anderson and Ball (1978) suggest that the appropriate degree of independence will very much depend on the functions the evaluation is to serve. In the case of a formative evaluation, where the objective is to develop the best possible change programme, they argue that the interests of evaluator and programme designers/implementers are likely to be similar, and a dependent relationship may promote the evaluator's responsivity to the latter's information needs. Furthermore the closer and more trusting the relationship, the better the information the evaluator is likely to get. At the very least, if the evaluator wishes to criticize aspects of the evolving programme, criticisms may be more acceptable if seen as coming from an insider rather than an outsider. The problem that the evaluator and programme developers may drift into a cosy mutually congratulating relationship of self-deception may be checked if they are aware that later a summative evaluation will consider the programme. In contrast, Anderson and Ball (1978) suggest that summative evaluations, to be credible at all, demand that the evaluator is financially and administratively independent of the programme to be evaluated. If this cannot be achieved, an independent research advisory board should act as a buffer, and, if necessary, as an adjudicator, between programme staff and the evaluator.

But although the relationship between researcher and those in charge of designing and running a change programme is important, we consider that the key relationship as far as maintaining independence goes (assuming the roles are separate) is with the sponsor/commissioner of the research. How independent is the researcher likely to be in this relationship and how can independence be protected?

Many American commentators (e.g. Anderson and Ball, 1978; Brickell, 1976; Cronbach *et al.* 1980) make the point forcibly that much depends on the evaluator's own institutional base. In Britain evaluators of programmes of planned change tend to be of two kinds—either the internal consultant, who is employed by the organization in which the change is taking place and who is in a relationship of dependence or relatedness to those conducting the change programme, or the external non-commercial researcher whose base is likely to be a university, and who has a substantial degree of both administrative and financial independence. (Bate and Mangham's comments, referred to earlier, are apposite here.) Although they may receive some financial support from the organization in which the change is taking place, their major funding is likely to come from their "home" institution (the university) or from an independent institution (a research council). Even the funds received from the organization are unlikely to come directly from those carrying out the change programme, but from their superordinates. This is not to argue that the "independent" evaluation researcher is consequently free of pressures. As Fineman (1981) graphically illustrates, the research councils and government departments from which a university based researcher is likely to seek funding of research into organizational change betray a marked preference for orthodox, positivistic research designs. In such cases, however, the pressures are brought to bear at the application stage (i.e. funds are less likely to be granted for "unorthodox" studies) rather than during the fieldwork stage. However, particularly when such funds are short, and competition for them is high (as during cut-backs in public spending) this implicit control can effectively encourage conformist research designs, while methodologically or politically radical researchers are likely to find funds short or under threat. In this context it is interesting that whilst an industrial relations research unit, funded by the British Social Science Research Council, recently has been obliged to submit to a formal inquiry following charges of "left-wing" bias (Berrill, 1983; Rothschild, 1982) no such inquiries have been made into institutions, in receipt of research council funds, commonly believed to adopt a conservative orientation.

In America, at least as far as much of the evaluation of social change programmes goes, the situation for nominally "independent" evaluation researchers is rather different, and, arguably more uncomfortable. For, in response to the enormous volume of federally mandated evaluation research into federally funded programmes of social experimentation (including change programmes in public service organizations, notably schools) many private, commercial and non-profit making evaluation firms have sprung up, highly dependent for their continued existence on winning competitive bids for such research contracts. Rubin (cited in Cronbach et al., 1980) estimated that for evaluations performed by representative firms in the San Francisco area, 85% of funds come directly or indirectly from a few federal agencies, such as Department of Health, Education and Welfare (HEW), Department of Housing and Urban Development (HUD), Department of Justice (DOJ). (Other funds come largely from state and local government authorities).

The relationship between private commercial firms who undertake evaluation research and federal agencies who sponsor it is characterized by the agency occupying the driving seat, specifying the problem to be studied, methodology to be employed, sample sizes and so on (Baker, 1975). If the R.F.Ps (requests for proposals/bids on proposed evaluation studies) specified a definition of the evaluation issues and research strategy that the contracting firm would have devised given a free hand, or if subsequent room for substantial re-negotiation was understood, this level of control might be accepted with few misgivings. As it is however, this appears the exception rather than the rule. On the quality of the general run of R.F.Ps the comments of Rossi (1979, p.21), an academic evaluation researcher, are worth repeating:

> In most cases it seemed to me that one would have to be methodologically naive, on the verge of slipping below the poverty line, a scientific hypocrite, or a combination of the above to have responded to most of the R.F.Ps we reviewed.

As far as re-negotiating the proposal goes, according to Baker (1975, p.214) there may be some room for manoeuvre, particularly if the agency is exploring a relatively new area and perceives policy alternatives, but once the final contract is drawn up, any departures in the research plan specified in that contract require official approval. Furthermore, it has been pointed out that subsequent alterations are as likely to come from the agency as from the evaluator. "The sponsor, responding to a new political wind, sometimes turns the study onto a new course in mid passage" (Cronbach *et al*, 1980, p.325). Indeed, whereas sponsors are prepared to condone flexibility in adherence to the evaluation design when it comes to responding to political pressures, they are far less prepared to do so in response to evaluators' developing awareness of new questions and issues in the research setting. Allowing evaluators flexibility in research design might lead to an overrunning of deadlines and budgets quite apart from the loss of control over what data are to be collected (federal agencies' preference for predetermined and, hence, positivistic designs may be seen in this light).

The agencies can demand this degree of control precisely because the vast majority of evaluation contracting firms are financially dependent on their contracts. This is particularly true of the smaller firms (Anderson and Ball, 1978, pp.136–137). The mushrooming industry, combined with the "competitive bid" approach to contracting, has meant too that firms face many competitors who may be prepared to respond to an inappropriate (in the eyes of the evaluators) or unrealistic R.F.P., if others will not. Cronbach *et al.* (1980) quote a government sponsor of evaluation funds as remarking

> I'd like, just once, to meet an evaluator who states honestly that in his opinion the agency's criteria aren't workable and who subsequently proposes an alternative. Instead, I meet evaluators who say (in confidence) that a particular activity is doomed to failure—but they are submitting a proposal anyway (Bernstein, 1977, p.8, cited in Cronbach *et al.*, 1980, p.199).

The dependency on and competition for government contracts have other effects, all of which are likely to undermine the evaluator's inclination or ability to confront agency wishes. First, continuity of employment is maintained by willingness to evaluate programmes in different areas, as federal concerns shift from one area to another. This means that individual evaluators may have to be shifted about before completing one evaluation if their specific skills are required on another. Alternatively they can be trained to become "interchangeable parts". In the first case, an evaluator's commitment to an evaluation whose conclusion will not be seen is undermined and, in the second, he or she joins the ranks of "technicians who exercise skills for a purpose someone else has chosen . . . (lacking) the perspective, the power and the incentive to turn out the best possible evaluations'' (Cronbach *et al.*, 1980). Secondly, in order to secure contracts, the firms use their most senior and prestigious researchers to write the proposals, and, because this can be a full-time activity given the number of contracts that have to be competed for in order to secure one, these members of staff are unlikely to be much involved in actually conducting the research. Hence it is the less experienced, less statusful staff who are left to cope with pressures in the field. This comment is also true of some research council funded research in Britain, where the ''principal investigator'' is simultaneously heavily involved in university teaching and administrative activities (Platt, 1976).

Ethical codes

Awareness of the role and value conflicts change evaluators may be subject to, particularly if he or she cannot secure financial and administrative independence, is one reason why they are increasingly arguing the need for an ethical code. In industrial organizations this is most notable among action researchers (e.g. Cherns, 1972) whether involved in programmes of work design and participation (e.g. Blackler and Brown, 1975; Clegg, 1979; Warr *et al.*, 1978) or in processual organizational development exercises (e.g. Argyris, 1971), and amongst those change agents committed to ''collaborative'' research (e.g. Herbst, 1976; Rowan, 1981). Possibly, even more vocal, is the concern evident among American researchers evaluating change programmes in public service organizations (e.g. Anderson and Ball, 1978; Cronbach *et al.*, 1980; House, 1980; Perloff and Perloff, 1980; Sieber, 1980). This is hardly surprizing because, many working from consultancy firms rather than universities and on contracts specifically for evaluation studies, they are the most conscious and articulate about their identity as professional evaluation researchers, rather than as academics *per se*. (Interestingly, though, their spokespersons are generally, but by no means exclusively, university based.)

However, in both groups there is much agreement about the nature of these ethical responsibilities and that they should be embodied in an agreement with the sponsor of the research before work is commenced. Most statements stress the need for an open participative ''joint'' approach and include such injunctions as the obligation to retain independence from any particular interest group, to insist on all stakeholders' informed consent to and veto on the research, confidentiality of sources, freedom to circulate reports to all interested parties and to publish findings. Additionally concern is generally expressed that the researcher should not undertake research which is incongruent with his or her values. Detailed statements of these codes may be found in Anderson and Ball (1978), Cronbach *et al.* (1980) and House (1980).

All this is very commendable, and if the codes were adhered to by researchers and their sponsors, would result in action, and collaborative, research and evaluations of a high degree of independence and integrity. The problem is though that the very reason why such codes are called for (particularly in the case of American social change evaluation researchers) — their dependency on sponsors who have the power to suppress findings they do not like — is also the reason why they will often not be adhered to. The evaluation firm or organizational development consultancy in danger of bankruptcy may feel compelled to undertake non-informational evaluations or spurious change exercises in order to preserve its staff until preferred contracts are secured. They may be obliged, for the same reason, to accept restriction on publication. Evaluators may have no power to prevent changes in the change programme that will impede their ability to conduct a rigorous evaluation (although the obligation to do so is stressed in the codes). No coercion of participants and informed consent may be difficult to achieve if the power of the various participants is unequal etc. It is argued that evaluators should reach agreement with potential sponsors that both parties will adhere to an ethical code (such as that suggested by Anderson and Ball, 1978) before the evaluator commits himself to the evaluation — but in situations where the code would be necessary to protect the evaluator's independence it is unlikely that the sponsor would agree to the contract, or abide by it if he had agreed to it. As all commentators admit, the only real sanction a researcher has if asked to conduct an unethical evaluation study or action research is to turn down the commission, making clear his or her reasons. But this only leaves the way open for the sponsor to offer the contract to a researcher with fewer scruples.

It is not surprising therefore, that calls for an ethical code have gone hand in hand with demand, among American evaluation researchers, for the development of professional self-regulation and support (Cronbach *et al.*, 1980). Is this the way for such researchers to confront the value conflicts to which they may be subject? While a fuller consideration of the whole question of professionalism and its relationship to the crises of verification (methods), utilization (functions) and accreditation (values) will be left to the final chapter, a few preliminary comments may be appropriate in the conclusion to this chapter.

Summary and conclusions

In this chapter it has been argued that much research on change and evaluation is inherently conservative and protective of the status quo. Furthermore this bias is exacerbated, particularly in the United States, by the evaluator's financial dependency on an instrument of government — the federal agency. In the U.S., evaluators who might initially have seen themselves as instrumental in improving or selecting the most worthwhile change programmes to produce a "Great Society" are now experiencing some disillusionment. Increasingly they have to cope with the realization that their activities at best ensure that change is a gradual accommodative process, at worst that such an approach to change, which they implicitly condone through co-operating in its evaluation, has little effect on basic social and economic inequalities. Although researchers in industrial organizations may be less disturbed by the implicit conservatism of their actions, particularly if they adhere to the managerial values of efficiency and so forth, there is evidence of similar disquiet (e.g. Baritz, 1960; Bate and Mangham, 1981; Blackler, 1982; Blacker and Brown, 1978b; Reason and Rowan, 1981; Tichy, 1974). The extent to which this causes the researcher disquiet will of course depend on how radical are his values. The true radical, as already suggested, is unlikely to touch evaluation research—or most action research (within the Quality of Working Life/organizational development tradition) anyway.

Perhaps in this context, American evaluation researchers' (in particular) calls for ethical codes should be seen as part of a wider strategy to secure recognition for their professional status—the *"sine qua non"* of "improving the evaluation enterprise" as Cronbach *et al.* (1980, p.352) put it. But this call, as such, may also be seen *as a rhetoric that serves both their altruistic and reformist intentions on the one hand and their pragmatic and conservative practice on the other*. In what way is this so?

Basically evaluation researchers can promote their reformist intentions— but justify their conservative practice—by simultaneously lending support to two very different models of professionalism, successively highlighting or backgrounding each model as appropriate. On the one hand there is the "trait" model which typifies an occupation as a profession if it possesses certain traits or characteristics, including altruistic intentions embodied in an ethical code (Greenwood, 1957). But the hallmark of this model is that professional status rests on high levels of technical expertise, of a type valued by, and to be utilized *largely at the behest of the client*. The professional is then the expert who works within the client's brief, critical if it appears ethically—or technically—inappropriate, but not primarily motivated to rewrite it. The ethical and technical pressures that the client may exert over the professional are both camouflaged and sweetened by the mediating notion of service in "the best interests of the client".

On the other hand there is the approach which defines professionalism not as an occupation but as a means of controlling an occupation (Johnson, 1972). In this model, if occupational control is seen in terms of the characteristic way in which the tensions in the producer (i.e. professional— the evaluator)—consumer (i.e. client—in the first instance, the sponsor) relationship are resolved, then professionalism may be considered as *existing in situations where the producer is able to define the needs of the consumer and the manner in which these needs are to be met.* In other words, the essence of professionalism may be seen in terms of a particular type of authority relationship existing between the "professional" and his client.

It is in examining the nature of this authority and how it might be achieved that the importance of evaluators' public adherence to ethical codes (along with claims to technical competence) should be seen. For, as has been argued elsewhere (Legge, 1978, pp.76–78), although *at the level of direct interaction between the client and the professional*, the latter's authority cannot be based on the persuasion of competent advice, strictly speaking, but on the exclusive legal right to operate and control access to goods and services (e.g. medical prescriptions, legal documentation) which the potential client needs in order to manage his own problem himself, independently of expert advice, persuasion *is* needed at another level. A profession needs to persuade some legislative body to designate it as the expert and responsible group in such a way as to exclude all other claimants.

> ... The leaders of an occupation persuade leaders of society that its members possess some technical competence so special and of such importance that the public should be prevented from using any other occupation with the same domain but assertedly lesser competence or *integrity*. The formal, institutionalized status of a profession is granted by society on the basis of having been persuaded that an occupation is competent and *responsible*. (Freidson, 1968, p.32, added emphasis)

Evaluators' demands for and claims to an ethical code may be seen in this light. On the one hand, it is part of the general attempt to obtain societal recognition of full professional status, such that authority may be exercised over the client through the control of "strategic accessories" (Freidson, 1968) rather than accorded by the client at his own discretion. (An example of such a "strategic accessory" might be the legal requirement for clients in receipt of public funds to have their programmes "validated" by "professional" evaluation researchers, if funding were to be granted and maintained.) On the other hand, it is part of a rhetoric designed to discredit potentially "unworthy" competitors in the supply of evaluation services by labelling them as either incompetent or unethical (see some of the earlier quotations cited by way of illustration).

Taking these two models of professionalism together it may be seen that whereas the "trait" model can be used to justify conservative practice (offering a service to the client according to the *client's* brief, acting ethically towards the direct client, rather than altruistically towards indirect clients) (Gowler and Legge, 1980), the "occupational control" model supports reformist aspirations. For this level of control, if achieved, would reverse the power positions of the researcher and his sponsor and guarantee the evaluator's freedom to state unpalatable truths. Indeed, in theory, it would place the evaluator rather than the sponsor in the driving seat in negotiating the evaluation contract. Such a contract could then be drawn up with an altruistic eye to the interests of the least powerful participants in the change programme—its direct (and the evaluator's indirect) clients—and to those of the public in general. The evaluator's obligation to his direct client, his sponsor, could be interpreted in the light of reformist principles. It is in this sense that the call for ethical codes—as part of a bid for professional status—may be seen as reformist.

Finally, this call can be seen from a rather different, if related, perspective. As has been argued in detail elsewhere (Gowler and Legge, 1980) professionals (and aspirant professionals) by their public adherence to ethical codes enshrining altruistic values, effectively cloak and thereby facilitate their exercise of a conservative pragmatism in the face of technical, economic and bureaucratic constraints on ideal type professional control of the professional–client relationship. Nor is this necessarily done cynically. The conservative evaluator may well argue that the present asymmetry in evaluator/sponsor relationships demands a conservative posture in order to achieve any utilization of his findings. In which case his reformist and altruistic intentions (expressed in his public call for an ethical code) are best achieved by aiming for the half loaf within his grasp rather than the whole one beyond his reach.

The popular call for ethical codes is hardly surprizing then, as it may serve as a vehicle for reformist aspirations and as both a justification and mask for present conservative practice.

What implications the demand for professionalization may have on evaluation research will be considered further in the final chapter. However, the tensions between reformist and conservative values which the rhetoric of ethical codes seeks to mediate must also be considered in the light of the utilization crisis. It is to this issue, touched upon in Chapters 1 and 3, that I now return.

Chapter 7

Reconsidering the Crisis in Utilization

As suggested in Chapter 1, much concern has been expressed by both American social change programme evaluators and by applied organizational researchers that their findings are not used by administrators and managers. This concern is evidenced among the American evaluators by a rash of publications bearing such titles as *Utilization-Focused Evaluation* (Patton, 1978), *Using Evaluations* (Alkin *et al.*, 1979), *Utilization of Evaluative Information* (Braskamp and Brown, 1980) and *Utilizing Evaluation* (Ciarlo, 1981). Furthermore in 1979 Sage established a new journal entitled *Knowledge: Creation, Diffusion and Utilization.*

Organizational researchers have not lagged behind in expressing misgivings about the usefulness of their work to practitioners. Indeed the development of "action research" in the 1960s and 1970s was in reaction to concern about the usefulness of basic descriptive organizational research to those involved in the management of organizational change (Cherns, 1972). However, not only have those committed to action research expressed some disillusionment in the long-term impact of such activities (e.g. Blackler and Brown, 1980; Klein, 1976; Tichy, 1974) but the concern persists that much research into organizations and organizational change has little impact on practitioners. Susman and Evered (1978) concluded that a "crisis of usefulness" existed in organizational sciences, and this fear has been echoed by Van de Vall *et al.* (1976), Gordon *et al.* (1978), Waters *et al.* (1978) and by Thomas and Tymon (1982). This growing unease culminated in the symbolic publication in the December 1982 and March 1983 issues of *Administrative Science Quarterly* (the bastion of basic organizational research) of a special issue entitled *The Utilization of Organizational Research*, in which the editor stated that "increasing numbers of organizational scholars have begun to express concern that organizational/administrative science has had little effect on life in organizations" (Beyer, 1982, p.588). Why is this so?

In Chapter 1, two propositions were put forward: that evaluation research findings appeared to have little impact at all on decision-making, particularly when they disconfirmed decision-makers beliefs (Carter, 1971; Weiss, 1975;

174

Zusman, 1976); and that this lack of impact was due to the perceived "irrelevancy" of much of the information generated to decision-makers' concerns. This "irrelevancy", it was suggested, reflected the deeper problem that organizational research, including the evaluation of change programmes, was failing to fulfil the functions that different stakeholders seek from it. Nor is this problem amenable to easy solution. To fulfil the functions just one audience desires an evaluative research study to serve, requires careful matching of research methods to those functions, so that appropriate "relevant" data may be generated. The problem is though that even for one party, the functions sought may be at odds with each other, requiring different "relevant" data, that can only be acquired by different and potentially incompatible research methods (see Chapters 4 and 5). Multiply this problem by the number of different groups which have a legitimate interest that the research serves the functions they demand of it and it can be readily understood that the evaluator has very difficult choices to make. This is particularly so because in attempting to resolve the utilization crisis, the research runs the risk of encountering crises in verification and accreditation (see Chapters 1 and 6 in particular).

Before concluding whether it is ever possible to fully reconcile the dilemmas posed by the three crises and what implications any attempted solution might have for the role of the evaluation researcher (see Chapter 8) it is necessary to reconsider how the utilization crisis might be overcome. Reasons for this reconsideration are three. First, in Chapter 1, in order to pose the issue starkly, in advance of consideration of evaluation functions, the meaning of utilization was treated as non problematic and almost as self evident. Evaluation findings were utilized if they "influenced" decision-making (Weiss, 1972b, p.11), if they had "impact" on policy (Williams and Evans, 1969, p.453). The key issue in the "utilization crisis", if commentators' statements were taken at face value, was one of information irrelevance. Hence an obvious approach to tackling this problem was to start with information irrelevancy and ask what information would be relevant and how it might be collected. Information was relevant if it fulfilled the functions an evaluation might serve, and hence utilization could be achieved by matching functions with methods. So far, so good. But in considering the many different functions evaluation research might serve, each requiring different information if to be deemed relevant, a uni-dimensional view of utilization seemed to lack the requisite variety to cope with the range of behaviours encompassed. If the concept of utilization requires re-examination, then so does its crisis.

Secondly, discussion of my preferred utilization strategy of matching evaluation functions and research methods was an incomplete account of how utilization might be achieved as it necessarily concentrated on only one part (if the most important part) of the task—namely the generation of data relevant to the concerns of potential users. Related issues were hardly touched upon—identifying who out of a range of possible users will be the people most likely to actually use evaluation findings; selecting whose and which of the competing evaluation functions should be served, particularly if resource constraints and potential incompatibilities rule out inclusive coverage; communicating and disseminating findings to those who can make use of them. These need to be considered in detail, but this can only be sensibly undertaken if the concept of utilization is developed.

Thirdly, as stressed throughout this text, the three crises in evaluation are so interlinked that it is difficult to discuss each separately without reference to the others. Reconsidering utilization—turning the wheel full circle—appears necessary in the light of the subsequent discussions of the other two evaluation crises. Moreover, although each crisis could now be reconsidered in the light of the others, utilization is arguably central. While the crisis in methods questions the technology of evaluation, and that in values, for and by whom it should be undertaken, the crisis in utilization questions whether the activity is worthwhile undertaking at all. As Weiss (1966, 1972c) almost two decades ago, put it

> The basic rationale for evaluation is that it provides information for *action* . . .
> Although it can serve such other functions as knowledge building and theory
> testing, unless it gains serious hearing when program decisions are made, it
> fails in its major purpose (added emphasis).

Unless this crisis is resolved, evaluation, including overtly normative as distinct from "pure" descriptive research, has no future. What further light then can be shed on the utilization crisis?

I start with the definitional question—what is meant by the "utilization" of evaluation findings?

Defining "utilization"

The two perspectives

Let's start by returning to researchers' and administrators' comments about the utilization of evaluation findings and juxtapose several typical and contrasting quotations.

> In the final analysis, the test of effectiveness of outcome data is its impact on
> implemented policy . . . by this standard, there is a dearth of successful
> evaluation studies (Williams and Evans, 1969, p.453).

> . . . There is little evidence to indicate that government planning offices have
> succeeded in linking social research and decision-making (Cohen and Garet,
> 1975, p.19).

Apart from the quotations cited in Chapter 1, similar comments may be found in Aronson and Sherwood (1967), Dexter (1966), Rossi (1972) and Thompson (1975). But compare these with the following quotation drawn from a respondent in a research study conducted by Patton (1978) on the utilization of evaluation studies sponsored by the Office of Health Evaluation.

> It [the evaluation study] served two purposes. One is that it resolved a lot of doubts and confusions and misunderstandings that the advisory committee had . . . And the second one was that it gave me additional knowledge to support facts that I already knew, and, as I say, broadened the scope more than I realized . . . the perceptions of where the organization was going and what it was accomplishing were a lot worse than I had anticipated . . . but I was somewhat startled to find out that they were worse, yet it wasn't very hard because it was partly confirming things I was observing . . . we changed our whole functional approach to looking at the identification of what we should be working on . . . none of these things occurred overnight, and in an evolutionary process it's hard to say, you know, at what point it made a significant difference or what point did it merely verify and strengthen the resolve that you already had (Patton, 1978, p.29).

In one sense the three quotations have something in common—an implicit assumption that *utilization is perceived exclusively in terms of the overt functions*—such as facilitating decision-making—*that evaluation findings can serve*. This is not surprising given that discussions about the utilization of evaluation findings tend to be cast in a prescriptive mould—"how to improve utilization etc." If such a discussion was extended to include the serving of covert functions, evaluators' claims for professional status would be undermined as altruistic values would be violated. In any case such utilization can be said to take care of itself.

In another sense, though, while not defining utilization precisely, these quotations do reveal two different perspectives (Alkin *et al.*, 1979; Patton, 1978). In the first set of quotations the criterion for utilization taking place appears to involve some immediate, measurable and direct impact on one or more important decisions about the change programme to which it is assigned. In Pelz's (1978, pp.347–352) terms, use is *instrumental*, (acting on research results in specific, direct ways) rather than conceptual (general enlightenment), or symbolic (using research to legitimate and sustain predetermined positions). Within this perspective clear evidence of the utilization of evaluation findings *is* hard to find. Indeed as Alkin *et al.* (1979) and Cronbach *et al.* (1980) point out, at least in relation to federally funded American social change programmes, refunding levels tend to remain constant from year to year with all projects, however evaluated, receiving similar percentage increases or decreases in funding.

The second perspective, embodied in the quotation drawn from Patton's research (1977, 1978), views utilization as a gradual influence process which, *combined with* other processes, may slowly change the course of decision-making, with in an organization, or in the broader environment by influencing the climate in which the decisions about the evaluated programme, and subsequent programmes are made. This is the "conceptual" use of research, referred to by Pelz (1978). As such the effect of evaluation is incremental and cumulative rather than dramatic, the influence being most marked on formative rather than summative decisions. Whereas the traditional perspective on utilization appears to demand that evaluation findings act as the major, if not sole informational input to important policy decisions about the programme directly under review, the alternative perspective suggests that evaluation findings are but one piece of information among many and hence can only exercise a confirmatory and cumulative impact.

If this perspective on utilization is adopted, many examples of *some* utilization of evaluation findings can be found, from the administrator in Patton's sample, who reckoned that evaluation findings had carried "about a third of the weight of the total decision" about the programme under review, to the examples of the cumulative influence of evaluation findings over a period of years in the five case study organizations, developing school curricula, portrayed by Alkin *et al.* (1979). An example of how diffuse and oblique the influence of evaluation findings can be is provided in Rein's (1976) discussion of how the evaluation by Stanton and Schwartz (1954) of the psychotherapeutic methods used in a private hospital, Chester Lodge, contributed towards a shift in the "dominant policy paradigm" away from individual toward "milieu" therapy. Although their evaluation report, which recommended such a shift, was not acted upon by the hospital administration, the book embodying these findings confirmed emerging doubts about individual therapy among the wider professional audience. The book became a vogue textbook on graduate courses and helped to establish the validity of "milieu" therapy among the new generation of psychotherapists. Such an example bears out Cronbach *et al.* (1980, pp.122–123) that "studies of prototypes and established programs have their greatest implications for programs that differ — perhaps radically — from the one actually surveyed". Similarly Rush and Wilkstom (1969, p.53) record that 72% of managers who responded to a Conference Board Survey, reported that behavioural sciences bring new and valuable insights to management.

So where does this leave one in defining "utilization"? Clearly the definition adopted will depend on the perspective taken. The more one leans toward the "cumulative, climate changing influence" view the more one is in danger of defining utilization so broadly (for example when "anyone uses anything from the evaluation for any purpose") that utilization is almost bound to be identified. Alternatively, if one takes the "dramatic impact" view one may define utilization so narrowly (for example, as requiring that "a single intended user make a specific decision immediately following the receipt of an evaluation report and solely based upon the findings of that report") that it is virtually impossible to find a single example of utilization (Alkin *et al.*, 1979, p.226). Perhaps the most useful way forward then, before deriving a definition, is to consider briefly which perspective most clearly accords with what we know about the reality of information processing and decision-making behaviours in organizations.

Dramatic impact or gradual influence in decision-making?

Given earlier discussions about information processing and decision-making in organizations, the "gradual influence" perspective on utilization appears the more realistic. As Cronbach *et al.* (1980), among many, have persuasively argued, the "dramatic impact" view of the utilization of evaluation findings appears to rest on images of "command" rather than "accommodation", of decision-makers uninhibited by the constraint of prescribed repertoires of behaviours (Weiss, 1981). Information is seen as presented to a single decision-maker, who is free to make the "correct" "rational" decision and act on it, subordinates complying to the letter.

But this picture of rational decision-making and unquestioned command, such that implementation mirrors the expert decision made, is at odds with what we know about the cognitive limitations on information processing, and the processes of decision-making when there is disagreement about appropriate ends and means–ends relationships (see Chapters 2 and 3). Limitations on information-processing as discussed in earlier chapters, results in startling, dramatic information often being more influential than dry "equivocal" evaluation statistics. If the findings are inconsistent with existing attitudes they may be rationalized away—the "wrong" outcomes were measured, the methodology was non-rigorous (Zaltman and Deshpande, 1982), the programme was given insufficient time to shake down—or simply not heard. Moreover Thompson and Tuden's (1959) classification of decision types (according to whether there is agreement about ends and means–ends relationships) suggests that expert testimony will only be conclusive where there already exists consensus on both ends and means–ends relationships. In other types "expert information" will be just one input in a process of bargaining and accommodation, in which satisficing and incrementalism are the order of the day. As decisions about change programmes generally involve some value conflict—if not about broad aims, then about priorities—and uncertainty about means–ends relationships, they fall squarely into a category where factors other than "expert" information are bound to weigh. The more radical and expensive the programme the more likely this is to be the case

(Cronbach *et al.*, 1980, pp.127–128). In these circumstances, the strength of the interest groups which choose to use, discredit or ignore research findings seems a more important factor in the decision-making process than the validity of the findings themselves (Bardach, 1976; Behn, 1978).

All this is consistent with the evidence, discomforting to the "dramatic impact" school, that the rigour (i.e. how close to the experimental model) of a research design does not appear to be *consistently* related to the utilization of its findings (Alkin *et al.*, 1979, p.241; Dunn, 1980; Patton, 1978, p.252; Van de Vall and Boyes, 1981). Evaluation findings stand as just one input into decision-making and in so far as methodological rigour makes for more equivocal, qualified, and diverse results, they may be the least persuasive of the informational inputs (Lindblom and Cohen, 1979, p.47). Their impact is likely to be greatest, when agreement on priorities exist, and they are seen as reducing the uncertainties about means–ends relationships and the "facts" in a situation. It is likely to be least when a "policy vacuum" exists. According to Corwin and Louis (1982) this occurs when there is an absence of an organized constituency of policy makers, identifiable policy issues and research questions, consistent policies and policy options, co-ordination between the different groups responsible for a policy area, and an on-going programme that can make use of the findings.

To summarize, if decision-making about organizational change is generally political and incremental, so it is only realistic to expect the impact of research findings, including evaluation studies, to be piecemeal and cumulative.

If this is so, though, why *were* commentators in the 1960s to mid 1970s so consistent in their expressions of disappointment at the lack of dramatic impact of evaluation research findings and why are organizational researchers so pessimistic today? Surely, it could be argued that a more realistic appreciation of how decision-making in organizations actually takes place would have alerted them to the over-optimism of their expectations? Is, in fact, a "crisis of utilization" merely a figment of some researchers overheated imaginations? Or do these charges serve other functions? These questions will be considered in the conclusion to this chapter.

A working definition

As the "gradual influence" perspective on utilization appears most consistent with the dominant view of how non-routine decisions are made in organizations, a definition broadly within this perspective seems sensible. One such definition, in fact, has been provided by Alkin *et al.* (1979), who ground it in the "middle range" forms of utilization which they observed to take place within their five case study organizations. The definition steers a middle course, for, in the words of its authors (1979, p.226) it seeks to be flexible enough to encompass the variety of types of utilization that actually occur without also capturing inconsequential spin-off effects of evaluation. Thus their approach is to identify "essential components" of utilization, namely, that (1) evaluation information must be communicated (2) to an "appropriate user" (3) who may use it in a variety of ways (4) for a variety of end purposes. The resulting definition (which given their interests is clearly directed towards the evaluation of curricula developments in schools) is as follows:

Utilization may be said to have occurred when
evaluation information is considered by
appropriate users ("a local client, sanctioned local users, external users') as
(*a dominant influence*   )
(*one of multiple influences*   )
(*one of multiple, cumulative influences*   )   *related to*
(establishment   )
(funding   )
(continuance of a component   )
(curriculum/instructional methods   )
(administrative/personnel operations   )
(community acceptance   )   (of)
a change programme (a local school programme).

I consider this definition useful for two reasons. Not only does it provide a checklist of factors that are likely to be crucial in the utilization process (the nature of potential users, the content and form of information, and the overt functions it may serve) but suggests that they are related. In other words a checklist of "factors" must be translated into and seen within a utilization process. It should be noted, though, that this definition follows the convention of defining utilization solely in terms of the *overt* functions evaluation findings serve. For the moment we will abide by the convention, but will reconsider this exclusion later in the chapter.

Within the framework provided by this definition the part played by these factors in the utilization process can now be considered further. From this description, prescriptions will be derived about how the utilization of evaluation research may be facilitated and augmented, and obstacles to such utilization overcome (1).

Achieving the utilization of evaluation research — key factors and processes

"Appropriate users" and the "personal factor"

For the utilization of research findings to occur, by definition *someone* must use them. If the definition of utilization is not to be so broad as to be unfalsifiable (to take a positivistic stance) the potential users, in general terms, must be designated at the outset. Three approaches to this problem have been suggested. Alkin *et al.* (1979) favour the identification of relevant decision-making roles within the formal structure of authority that is authorized to oversee the evaluation. This group, whom the authors designate as "clients", may explicitly sanction others to use the information—for example, those actually implementing the change programme. A further group, the "external users" (for example, members of external organizations who are recognized by the clients to have some legitimate right to use the data, for decision-making, planning or research purposes) is identified, but as Alkin *et al.* (1979, p.228) admit this category verges on the problematic: "the difficulty is in establishing some threshold of salience; at some point, the user and the use become so attenuated from the program as to seem insignificant".

A second approach is to define as appropriate users the "stakeholder audiences" identified in Chapter 3 (Guba and Lincoln, 1981, pp.307–309; Stake, 1975). One problem with this approach though is it encourages the attenuation that Alkin *et al.* (1979) fear.

Patton (1978), I feel, offers a more constructive approach by concentrating on the notion of salience. In the course of his research into the utilization of Office of Health (H.E.W.) evaluations, he asked his respondents, administrators and evaluators alike, to "pick out the single factor you feel had the greatest effect on how this study was used". A range of factors were offered from which a choice could be made: methodological quality, methodological appropriateness, timeliness, lateness of report, positive or negative findings, surprise of findings, central or peripheral programme objectives evaluated, presence or absence of related studies, political factors, decision-maker-evaluator interactions, and resources available for the study. Only two factors emerged as consistently important in explaining the degree of utilization achieved, political factors and what Patton terms "the personal factor". It is this "personal factor" which Patton argues is salient in identifying appropriate users.

But what is this "personal factor"? To quote Patton (1978, p.64) the term refers to

> . . . an identifiable individual or group of people who personally cared about the evaluation and the information it generated . . . The personal factor represents the leadership, interest, enthusiasm, determination, commitment, aggressiveness and caring of specific individual people . . . these are the people who are actively seeking information to reduce decision uncertainties so as to increase their ability to predict the outcomes of programmatic activity and enhance their own discretion as decision-makers.

Interestingly, the importance of their potential users' ability to get new things done, to be willing to take responsibility and initiate changes, to be adept at "intelligent risk-taking" is also recognized by Alkin *et al.* (1979) as crucial in the utilization process. Indeed, it is they who provide detailed case studies (e.g. "Garrison" and "Rockland") highlighting the importance in utilization of decision makers' genuine commitment to the evaluation and their administrative and political skills to use the findings effectively.

In both these cases the expectations and initiatives taken by users of the evaluation played a key part in the utilization of the studies—a finding that concurs with the Patton study already cited. The corollary, borne out by both studies, is that when the potential users have no enthusiasm for evaluation, play little part in the conceptualization and design of the study, are not, or no longer, interested in the focus of the study, little utilization of the findings in decision-making occurs (Corwin and Louis, 1982). Alkin *et al.* (1979, pp.81–108) Valley Vista case study provides an illustration of this.

The "personal factor" does not stop at the potential users of the evaluation study. The enthusiasm and commitment of users (or lack of it) is in many cases a reflection of their experience of evaluation, which in turn is very much influenced by their experience of researchers. Alkin *et al.* (1979) in their Bayview case study show how the personal qualities of the researcher converted project decision-makers from apathy about evaluation into developing a conviction that evaluation could provide some answers to questions they wanted answering. In this case the evaluator was extremely committed to the philosophy that evaluation should meet the needs of project staff, and worked hard to gain their confidence.

An important factor in developing a good working relationship between researchers and potential users of evaluation studies is, of course, that the former must appear credible to these users. In part, of course, such credibility is likely to rest on researchers possessing the technical expertises appropriate to generate valid data. But this is not the whole story and we have already referred to the finding that methodological rigour does not invariably appear strongly related to utilization. This is not surprising as many users will themselves lack the expertise to judge a researcher's technical competence—in which case trust must be based on judgements of the researcher as a person. Here the evaluator's degree of commitment and enthusiasm appears an important factor in establishing trust and rapport with potential users. Accounts that indicate the importance of such factors in action researchers' success or failure in implementing and evaluating change programmes may be found in Bate and Mangham (1981) and Klein (1976). McGivern's (1983) study of the relationship between consultants and clients similarly indicates the importance of mutual trust and the consultant's perceived high level of personal commitment, in developing a successful relationship.

The emphasis on the importance of the "personal factor" in defining appropriate users, shifts attention from roles (the Alkin *et al.* approach) to the people who occupy them. This is clear in Patton's (1978, p.284) approach to identifying potential users, which involves the researcher in asking the following questions:

(1) Which are the people who can use information?

(2) Which are the people to whom information makes a difference?

(3) Which are the people who have questions they want to have answered? and

(4) Which are the people who care about and are willing to share responsibility for the evaluation and its utilization?

The questions are as relevant to action researchers working in industrial and commercial organizations, as they are to evaluators of social change programmes.

The first question suggests that an individual's formal position in the authority structure may be a guide in identifying potential users, but only a guide. Obviously, even if not a key decision-maker, a potential user still requires the access to key decision-makers in order to have the findings used, and resources to facilitate the research process—both of which are partially determined by his or her organizational position. But power and influence in an organization does not rest solely on position in the hierarchy—how strategic an individual's department is perceived to be to organizational success, whether superiors depend on his or her expertise, the individual's charisma, will all affect the degree of influence he or she is able to exert in decision-making (Legge, 1978). In which case, Patton argues, an individual with enthusiasm for evaluation or action research but (relatively) lower down the hierarchy, may constitute a more appropriate user than a disinterested superior. Patton's remaining questions are directed at identifying those who possess the motivation for using evaluation findings.

While I would basically support Patton's approach it is not without problems. First, what are researchers to do if none of the potential users displays "the personal factor?" Presumably there are two options. Either they can treat as appropriate users those occupying the roles identified as relevant by Alkin *et al.*, and attempt, through their own commitment and enthusiasm, to open the latters' eyes to the potential usefulness of research and so bring about an attitude change in the more susceptible individuals. (Alkin *et al.* Bayview case illustrates this approach). Or they can question whether it is really worthwhile undertaking the study at all except for academic learning purposes. The first strategy is probably appropriate in situations where the researcher is highly committed and has sufficient resources, particularly of time and processual skills, to convert the potential users. If he or she lacks such commitment and resources, the second strategy would seem sensible—particularly in the case of the action researcher, where support by decision-makers with the power to allocate resources is crucial for the research to get off the ground at all. But this is to assume that evaluative research serves only the overt informational functions discussed in Chapter 3. The fact that matters are rarely so clear cut and apolitical may result in the researcher undertaking a study having "symbolic" uses (Pelz, 1978) such as legitimizing the status quo (e.g. Trice *et al.*, 1969) or justifying a decision already made (e.g. Sabatier, 1978). Such studies, at least, are guaranteed a form of "misutilization", as Cook *et al.* (1980) put it.

A second problem is if the researcher identifies several potential users with the "personal factor" but who each have different questions that they want answering, which logically require different and possibly incompatible evaluation designs. Or, even if the questions and the potential designs are compatible, they are so numerous that, given limited resources, choices have to be made. Here the evaluator is presented with the recurring problem of selection rather than identification, and several options may be considered. Either the users can be encouraged to mutually negotiate and agree a set of priorities which could be evaluated within one, or compatible, research designs. This is the preferred option, if feasible, as no potential user is lost. Or the researcher can select from the group on the basis of such criteria as: whose questions appear the most worthwhile or urgent; who appears to possess the "personal factor" in the highest degree; which individuals appear to have the most say, at present, in organizational decision-making? Such a selection is easiest when a few individuals emerge as scoring significantly higher than other possibles on all three criteria. And while such a selection might alienate some potential users, it serves to concentrate the researcher's efforts in directions where utilization might have the largest pay-off. If different individuals score variably on the criteria then the researcher's own values come into play—including pragmatism. It may be politically more acceptable to tailor the study towards the questions sought by an individual who scores only moderately on the "personal factor" (while not being devoid of it) but who already has a reputation for being influential in decision-making. (Of course, this is to assume that evaluators perceive some choice in directing their studies towards potential users with the "personal factor". They may feel so constrained by the terms of funding/sponsoring that they can see only one audience—the funders/sponsors—however low they, as individuals, might score on the "personal factor".)

But the process of selection raises a more fundamental problem. Alkin *et al.* (1979, p.260) criticize Patton's approach through its very emphasis on the evaluation researcher selecting particular individuals rather than focusing on pre-specified roles, irrespective of the characteristics of their incumbents. They argue that, without additional constraints on the manner in which appropriate users are selected, the approach would allow a "Machiavellian" researcher to select potential users and target the evaluation in highly biased ways. For example, if the researcher's own values dictate a certain position (for example, if he (or she) is highly partisan pro or anti a particular change programme) he may deliberately select as appropriate users those felt to be sympathetic with his position, perhaps using attributions of the "personal factor" by way of justification. Nor need so extreme a case be made. If evaluators identify and select certain individuals as potential users, and mould their research around their information requirements (implicit in Patton's questions 2 and 3) are they putting other participants at a potential disadvantage in subsequent debates about findings? Are they essentially acting undemocratically?

The answer would depend on how one defines democracy and what arrangements the researcher makes for the dissemination of findings — points that will be taken up later in the chapter. But what should be recognized here is that this criticism returns us to the broader issue of the values inherent in an emphasis on utilization, of which the "dangers" inherent in Patton's approach are but a reflection. Selecting individuals with the "personal factor" who are keen and able to use research findings in decision-making will tend, by definition, to rule out the silent majority — and the deprived minorities — and to rule in those who have a vested interest in the status quo — if, as Patton would assume with the best of intentions about reforming it.

Evaluation information and study design

It is, of course, a truism, that for research to be used, the information it generates must be perceived as useful, and, indeed, there is a general consensus that perceived usefulness *does* increase the chances that information will actually be used (other things being equal) (Alkin *et al.*, 1979; Cronbach *et al.*, 1980; Guba and Lincoln, 1981; Hakel *et al.*, 1982; Patton, 1978; Weiss and Bucuvalas, 1977). So what are the ingredients of perceived usefulness? Dunn (1981) suggests three criteria are used to assess the usefulness of information: is it *relevant*, i.e. is the information appropriate to a given problem, is it timely?; is it *adequate?* i.e. is it truthful?; is it *cogent*, i.e. is it persuasive? But, how, in fact, do information users judge research reports and academic articles to be useful? What criteria do they employ?

Weiss and Bucuvalas (1980a) throw some light on this question. In an empirical study (2) exploring the frames of references that decision-makers employ in assessing the usefulness of applied social science research generally for their work, Weiss and Bucuvalas found that they used three tests: was it relevant (i.e. did it deal with issues that concerned the decision-maker's job responsibilities); was it trustworthy and did it provide guidance — either for immediate action or for considering alternative approaches to problems. In assessing whether a study was trustworthy decision-makers rated studies against two criteria: "research quality" (judged in terms of methodological rigour) and conformity with prior knowledge and expectations. Utility was assessed in terms of the research's ability to assist practical problem-solving or to offer alternative perspectives. The items operationalizing practical problem-solving, or the "action orientation" included: explicit recommendations, manipulable variables, targeted set of dependent variables, direct implications for a course of action, applicability within existing programmes, and addition to practical knowledge. The second utility criterion, termed "challenge to the status quo", included such items as "challenges existing assumptions and institutional arrangements", "raises new issues and offers new perspectives".

Weiss and Bucuvalas (1980a) found that decision-makers did indeed judge the usefulness of a study in terms of its relevance, truthfulness and utility. However, the real interest in their findings is in the evidence of the strength of and trade-offs between these criteria. For example, somewhat surprisingly (and in partial contradiction to the findings of Alkin *et al.*, 1979; Komarovsky, 1975; and Patton, 1978), research quality was found to be more important than all the other criteria in explaining respondent's own likelihood of using research — although the same respondents were not so sure that this was true of their colleagues. But the importance attributed to research quality was particularly marked if the study was to be used for mobilizing support for a point of view, or debating new approaches to an issue. Weiss and Bucuvalas' interpretation is that if a study is to be used in an adversarial decision-making process, not only do decision-makers need assurance that the evidence is firm, but protection from methodologically based criticism. Where research quality seemed of less importance was when the results were in accordance with decision-makers' prior knowledge and expectations. [This, of course is consistent with Patton's (1978, p.255) evidence that decision-makers are more likely to criticize the methodological quality of an evaluation if they do not like and have not anticipated the findings; also with Zaltman and Deshpande's (1982) evidence that managers frequently examine the methodology of a market research report if the results are surprising, not if they are expected, and in order to find out what was wrong with it, not to determine if it was sound.]

A second important point to emerge from the study is that the "action orientation" ("does the research show how to make feasible changes in things that can be feasibly changed") and the "challenge to the status quo" ("does the research challenge current practice, does it offer new perspectives") represent alternative functions that a study can serve. In other words, a study can be rated high in usefulness if it scores highly on one factor but low on another. Thus

> when a study's results are feasible to implement, evidence of major deficiencies in practice or fundamentally new perspectives do not add much to its usefulness. When a study suggests radical redirection of policy or program, explicit

> direction for implementation adds relatively little to usefulness; respondents
> are receptive to its ideas, but they are not prepared to take immediate steps
> to carry out its recommendations. (Weiss and Bucuvalas, 1980b, p.704)

Interestingly, and contrary to appearances, this finding is *not* inconsistent with the evidence of decision-makers' reluctance to accept surprise or counter-attitudinal findings. Weiss and Bucuvalas point out that, as the correlation between factor scores for "challenges to the status quo" and "conformity to user expectations" is virtually nil, it is reasonable to infer that research findings that challenge current practice are as likely to accord with decision-makers' beliefs as to contradict them. Decision-makers, like evaluators, can be reformist in their intentions—indeed, their very willingness to initiate change programmes is indicative of such predispositions. According to Weiss and Bucuvalas, the studies that provided a "challenge to the status quo" and which were rated highly for usefulness were indeed reformist *not* radical—none seriously challenged existing social and economic institutions. Furthermore one measure of "usefulness" used in this research—"the likelihood of taking a study into account in the work of one's office"—is consistent with the probable use made of challenging studies. That is, it does not demand that respondents implement or act immediately upon the findings, merely that they are useful for stimulating thought, "enlightening" the decision-maker.

In Weiss and Bucuvalas' (1980a) research study tests of relevance and utility are separated out—relevance being seen in terms of whether the substantive content of information maps onto the decision-maker's job responsibilities, utility in terms of two alternative functions a study can serve (guidance for immediate action vs enlightenment about different and new approaches to problems). Most commentators though tend to conflate the two concepts defining information as relevant to decision-makers if they recognize it as being useful to them. (Effectively this was my approach in treating information as relevant if it could serve the various functions stakeholder audiences sought from evaluation research.) This approach has also been adopted notably by Thomas and Tymon (1982) and by Beyer and Trice (1982) in considering how organizational research generally can be made more useful to managers and administrators, and their conclusions may be usefully summarized.

Thomas and Tymon (1982) argue that much organizational research at present lacks *descriptive relevance*, in that findings fail to capture phenomena as experienced by the practitioner in his or her organizational setting. This, they suggest, is particularly true of experimental studies whose controls to protect internal validity renders them artificial, and whose emphasis on simple unidirectional causal notions distorts important aspects of organizational reality (Cummings, 1978; Kilmann, 1979). This concurs with several commentators conclusion that, generally speaking, qualitative research produces data that are more recognizable and accessible to managers (Beyer and Trice, 1982, p.612; Dunbar, 1983; Van de Vall *et al.*, 1976).

Secondly, they suggest it lacks *goal relevance*, in that dependent variables do not correspond with outcomes which concern practitioners (see also Cheng and McKinley, 1983). While this may be true of some basic descriptive and explanatory organizational research, this seems an inappropriate criticism of much evaluation and action research into change, where as already suggested researchers are perhaps overly ready to incorporate managerial values into their selection of dependent variables (see Chapter 6). A greater problem is in identifying and selecting specific goals as dependent variables where conflict between different groups of "practitioners" exists.

Their third criticism of organizational research is that it lacks *operational validity*, in that practitioners are unable to manipulate what are suggested to be causal variables. This criticism, in relation to the evaluation of social change programmes has been echoed by Riecken and Boruch (1974, pp.239–243) and Weiss and Weiss (1981) and by Beyer and Trice (1982, pp.613–614) about organizational research generally. Beyer and Trice however suggest that focusing on manipulable variables, while improving utilization, carries dangers. It can lead to research with little explanatory value, if the variables considered non-manipulable best explain and predict phenomena of interest. It also tends to focus researchers' attention on those variables that are under control of the levels of the organization to which they have gained access (usually lower or middle) rather than the highest levels. Hence again this may result in research taking on an overly conservative stance (see Chapter 6).

Thomas and Tymon (1982) identify two further problems with the potential utility of much organizational research: it lacks *non-obviousness* (findings are considered trivial or commonsense) and *timeliness* (findings arrive too late to influence the decisions to which they might relate, while the phenomena under study change faster than research designs can cope with). We will consider the whole question of timeliness in the next section. As for the charge that much organizational research is obvious, Thomas and Tymon cite Gordon *et al.* (1978) evidence that when a sample of non-psychologists were asked to predict the findings of 61 published studies, on average they correctly predicted three out of four findings! This they attribute, following Kilmann (1979), to the oversimplifications that arise through the need for experimental controls.

If there is a general consensus that information relevancy/perceived usefulness does increase the chances that research will actually be used, what are the specific tactics a researcher can employ to produce a "relevant" study?

The general approach of action researchers in implementing and evaluating change, emphasizing as it does the iterative processes of data-gathering, diagnosis, further data gathering, feedback to client group, joint setting of objectives and designing of a programme of activities to achieve them, implementation, joint data gathering and evaluation and so on, is designed to facilitate utilization and often does so (Dunn, 1980). Its success, in terms of utilization, depends on the sort of factors which Patton (1978) illuminates in his discussion of the application of a similar approach to the evaluation of change programmes in public service organizations.

Patton (1978) suggests the following series of steps in designing a "utilization-focused evaluation study". First, having identified the relevant decision-makers and information-users (those high on the personal factor) the researcher should "identify and focus the relevant evaluation question". This involves finding out what the *potential users* see as the purpose of the evaluation, what information they want and how they intend to use it. This entails, first, getting members of the evaluation task force (identified and organized decision-makers and information users and evaluators) to agree on the purposes and emphasis of the evaluation (for example, whether it is to be formative or summative, which components and programme activities are to be examined). Secondly, it involves them considering the alternative approaches to focusing evaluation questions — whether in terms of programme goals, its implementation, the programme's theory of action, the stage in its development or in the context of the programme's organizational dynamics (Patton, 1978, pp.285–286). The third step is for the evaluation task force to derive the evaluation questions it wants answering in the light of positions adopted about the evaluation's purpose and focus. Patton (1978, p.83) suggests that when formulating these questions the evaluation task force should ask whether they satisfy the following "utilization-focused" criteria:

(1) It is possible to bring data to bear on the question.

(2) There is more than one possible answer to the question, i.e. the answer is not predetermined or "loaded" by the phrasing of the question.

(3) The identified decision-makers *want* information to help answer the question.

(4) The identified decision-makers feel they *need* information to help them answer the question.

(5) The identified and organized decision-makers and information users want to answer the question for themselves, not just for someone else.

(6) They care about the answer to the question.

(7) The decision-makers can indicate how they would use the answer to the question, i.e. they can specify the relevance of an answer to the question for future action.

Elaborating on these criteria, Patton makes the following points. In his view evaluation *research* questions are empirical questions about impact or change, not judgemental questions about whether what is observed should be labelled as good or bad. Questions that cannot be answered empirically he argues do not provide a clear focus for utilization. Evaluators should avoid questions where they do not really want the information—for example, information that is too sensitive to act upon. "Needing" information points to the fact that it should be information that is not already known. The personal interest criterion relates back to the identification of relevant decision-makers and information-users—evaluation questions should focus on *these* individuals' information requirements—not on questions which those uncommitted to utilization might suggest should be answered. Finally, Patton (1978, p.88) suggests that the evaluation task force, during the conceptualization of the research questions, should be able to say how they plan to use the resulting information, for, if they cannot indicate future usefulness at the outset, there is no reason to believe they will be able to do so after the evaluation. In order to facilitate this, collecting information about malleable variables is advised.

Having identified and focused the evaluation questions, Patton (1978, pp.198–238) then proposes that evaluation methods are selected which are most appropriate for generating the type of information required to answer the evaluation questions. Without doubt, this is a powerful approach for generating information that the identified decision-makers and information users will find relevant/useful. However, Patton tends to skate over such potentially problematic issues as whether it is always possible to get decision-makers to agree a consistent set of evaluation purposes, let alone priorities; whether empirical questions can ever be truly value free (see Chapter 6); whether it is ethical for an evaluator to avoid some questions solely because potential users do not want them answering. Furthermore, when he speaks of matching method to evaluation questions and situations, some confusion is evident. Patton, on the one hand, advocates an epistemological and methodological pluralism, but in speaking of "malleable variables", "empirical questions" seems unaware that such concepts are inconsistent with interpretive epistemological and ontological positions. Perhaps most problematic from the utilization point of view, though, is his reliance on the ability of his identified decision-makers to formulate the evaluation questions they want answering. For there is evidence that decision-makers, in fact, are often unable to define their research needs (Weiss and Bucuvalas, 1980a).

The approaches advocated by Stake (1975), Alkin *et al.* (1979) and Guba and Lincoln (1980) are in the same mould as Patton's. Stake (1975) advocates that a "responsive approach" to evaluation should involve the identification of the problems and concerns of stakeholder audiences about the change programme and that the evaluation should be designed to elicit information "responsive" to these concerns. Alkin *et al.* (1979, p.238) likewise suggest that potential users have many "questions or concerns" about the programme being evaluated, and that these should serve to focus the study. However, Guba and Lincoln (1981, pp.311–320), elaborating on Stake's suggestions, indicate in more detail how this might be done.

They suggest that the "concerns" and "issues" of stakeholders in the evaluation can initially be identified using the "naturalistic" research methods discussed in Chapter 5 (see pp.177–178). (It should be remembered that their definition of a "concern" was "any matter of interest to one or more stakeholders about which they feel threatened or think will lead to undesirable consequences, or that they wanted substantiated or refuted", an "issue" was "any statement or proposition that allows for the presentation of different points of view".) However, they recognize that for focusing an evaluation study, the concerns and issues initially identified need to be prioritized, and, to the extent that their initial sample of respondents may be unrepresentative, tested for relevance to a wider sample of each "stakeholder" audience. To this end they suggest the use of a questionnaire, sent to a larger sample of each audience, listing descriptors (see Chapter 5), issues and concerns that have already been identified with the smaller sample. Respondents would then be asked to rate on a three point scale "whether each statement validly describes an element in the situation or phrases a concern or issue in realistic terms" and to indicate on a five point scale the absolute priority (1 = highest priority, 5 = lowest priority) of each issue and concern. Guba and Lincoln (1981, p.320) suggest that a descriptor, concern or issue should be treated seriously in subsequent research if (1) all audiences agree about its reality and/or high priority or (2) disagree about its reality or priority. An item should be considered unimportant and irrelevant to the audiences' interests if all audiences agree that it lacks validity or is of low priority. Subsequent research design will depend on which concerns and issues are validated and prioritized, and hence what information will count as relevant (Guba and Lincoln, 1981, p.361). Again the design appropriate to generating relevant information is called for.

It remains to consider a further factor of information relevancy/utility—timeliness—and the whole question of its persuasiveness. As these factors also concern the broader questions of information communication and dissemination, they will be discussed in the next section.

Information communication and dissemination

There is a general consensus amongst evaluation commentators that the nature of communications during the evaluation research and the manner and form in which findings are disseminated are crucial factors in the utilization process. As this consensus, broadly speaking, extends to how communications and dissemination should be conducted, a brief summary may suffice. However, before embarking on this, it may be useful to clarify the difference between "communication" and "dissemination". "Communication" is used to refer to the verbal interactions and exchanges which take place between the researcher and appropriate users during the period in which the evaluation research is conducted, and "dissemination" to refer to the reporting of findings after the study has been conducted. It should be noted though that this distinction is not completely clear-cut—preliminary findings, "early warnings" are often conveyed to users during the communication process. That said, what factors in the design and organization of the communication and dissemination process appear to facilitate the utilization of evaluation research?

There is general agreement that, during the research programme, the evaluator or action researcher should maintain on-going and two-way communications with those to have been designated as "appropriate users"—be they Alkin et al. (1979) and Patton's (1978) "appropriate decision-makers and information users", Anderson and Ball's (1978) "agents in the evaluation process", Stake's (1975) and Guba and Lincoln's (1981) "stakeholder" audiences, or Cronbach et al. (1980) "policy shaping community". At the very least such communication is necessary to establish what would count as relevant/useful information to the "appropriate users", to establish priorities in issues and concerns and about which functions are to be served. How frequent, and the nature of subsequent communications, is more a matter of debate. Patton (1978) probably goes further than most in advocating the evaluators and "the relevant decision-makers and information users" organize themselves into a task force to jointly debate, evolve and oversee every subsequent stage of the evaluation, including design, data analysis, interpretation and dissemination. However, whether such a participative relationship is appropriate in all cases has been questioned. Alkin et al. (1979, pp.242–243) argue that many of the users will not wish nor have the time to be so closely involved, and that the evaluator should match the frequency and nature of his or her communications to their requirements.

My view is that, following the evaluator's initial efforts to establish what counts as relevant/useful information to the various potential users, the nature and frequency of communication should follow from the functions sought, and subsequent design of the study. If, for example, policy-makers wish the evaluation to serve a control function ("is X programme failing to produce anticipated results, and are Y managers responsible") and the evaluator agrees this function should take priority and that a quasi-experimental design is appropriate to produce relevant information, this will have implications for his subsequent communications with potential users. For example, his communication with programme implementers and clients will be constrained by the validity requirements of his design, while those with the group whose functions the evaluation is designed to serve are likely to increase in frequency. Furthermore, potential users whose evaluation functions, issues and concerns are not considered to have as high a priority as others may be less involved in communication with the evaluator than those whose functions, issues and concerns form the core of the evaluation study.

As a broad generalization, it seems agreed that a more participative style of interaction, involving more frequent and informal communication with programme designers, implementers and clients will be more consistent with formative evaluations of a non-experimental design, while a less participative style, involving less frequent and possibly more formal communications with policy-makers and funders will be consistent with experimental and quasi-experimental designs. This view, in fact, accords with the evidence of Alkin *et al.* (1979, p.242) who suggest that evaluators who defined their role as that of "facilitator" or "colleague" of programme staff, generally while conducting formative evaluations, did tend to be more participative than those who defined their role as "judge" or "researcher", and who conducted experimental or quasi-experimental studies. Given the range of alternative communication patterns and styles which may emerge, the consensus appears to be that communications during the research should be conducted in a "timely and appropriate fashion" (Anderson and Ball, 1978, p.93), that they should be responsive to user requirements for information and explanation, and compatible with the evaluation design — but that detailed prescription is impossible due to the necessity of a contingent response.

The question of the timing and timeliness of communications as a prerequisite of their relevance has already been mentioned. While the two concepts are closely related, they are not identical. The "timeliness" of information, that is its temporal relevance, may be a function of "good" timing in its submission, but information deemed irrelevant one day may be considered highly relevant the next due to changes in circumstances, unanticipated events quite outside the evaluator's knowledge or control. This said, there is a growing view that while the submission of the final report to schedule is important, its importance can be overrated. Far more important in ensuring the "timeliness" of information is that it should be delivered when use can be made of it and, as Weiss (1972a) points out, if evaluators have given regular informal feedback, the evaluation report in any case should contain little that users have not heard already. Furthermore, there is agreement that springing "surprise" findings in a final report hinders rather than facilitates their utilization, as it tends to increase rather than decrease decision-makers uncertainty, besides drawing fire if the "surprise" findings are counter-intuitive (Patton, 1978, pp.264–265). But in timing the release of preliminary findings the evaluator needs also to be aware that his audiences may place too much reliance on what are only tentative results. Precisely when it can be deemed appropriate to communicate results will depend, to a large extent, on the questions being asked (and therefore what constitutes "real" answers) and, consequently, on the study design. But a consensus does exist that communication, particularly of "early warnings" about problems in implementing the change programme, deviations from its original design and so on should occur well before the final report is written (Cronbach *et al.*, 1980, pp.178–182).

Finally there is the question of the dissemination of findings via reports and presentations—what information should reports contain and how should that information be presented in order to facilitate utilization? As far as information content goes—this should be determined by what has already been identified as potentially useful information at the outset of the study. That is, information that is responsive to the issues and concerns of appropriate users and which fulfils the functions sought of the evaluation. What this information will comprise in substantive content will of course vary according to the focus of the evaluation and the nature of the design that was considered appropriate to generate "useful" information. Guba and Lincoln (1981, pp.364–365), for example, provide a useful outline of what a report based on a "naturalistic" evaluation, should contain.

In what style should the information be presented in order to facilitate utilization? Should reports present findings quantitatively or qualitatively, should jargon be used or avoided, should brevity or comprehensiveness have the higher priority; should presentations be formal or informal? Again a consensus emerges. There is no one "right" stylistic approach—style of report or presentation, while being constrained ultimately by the study design, must be matched to the requirements and preferences of the audience, and be fashioned with an awareness of the "natural language" of the audience (Alkin *et al.*, 1979, pp.257–258; Guba and Lincoln, 1981, pp.366–367). Underlying this contingent approach to style of presentation though are two widely espoused principles: that the report should be intelligible to the audience to which it is addressed, and that it should be persuasive.

What then makes an evaluation report persuasive, that is, believable to the audience to which it is directed? First, evaluation researchers agree that credibility is in the eye of the beholder and hence for a report or paper to be persuasive it must be written for a specific homogeneous audience whose evaluation functions, issues, concerns and values it addresses (Alkin *et al.*, 1979, pp.252–254; Anderson and Ball, 1978, p.104; House, 1980, pp.74–76). It is therefore highly unlikely that one research report or paper will suffice to cover all potential users, if its utilization is taken seriously. Each user audience may require its own report.

Certainly, there is plenty of evidence to suggest that publication of research findings in academic journals and books, while appropriate for influencing fellow researchers (and securing career advancement) makes little impact on practicing managers in industry, particularly if they are presented in the highly quantitative and non-prescriptive style generally favoured by such journals (Dunbar, 1983; Van de Vall *et al.* 1976). For example, Watson (1977) in his study of personnel managers, found that few were familiar with any of the recent organizational behaviour research "relevant" to their function. Beyer and Trice (1982, p.603) reports that when Dunnette and Brown (1968, pp.180–183) surveyed executives perceived to be "acutely attuned to contributions by behaviour scientists", they found "only a small portion" of them had even heard of many of the studies nominated by industrial psychologists as "most significant". In contrast, researchers whose names, and to a lesser extent, work, was recognized were those such as Herzberg or Drucker, who have been highly active in proselytizing their work via public lectures, in-company courses and "popular" short articles in newspapers and professional magazines. This finding is, of course, totally consistent with the verbal nature of managerial work, referred to in Chapter 2 (see also Gowler and Legge, 1983). In contrast, though, it would appear that administrators in public service organizations, particularly those with a professional background in education or medicine, are somewhat less deterred by an academic presentation of material (Weiss and Weiss, 1981).

Assuming a report or paper is written for each audience and contains the information relevant to its own evaluation functions, issues and concerns, expressed with an awareness of its "natural language" what else can be done to enhance its persuasiveness? House (1980, Chapter 5) makes some interesting suggestions. He argues that persuasiveness and credibility go hand in hand, and that the credibility of a research report may be heightened if the information it contains is presented with optimum coherence. Coherence results from following the six classic principles of aesthetic form, namely organic unity, theme, thematic variation, balance, hierarchy and evolution. In practical terms adherence to these principles, first and foremost, demands that the report "tells a story", that it has a theme such that "inferences and interpretations of events are integrated with each other, and parts are ordered to the whole". The theme "must not only persist but reappear in variations if the total effect is to be achieved". Coherence will be obtained by following the organic unity principle—that the report contain only the "necessary elements" for explicating the theme. The same can be said for "balance" which involves the creation of dramatic tension by maintaining a dialogue between opposing elements, and for hierarchy, as a means of ordering the separate parts. Finally, "evolution" which involves the idea that "a total meaning can be created by an accumulation in which earlier parts determine that which happens later" is an important element in achieving coherence. Again, practically speaking, this suggests that the conclusions of a research report should seem to evolve inevitably from the preceding presentation of data and interpretation.

How these aesthetic principles are applied, and the ease of application will, of course, depend on the design of the study. For example, the organic unity principle may be expressed in an experimental design by its parsimony, elegance and power. As House (1980, p.107) puts it, "consider, for example the aesthetic appeal of a multivariate analysis as compared to a long string of bivariate data analyses". But a poorly designed study, whether positivistic or interpretive, will place constraints on the report writer—inappropriate or poorly executed method may result in a temptation to "fudge" data in order to achieve coherent presentation.

The importance of adhering to these aesthetic principles in report writing, according to House, is that the resulting product will have a power over and above its appeal to cognitive understanding. Following Langer (1942) he suggests that a report which abides by aesthetic principles will have an "artistic meaning". In other words it will communicate tacit knowledge and feelings, "vibes", quite apart from any literal meaning that is conveyed by its propositional statements. A good example (cited by House, 1980, pp.100–101) of the power of such tacit knowledge is provided by Schön (1979), who suggests that the metaphors we use in framing social problems guides the solutions that emerge. For example if a problem of social services is that they are "fragmented", the implicit solution is that they should be co-ordinated. But a different solution would emerge if the image of "autonomy" substituted for fragmentation. Similarly, in industry, if a problem is defined as worker "restriction of output", the solution might appear to be in enhancing motivation, if it is defined as "poor machine utilization" the solution might lie in increased automation.

While the report's coherence in "telling a story" is likely to add to its persuasiveness, the "telling" should not be overextended. There is a general consensus that while weighty appendices may fulfil various covert functions in evaluation, information overload is self-defeating and brevity and summarization a virtue if the report is to be used to serve overt informational functions (Berke, 1976; Cronbach et al., 1980, pp.186–187). Just as a short report stands a better chance of being read than a long one (other things being equal), the evaluator should be guided in all his communications with potential users by what he knows of the ways in which managers typically gather information. That is, from brief and frequent conversations rather than from the occasional reading of long reports; from anecdotal rather than abstract presentation of information; from trusted, accessible insiders rather than from inaccessible, scarcely known outsiders (see Chapter 3).

Finally, although the importance of effective communications in facilitating the utilization of research is the received wisdom, a sobering cautionary note should be sounded. As Weiss and Bucuvalas (1980a, pp.244–245) warn, if decision-makers cannot articulate their research needs, there is a limit to what the often advocated "face-to-face" communication can achieve. Also, while it may increase decision-makers' understanding of research, trust in its validity, ability to interpret its results, it may also increase their awareness of its limitations and so enhance any initial scepticism. Furthermore, if findings from different studies are contradictory, "good communications" on the part of a persuasive communicator may result in the acceptance of results from a weaker study and rejection of those from a stronger, but inadequately communicated study. However, the latter observation perhaps only serves to emphasize the importance of effective communications.

Summary and conclusions

In this chapter I have discussed whether research findings are used in decision-making, and concluded that they are and they are not — depending on how both utilization and decision-making are defined. But if it is acceptable to define utilization in terms of enlightenment rather than dramatic impact, and if the indeterminancy of much decision-making is recognized, then not only can it be acknowledged that utilization *does* take place, but the way is cleared for suggestions to be offered about how this process might be facilitated. The suggestions which have been made — about getting the appropriate information to the appropriate people in an appropriate form and at an appropriate time — are to a degree trite and self-evident. How to implement them is not. The strategies proposed admittedly contain problems, but at least provide a starting point.

Throughout, utilization has been discussed in informational terms, but, if the discussion in Chapter 3 is accepted, evaluation research is often used to fulfil symbolic and covert functions. For reasons already given, the utilization debate is not cast in these terms — as far as enhancing a study's ability to serve the covert functions goes, the approach is either to ignore the possibility or to refer to "misutilization". Yet the evidence we have about "misutilization" (e.g. Brickell, 1976) in one sense confirms the major prescriptions discussed in this chapter. When such "misutilization" occurs it is marked by the determination of the "misusers" to make their own use of the evaluation and by the attention they pay to persuasive communications.

So was my suggestion, and that of other commentators, that a "crisis in utilization" existed, misguided, or a misrepresentation of the true state of affairs? In a very literal sense — yes. Evaluators' concern that their research findings were not utilized, at least for overt informational purposes, can be seen to have arisen from their unrealistic expectations about the nature of much decision-making and of the potential impact of research findings in that process. The more recent cries of applied organizational researchers (e.g. *Administrative Science Quarterly* December 1982 and March 1983), one may suspect, are evoked by more pragmatic concerns. Having tackled the utilization problem through the development of action research in the late 1950s and 1960s, and achieved a measure of success, (Dunn, 1980) the issue has returned to prominence because the cold winds of recession are drying up research council funding and erstwhile plentiful action research-consultancy contracts alike. Researchers' concern with utility, if unconsciously, may well be in reaction to managers' increased reluctance to grant access without a clear quid pro quo, and their reported decreased interest in humanistic experiments, when high levels of unemployment ensure employees' ultimate co-operation (Purcell, 1982). Even so, it should be noted that the loudest cries of distress were heard in the late 1960s and early 1970s in the U.S.A. among social change programme evaluators, when the high hopes that a "Great Society" could be created by following the advice of the new philosopher kings, the social scientists, were being dashed. Such disillusionment was perhaps one step towards a realignment of expectations and a new realism. However, at the time, the concern was genuine, if unrealistic, and in this sense a crisis— *of disillusionment about the utilization* of evaluation research, rather than its *actual utilization*— could be said to exist.

But, this is to look at the surface level of the "crisis" only. I would suggest an alternative perspective. In order to resolve their disillusionment, social change programme evaluation researchers, in particular, have had to redefine what they mean by utilization and the gradual influence/enlightenment definition is now the new orthodoxy (Alkin *et al.*, 1979; Patton, 1978; Weiss and Bucuvalas, 1980a). But, there are real problems with this "soft" definition at least for positivists, as, with this enlightenment definition the proposition "utilization occurred" becomes virtually impossible to falsify. It is noticeable that whereas the "dramatic impact" view of utilization sought as evidence measurable changes in policies and programmes (for example, termination, re-funding, re-designing a programme component), the gradual influence view relies on respondents' opinions and attributions of how the research influenced their own and others' internal thought processes. This can result in attributions of utilization which appear to strain a meaningful definition to the seams. For example, Alkin *et al.* (1979, p.31) speak of utilization occurring when decision-makers chose to act contrary to the clear implications of evaluation findings, after giving them a "serious hearing". "Evaluations can be utilized, in the broader sense of being 'listened to', without being obeyed." So it would seem that a real problem remains with the notion of utilization.

It is from this standpoint that an alternative perspective on the "utilization crisis" may be offered. I suggest that, in the late 1960s and early 1970s, it was evaluation researchers' commitment to positivistic research designs that led them to define utilization in terms of "dramatic impact". Positivistic designs, carefully controlling for internal and external validity, would produce "the" truth about a change programme, and that truth should be acted upon as it provided better guidance than the "less valid" information from other sources. Decision-makers were rational people and would therefore make decisions rationally on the basis of the "best" information. Because they would act on evaluation findings, it was reasonable to define utilization in terms of impact and look for it accordingly in changes in policy and so forth. When these could not be identified the proposition "utilization occurred" was falsified and hence a "crisis in utilization" was proclaimed. For, as Alkin *et al.* (1979, p.27) comment:

> Where evaluators view themselves in some way as the "determiners of truth", the expectation is that "we have found the truth and the truth shall set you free" . . . The most traditional approaches to the determination of truth are so-called scientific methods — and evaluators who have scrupulously followed each of the steps on this path feel justified in their indignant feelings when their findings are not heeded.

But, in so doing, such researchers found themselves on the horns of a dilemma. Adherence to positivistic methods meant that, given the indeterminancy of decision-making, they inevitably identified a utilization crisis — no "impacts" were "observed", or if observed, their size was "measured" as disappointingly small. But if evaluation research was not utilized, by definition, it ceased to be worthwhile. For, as already suggested earlier in this chapter, "utilization" is the *sine qua non* justification of overtly normative research. If it is not utilized, it is not worth doing. This was a difficult conclusion for an evaluation researcher to accept.

The answer, of course, was to redefine utilization, and to accept the validity of a "gradual influence" definition. This could reasonably be done, given increasing evidence of the real "incremental" — or even "garbage can" — nature of decision-making. But to assert that "utilization" did after all occur, immediately called into question the validity of those methods that by observation and measurement of *behaviour* and the falsification of operationalization propositions, had demonstrated that a crisis *did* exist.

In a nutshell, then, the crisis in utilization may be seen as precipitating a crisis in methods, at two levels. At the surface level there is the comparatively straightforward concern that the information generated by positivistic methods is not relevant to many of the evaluation functions sought by potential users, and hence, if "useful" information is to be obtained other methods must be employed. At a deeper level, though, the redefinition of utilization is, in itself, a denial of the ontology on which positivism is based. To accept that utilization "really" exists if people say it does, rather than its existence being recognized by the observation and measurement of behavioural impacts, is to have abandoned the ontological assumptions of positivism even if the empty shell of its methods is ritually maintained.

The utilization debate has placed the unreformed positivist in a series of double binds. If he maintains that the "best" information is produced by experimental and quasi-experimental designs, then he has the problem that these same methods suggest a genuine utilization crisis exists — the "best" information is not used. If to protect his chosen methods he asserts that the information emanating from such studies is in fact used, he has to redefine utilization in terms unacceptable to his epistemological position. In attempting to justify continued adherence to traditional evaluation research methods, he has, in fact, denied the assumptions on which they are based. It is ironic that it is far easier for the non-positivistic researcher to maintain an ontologically consistent position, as he can accept a very broad attributional definition of utilization.

At a practical level, though, will this create difficulties with the bodies who fund such applied research? Will they be prepared to accept such a "soft" definition of utility? This is an open question, but should perhaps be considered in the light of the following speculative comments.

The redefinition of the "utilization of evaluation research" is not unconnected with the value issues discussed in the previous chapter. At a surface level, as already discussed, a concern with utilization encourages an evaluator to serve decision-makers rather than other potential audiences, and hence, some might say, sell-out to vested interests (Joyce, 1980). At a deeper level though the redefinition of utilization may be seen as similarly protective of the status quo. The argument might run as follows.

The old "dramatic impact" definition in a sense could be as embarrassing to decision-makers as researchers, as it revealed only too clearly that evaluations were more likely to impact directly on action if their findings and recommendations were minimally disruptive to the existing programmes (including institutionalized change programmes) (e.g. Beyer and Trice, 1982, pp.607–608). For example, it is noticeable in the case studies that Alkin *et al.* (1979) recorded, that where an evaluation was considered to have had a "dominant influence" on decision-making (e.g. the "Rockland" case), its recommendations involved merely discontinuing a peripheral aspect of an otherwise validated programme, without loss of jobs or even status of those involved. Indeed, it could be argued that the very implementation of such recommendations, through contrast with what was *not* recommended—changing the core programme—served to underwrite the latter. Rich (1979) makes a similar point about the circumstances in which "impact" can be identified, when he suggests that low political and financial costs, or high potential rewards are key factors in evaluation studies' recommendations being implemented.

Now admittedly by simply ignoring threatening research studies, and only implementing minimally disruptive recommendations (or recommendations decision-makers welcomed *or had already decided upon* (Feldman and March, 1981, pp.175–176)) decision-makers could be said to be protecting the status quo. Yet the publicity resulting from the "crisis of utilization" could be seen as offering a direct challenge, through highlighting their unwillingness to accept or act upon criticisms that were reformist rather than radical in intention. It could be argued that by apparently not responding to evaluation—by not clearly utilizing the studies particularly of social change—decision-makers were courting the danger of turning frustrated reformers into radicals. The redefinition of utilization then is highly functional for decision-makers as well as for evaluators, because it provides them with a rhetoric through which to claim that they *do* utilize evaluation studies, if in ways that are not expressed in immediate action. Because the redefinition of utilization serves the interests of both decision-makers and evaluators it is hardly surprizing the speed with which the redefinition is becoming the new orthodoxy. To echo Voltaire, if it did not exist, it would have to have been invented.

So the redefinition of utilization vindicates both researchers and decision-makers. Whether this speaks of co-optation and mutual collusion rather than growing co-operation and understanding will be considered in the final chapter, when the themes developed in preceding chapters will be drawn together, in a consideration of the future development of the evaluation profession.

Notes

(1) In the light of earlier discussion in Chapter 1 and frequent implicit references to utilization problems throughout the book, a separate section devoted to listing "utilization obstacles" would be repetitive and hopefully superfluous. Moreover, I have the slight reservation that such a listing, outside the context of a broader discussion, could be misleading as "lists" tend to concentrate on context-free "factors" and ignore context-related processes. Also there is the problem that the research studies which identify the obstacles tend not to make explicit the definition of utilization with which they are working. However, for readers who wish to refer to such lists, those provided by Weiss and Bucuvalas (1980a, pp.16–23 and pp.241–242) based on their own and others' research into the utilization of applied social science findings, are recommended.

(2) Some methodological caveats must be entered about this study, for the data, as in many positivistic studies, were in a sense contrived. The research was based on interviews with 155 officials in senior positions in U.S.A. federal, state and local agencies in the fields of mental health, alcoholism and drug abuse, and concerned their responses to 50 actual research reports. Each person read two of the 50 research reports, which had been summarized in standard format two-page abstracts. Then, using a six-point scale, they rated each one on 29 descriptive dimensions, derived from the literature and "considerably pre-tested" by the researchers. From their ratings of the studies, the researchers derived the decision-makers' frames of references by means of factor analysis. Having located the five frames of reference (relevance, research quality, conformity to user expectations, action orientation, challenge to the status quo) the researchers used regression analysis to test what effect each factor had on the perceived usefulness of the research. The measure of usefulness lacked specificity; (in the words of the authors it "lacked the crispness of the traditional (i.e. dramatic impact) formulation of research utilization"). The measure was the question, "Assuming your office had to consider the issues discussed in the study, how likely is it that you would take the study results into account?" Respondents rated each study on a five-point scale from "very likely" to "not likely at all"). Hence, although empirical, this study is dealing with a hypothetical rather than actual situation and, it must be recognized, is subject to the criticisms of positivistic research designs raised in Chapter 5.

Chapter 8

The Future of Evaluation Research

In the preceding chapters, it has been suggested that, in recent years, evaluation research has been confronted by crises concerning its verification/methods, accreditation/values and utilization/functions. In essence the nature of these crises was characterized as follows:

(1) *Verification/methods.* It was suggested that disillusionment with traditional positivistic methods has been triggered by their tendency to produce "weak" or uninterpretable findings about the effects of change programmes. This problem appears to have resulted from: (a) difficulties experienced in maintaining internal validity (confidence with which conclusions can be drawn from a set of data) in organizational settings; (b) conflicting requirements of internal and external validity (the confidence with which conclusions can be generalized) in such settings.

At a more fundamental level, this has provoked doubts about positivism's ontological assumptions.

(2) *Accreditation/values.* It was suggested that, while many researchers' personal values are liberal and reformist, normative research in organizational settings, including the evaluation of change programmes, tends to have an in-built conservative bias. This can raise moral and value dilemmas for researchers.

(3) *Utilization/functions.* It was suggested that a fear exists that evaluation research is not being used, and does not fulfil the functions demanded of it, by administrators and evaluators.

In exploring the nature of these crises, strategies for overcoming, or at least circumventing them, have been proposed, and now need to be considered further (1). And, more generally, what of the future of evaluation research as an organized activity?

The crises resolved?

In a nutshell, the argument has been presented that the crises may be ameliorated by undertaking a "matching" process, to achieve compatibility between evaluation functions sought and evaluation design employed, *within the constraints imposed by the nature and conceptualization of the change process.* If the evaluator can "match" the evaluation functions to be served, with the methods that stand the best chance of generating data that will fulfil these functions, then some of the difficulties with utilization and methods should be eased. For, if stakeholders in the evaluation are provided with information that is relevant to their concerns—in whatever sense—it stands a good chance of being used—even if we have to accept a broad definition of utilization. And, if utilization is increased, then the disillusionment with traditional methods that arose from a belief that they were not capable of generating "useful" data should also be relieved. But how might this be done?

A contingent approach

It is suggested that the following procedure—effectively a decision tree— may be usefully employed for contingently matching evaluation functions and research methods. In effect, the procedure involves the application of a series of questions varying depending on whether the decision to evaluate (in principle) is taken *before* the detailed planning and design of the programme—as in action research (procedure A) or after the programme has been implemented (procedure B) (2). It should be noted that such a normative contingency approach has a well tried pedigree in applied organization studies. Similar "funnelling" procedures, for example, have been successfully developed by Lupton and Gowler (1969) in assessing the appropriateness of a wage payment system to the context in which it operates, and by Vroom and Yetton (1973) in matching decision-making styles to organizational context.

Procedure A

The researcher might pose the following questions to the major stakeholders in the change programme. (If the person conducting the evaluation has adopted the "trait" model of professionalism—see later in the chapter—it may be appropriate to confine these questions to those (a) funding the programme, (b) funding the evaluation.)

(1) *Do you want the proposed change programme to be evaluated?* If the answer is *No*, those planning, designing and implementing the programme are not constrained in how they undertake these activities, on account of the requirements of an evaluation design. If the answer is *Yes*, the researcher should proceed to question 2.

(2) *What functions do you wish its evaluation to serve?* What those involved with the change programme have to consider is: (a) Is there agreement between the different stakeholders in the change about what function(s) its evaluation is to serve and, if different functions are identified, are these mutually

compatible? (b) Is there agreement between the different stakeholders on what functions the evaluation should serve, but recognition that the functions identified appear incompatible? (c) Is there disagreement between the different stakeholders in the change programme about what function(s) its evaluation should serve?

If the answer to 2(a) is *Yes*, the researcher should proceed to question 3.

If the answer to 2(b) is *Yes*, the researcher may then negotiate which function is to take priority and, while including subsidiary functions that are compatible, exclude those which are not. He or she may then proceed to question 3. If the answer to 2(c) is *Yes*, the stakeholders involved must either, through a process of negotiation, or through the exercise of power, achieve the position implicit in 2(b), or, if this is impossible, recognize that a basic requirement for a successful evaluation exericse (in the terms discussed in this book) is not present and abandon the idea.

(3) *What are the alternative approaches to evaluation?* This is a question the researcher needs to ask of him or herself, exploring the design principles that these approaches embody. Depending on which model of the professional role is adopted (see later in the chapter) the researcher may also wish to consider the ontological, epistemological and general value assumptions underlying different evaluation designs. He or she may then proceed to question 4.

(4) *Which of the identified alternatives best matches the functional requirements of the evaluation exercise?* Here the researcher needs to discuss with the stakeholders in the change programme which approach to evaluation is most likely to generate data that will serve the evaluation functions they have prioritized. The discussions in Chapters 3–5, in particular, provide some direction as to appropriate choices. Having selected the basic approach that the evaluation design will embody, the researcher and stakeholders may consider question 5.

(5) *Given a particular approach to evaluation has been selected, can an evaluation design embodying the principles of this approach be evolved that is practical and appropriate to implement given the way the change programme is likely to be planned and implemented, and how it is conceptualized?* Basically the point of this question is to alert those designing and implementing the change programme, that some forms of planning and some problems that may be anticipated in implementation are likely to undermine the control that experimental forms of evaluation demand (see Chapter 2). In which case they need to consider (a) what evaluation design is practical to implement, if the change process is likely to be "messy" and difficult to control (b) what evaluation functions such a design may serve. If the stakeholders are not interested in the functions a feasible design can serve, they may wish to abandon the exercise. Alternatively they may wish

to examine the constraints that are likely to impede their preferred alternative and see if these can be overcome. In other words, once committed to a particular form of evaluation design, the change agents need to be aware that this will have implications.

Procedure A would appear particularly suitable for use by action researchers involved in designing and implementing, as well as evaluating, programmes of planned change. The work undertaken by action researchers designing new work systems (such as Mumford and Clegg and Wall in Britain, or Lawler and Davis in the U.S.A. or Thorsrud in Scandinavia) or introducing participation (such as Bate and Mangham and Warr and his colleagues in Britain) would be able to incorporate and, to some extent, implies, this approach.

Procedure B

In many situations the researcher may only be called in, or achieve access, *after* the change programme has been implemented. In these circumstances, which often occur in applied research (see Chapter 4), while the questions posed will be essentially the same, the ordering will be reversed. In other words, his or her first task will be to point out, given the post facto nature of the study, what designs have been ruled out (i.e. experimental and some quasi-experimental), what data cannot be generated, and what questions therefore cannot be answered. At the same time the researcher needs to point out what designs are still feasible, and what functions such designs can realistically serve. If the stakeholders in the change programme then consider that these are not functions they wish to have served, then there is little point in the evaluation proceeding, as the chance of "irrelevant" information being used is not high. However, the researcher may still deem it worthwhile to conduct research to fulfil the learning functions of an academic peer group or his or her own career advancement functions.

The difference between the two "matching" processes is essentially that (a) is (ideally speaking) *evaluation-proactive* (the logic being that choice of evaluation function → choice of evaluation design → constraints on how the change programme may be planned and implemented) while (b) *evaluation-reactive* (the logic being that how the change programme was planned and implemented → constraints on what evaluation designs are feasible → constraints on what evaluation functions may be served).

Organizational design strategies?

But the application of a "contingency" approach does not end here. It was suggested in the previous chapter that a further reason why research fails to be used by managers and administrators is that it falls into "policy vacuums" existing in their organizations (Corwin and Lewis, 1982). If, as they suggest, such vacuums emerge in the absence of an organized constituency of policy-makers, identifiable policy issues and research questions, consistent policies and clear policy options, co-ordination between departments responsible for a policy area and so on, it is clear that part of the problem can be laid at the door of faulty organizational design. The problem would appear to be the old one of achieving optimum differentiation to develop the knowledge necessary to cope with environmental complexities and uncertainties, but with the requisite integration to safeguard against such "policy vacuums" (Galbraith, 1973; Lawrence and Lorsch, 1967). This is not easy. For the very organizational design decisions aimed at promoting, through high levels of differentiation, an adaptive change-oriented organization—such as appointing management staff on temporary project-specific contracts, decentralizing control over resources, fostering overlapping competitive relationships between departments—create problems of integration and co-ordination, which in turn act as barriers to the dissemination and utilization of information—including research findings (Corwin and Lewis, 1982, pp.636–637). Indeed, Klein's (1976) experience as an action researcher in Esso Petroleum illustrates just how disruptive divisional independence and managerial turnover can be to the wider dissemination of pilot projects.

Ironically, too, the highly differentiated organizations in which "policy vacuums" are likely to occur are precisely those which tend to facilitate the "misutilization" of research findings for covert purposes. For as Pfeffer (1981, pp.67–96) points out, high levels of differentiation (but with a requirement for departmental interdependence) combined with environmental heterogeneity and scarcity (the rationale for evaluative research), provide the conditions which encourage the exercise of power and politics in decision-making.

While organizations cannot be designed to *guarantee* the use of research findings—for that involves broader motivational issues—existing organizational barriers to their use can be ameliorated. Organizations can be designed to facilitate integration through enhanced information processing capacity (Galbraith, 1973). Managers and administrators can also use strategies to reduce the use of power and politics in decision-making (Pfeffer, 1981). These, however, are both vast subjects which it would be inappropriate to explore in detail here. Suffice to say that, in the first case, the nature of the strategies adopted will depend on how intensive the exchange of information between groups and departments needs to be in order to achieve the requisite degree of integration, which in turn will depend on the degree of environmental uncertainty experienced. Potentially, though, in a change oriented organization, operating in an uncertain environment, integration may be facilitated by the use of liaison roles, temporary task forces and so on, who may be charged with the additional responsibility for disseminating the results of evaluative studies in their areas to other departments and groups with which they routinely share information. Corwin and Lewis (1982, p.638) go as far as suggesting that distinct organizational units might be set up to disseminate the results of research throughout an organization, and (between government agencies) interorganizational task forces, but the costs of such a suggestion would need to be explored in the light of expected benefits. Much would depend on just how much research was being undertaken within an organization. Furthermore, it cannot be ignored that if managers and administrators show little interest in research findings they are unlikely to display much more in setting up new units to disseminate research. A chicken and egg problem may have to be confronted.

As for reducing the use of power and politics in decision-making (and with it the "misutilization" of research), Pfeffer (1981, pp.88–94) suggests a range of strategies which might be employed. Generating slack resources, by reducing the interdependence among departments, and scarcity *per se* is likely to reduce the potential for conflict and, hence, the use of power and politics. Fostering greater homogeneity in goals and beliefs about means–ends relationships, via recruitment and socialization practices, and by rewards and sanctions, is another strategy for reducing conflict. Making decisions appear less important than they are, by avoidance, by labelling them as "unimportant", and by decomposing them into a range of smaller, piecemeal decisions, is a further strategy for avoiding conflict, and hence reducing the use of power and politics in decision-making. Again, though, there is the chicken and egg problem that circumstances in which use of such strategies might be most appropriate (if reducing the use of politics is *the* objective) are precisely those in which their implementation might be most difficult to achieve. And, this is quite apart from the direct and indirect costs (e.g. costs of extra resources, less diverse information represented in decision-making, decisions avoided) which in themselves may be as inimical to the "proper" use of research findings as those political behaviours the strategies are designed to prevent.

So are these contingent "matching" strategies the answer to the crises in evaluative research? Unfortunately a problem remains, because, *per se*, they do little to resolve the crisis of *values*. Now admittedly, on the surface, utilization would appear the most pressing crisis to resolve as thereby rests the very *raison d'être* of evaluative research. But, at a deeper level, none of the crises can be truly resolved unless some resolution of the value crisis is arrived at. This is because values lie at the heart of those very acts of "matching" by which problems with utilization and methods are ameliorated. To match evaluation methods with evaluation functions requires choices. Different stakeholders in a change programme wish different (or differently interpreted) evaluation functions to be served. These may be conflicting and incompatible, both in terms of the set each stakeholder holds and as between stakeholders. The different methods required to generate data to fulfil these functions make incompatible demands in the fieldwork situation. *Values permeate the choice of whose functions are to be served when such conflict arises.* Furthermore, when disillusionment with traditional methods arises less from their perceived inability to produce "relevant" data (i.e. data that matches the evaluation functions to be served) but from doubts about their ontological and epistemological validity, value issues are also at stake. Finally choices about organizational design and the weighing of associated costs and benefits cannot be otherwise than normative, value laden acts.

Leaving aside the broader issue of organizational design, in an ideal world the solution to this problem would seem to be the achievement of a compatibility between researchers' value positions, the evaluation functions they wish their data to serve and the evaluation design consequently adopted. If values underlie choices about whose and which evaluation functions are to be served and about commitments to particular methods, *then researchers' value positions must take priority in this matching process*, rather than be moulded by it.

It has been argued that a value crisis exists because those in the best position to make use of evaluation findings tend to be more conservative than many researchers might choose. Those individuals who might be sympathetic to the more liberal evaluator tend to lack the funds to sponsor research and the power to implement the findings. This, in essence, is the double bind situation identified in Chapter 1, that in trying to resolve dilemmas about utilization the researcher can encounter problems about values, and vice versa. So, what are the ways round the dilemma that the evaluation researchers (including applied normative organizational researchers) as a whole might adopt? As indicated in Chapter 6 professionalization has been regarded as an answer, and it is to this issue that we now return.

The professionalization of evaluation researchers

Can professionalization resolve the value crisis? I consider that although it is not the complete answer—and, indeed, that may not exist—it has much promise. Why is this?

It must be borne in mind that the value crisis has two aspects. The first is the problem already discussed in terms of evaluation's (and much normative organizational research's) conservatism and the demoralization it may give rise to in those committed to more humanistic organizations and even moderately reformist social change programmes. The second aspect is more insidious, and is interwoven with the crisis of verification. That is when methods are questioned not simply because of their perceived inadequacy in obtaining "useful" data, but because their ontological and epistemological assumptions are deemed to be wrong irrespective of issues of utility. These two aspects of the value crisis come together when researchers are confronted by the conservative implications of positivistic designs. The "sourcebook" of the New Paradigm Research Group, *Human Inquiry*, makes this link (Reason and Rowan, 1981, pp.xiv–xvi). I consider that professionalization can alleviate both these aspects of the value crisis, although different models of professionalism speak to different aspects of the crisis and suggest different approaches.

To consider first the disquiet over the epistemological and ontological assumptions of particular evaluation designs. I suggest that part of the problem arises from the fact that the evaluator's occupational role has been labelled in terms of "research". Many prominent evaluators have backgrounds in purely academic research and, not unnaturally, are aware of and have entered into ontological and epistemological debates that have been part of social science over the last decade. The more the evaluator sees himself in the role of a researcher the more concerned he has to be with using methods according to their ontological and epistemological assumptions and avoiding charges of abstracted empiricism and so forth. This reflects the fact that *as researcher* the evaluator is essentially peer-serving, and peer-evaluated—often by colleagues in "purer" applied research.

But suppose the evaluator modelled his or her role on that of the client-serving professions? This would provide him or her with a different definition of what constituted technical expertise. Namely, the knowledge and application of techniques and methods *whose validity is justified in their ability to mediate their client's problem* rather than in the epistemological consistency with which they are applied. In other words, to the extent that client-serving professions see their methods as technologies rather than expressions of a scientific paradigm, a justification is provided for methodological flexibility and a divorce of methods from their ontological and epistemological assumptions. If the evaluator redefines his role as a client-serving professional rather than as a researcher, he may find that epistemological concerns dissolve and methodological pluralism presents no problems. Adopting the role-model of the professional allows the concurrent use of quantitative and qualitative techniques without a qualm. Fashioning the information from an interpretive design into an input for decision-making would no longer be problematic as any epistemological contradictions involved could be dismissed as irrelevant in mediating the client's problems. But, as this indicates, in order to adopt this role, the evaluator would clearly be placing a higher priority on methodological utility than on epistemological consistency. *But at least professionalism provides a justification for doing this that research, or the role of a researcher, lacks.*

Perhaps it is in this light that social change programme evaluators recent search among the professions, in particular law and art criticism (3) rather than in the social sciences, for metaphors on which to base new approaches to evaluation design, can best be understood (Smith, 1981).

The implication is that this verification-value crisis might be resolved if evaluators were to be trained as professional evaluators, rather than recruited after a socialization in academic research, as essentially researchers competent to turn their hands to normative applied research, including evaluation studies. But, if this is the case, which model of professionalism might most appropriately be used—the "occupational control" or the "trait" model? Also, how might adoption of these models resolve the other aspect of the value crisis? It is to these questions that we now turn.

The "occupational control" route

In Chapter 6 it was suggested that the "occupational control" model of professionalism could be used to support reformist aspirations. For this, *par excellence*, is the ideal type model of the professional client relationship in that it posits an asymmetrical relationship between the professional and the client, in which the professional (the evaluator) is seen to be the dominant partner. Consequently, the relationship, in theory, is characterized by the professional, on the basis of expertise derived from a body of knowledge, having autonomy to define the needs of his client and the manner in which these needs are to be met. The client accepts the direction and authority of the "expert" in the belief that the latter has an exclusive competence, obligation and commitment to act in his (the client's) best interest. The client "trusts" the professional to use his expertise to evaluate the nature of his "real" needs and how these might best be met; in return the professional demands the client's *trust in his judgement* and compliance with his advice.

If evaluators could gain acceptance of their professionalism in terms of this "occupational control" model, then their values would dictate what evaluation functions their clients could reasonably expect them to serve, and, in theory, the latter would recognize this. In this way their value positions could then guide the matching process required to overcome the methods and utilization crises.

That such an ideal-type model of a professional client relationship is attractive to some of the leading commentators in evaluation research is in no doubt. Perhaps Cronbach *et al.* (1980) make the clearest statement of such aspirations. The tenor of their argument is that the role of the evaluator—at least those evaluating U.S.A. government funded social programmes—should be less that of the "captive" serving one decision-maker than of the expert providing information to the "policy-shaping community" as a whole to raise questions and mould thinking about the nature of, and solutions to, pressing social problems. They suggest that the power of evaluation researchers to negotiate such a role *vis-à-vis* their potential clients (notably funders/sponsors of the evaluation) may be enhanced by seeking a stronger professional base. This they argue might be achieved by developing the classic attributes of professionalization: an expertise grounded in a professional training, and collegial review and control. The professional training ideally might constitute a disciplinary preparation in one of the social sciences, participation in interdisciplinary seminars that examine evaluations, apprenticeship to practicing evaluators and an internship in an agency (or any organization) where policy is formulated. Ethical standards and peer review might be provided by a National Evaluation Federation, to which existing membership groups might be federated, while the equivalent of scientists' "invisible college" might be provided by social problem study groups. Both groups would act to persuade the "political community" that a "professional, sophisticated evaluation community" should be "free to do its best work" in order to "educate all sectors of the political community".

If evaluators could achieve such a relationship with their potential clients the way forward to resolving all three crises would be well within their reach. But is this "occupational control" model of professionalism attainable? Elsewhere it is argued that in real life, even in those established professional occupations such as medicine and law, this model is becoming increasingly problematic, partly due to organizational and administrative constraints, and partly due to clients' reluctance to take professional expertise and values on trust (Gowler and Legge, 1980). If this is so for established professions, dealing with relatively powerless or submissive groups of clients (e.g. patients, litigants), what chance do evaluators of organizational change stand?

The key question would seem to be: on what basis can evaluators persuade society to recognize their right to exercise such direction over their direct clients, the funders or sponsors of an evaluation? How can the "profession" persuade some legislative body to designate it as the expert and responsible group in such a way that authority may be exercised over the client through the control of "strategic accessories" obtainable only through accredited members of the profession? The answer is reflected in the activities which prestigeful evaluators are at present undertaking and which have already been mentioned. The first step is internal organization of evaluators, so that the profession may speak with a united public voice. The second step is developing an appropriate rhetoric in order to make "the potential contribution of evaluative work so clear that those who want excellent programs will join the battle on their side" (Cronbach *et al.*, 1980, p.353).

That these strategies are clearly in the minds of leading American social change programme evaluators is evident from developments over the last decade. First came the organization of small bodies of evaluators working in specific fields (e.g. the Evaluation Network, concentrating on educational evaluation), then the broader groups (e.g. the Evaluation Research Society), and now there is a call that these groups should be federated, in order to provide a "public meeting" of the evaluation community (Cronbach *et al.*, 1980, p.355). Like all such professional federations it would be concerned with training, laying down standards and accrediting neophytes, in order to control the supply of "professional" evaluators. Furthermore similar groupings of action researchers and organizational development consultants are emerging in Britain (e.g. The "O.D. Network").

As Cronbach *et al.* (1980, p.353) state, organization is an essential prerequisite to developing and using any rhetoric effectively.

> Coalition starts at home. Before allies can be enlisted, evaluators have to thrash out their own main ideas and become clear about priorities in their own minds and hearts . . . Only after evaluators know what, by and large, they do agree on can they co-ordinate their actions . . .

The rhetoric to be employed is emerging. That properly trained and accredited evaluators stand the best chance of generating information that may illuminate the policy shaping community in its attempts to mediate pressures for change in a world of scarce resources. Cronbach *et al.* (1980, pp.373–383) justifications for proposed "social problem study groups" are an example of the use of this rhetoric. The interesting thing is the implicit reliance on utilization as a justificatory principle— but utilization defined in its broadest sense, as in accordance with the new orthodoxy. This is hardly surprising, confirming as it does earlier comments on professionalization acting as a justification for methodological utility's priority over epistemological consistency.

How successful is this bid to gain acceptance of an "occupational control" model of professionalism likely to be? It is too early to say. One problem is that what could be a powerful weapon in the hands of an organized profession is already tainted. Researchers are fortunate in the U.S.A., and in evaluating "social" change programmes, that an evaluation is often a mandated requirement of federal funding. If they could persuade the legislature that only those accredited by their professional organizations could be employed on such evaluations, they would gain some control over an important strategic accessory. But this control is disabled as long as the funders can specify the design of the evaluation. For by doing so, they are implicitly controlling what functions it can serve, placing constraints on the potential utility of the data, and hence, are in a position to undermine the evaluators' own rhetoric. This problem is a reflection of the central difficulty.

It is easy enough to imagine what would constitute the evaluation profession's "real" control over the strategic accessory of mandated evaluations attached to publicly funded change programme. A properly accredited evaluator, as a condition of funding, would have to be appointed to undertake an evaluation, with the right to freely negotiate what functions are to be served, and what designs are to be employed, with the right of appeal to some arbitrary body if deadlock is reached. But the individuals who could exercise most influence in either promoting or impeding legislation to give accredited evaluators this degree of control would tend to be precisely those experts involved in funding and sponsoring such evaluations, and who at present exercise asymmetrical control over evaluators (see Chapter 6).

One way round this, of course, is for evaluation researchers to seek to mobilize the potential influence of the direct clients of change programmes rather than evaluations in support of their aspirations. But, as already argued, in Chapters 3 and 6, such groups tend to be relatively fragmented and powerless—certainly as compared to the funders and sponsors of evaluation. And, whether the focus is on industrial or public service organizations, the economic recession of the 1980s has, if anything, undermined such influence as they possessed in more affluent times.

Up to this point, by implication, we have been referring to those situations where an "independent" evaluation (at least nominally independent—see Chapter 6) is a condition of the public funding of a change programme. But what of the other situations when the evaluator is both voluntarily hired but financially dependent on the funders or sponsors of the evaluation? For example, as in those cases where an external—or even internal—consultant evaluates a plant's O.D. programme at the instigation of Head Office? Here the control the evaluator will be able to exercise in relation to the sponsors can only rest on the persuasion of competent advice, as he has no strategic accessories he can withhold. His or her only sanction is to refuse to proceed with an evaluation judged to be inappropriate or unethical and this sanction has little weight so long as the evaluation "profession" lacks the right and ability to exclusively accredit and control the supply of researchers. While anyone is free to sell their service as such, and the "independent" funder is free to acquire an evaluator who will provide the service he dictates, something resembling a customer–retailer relationship will exist rather than a professional–client one. Realistically speaking, it is difficult to see how any other relationship can exist between the evaluator and funder, when the evaluation is being financed by money over which the funder has complete (i.e. not governmentally constrained) control.

If the achievement of an "occupational control" model of profession-alism appears largely unrealistic at present, what of the less ambitious "trait" model? And, could the development of professionalism along this path facilitate the "matching" process by which we have suggested all three crises may be resolved?

The "trait" route?

As suggested in Chapter 6, the "trait" model of professionalism typifies an occupation as a profession if it possesses certain traits or characteristics, in particular, high levels of technical expertise, of a type valued by, and to be utilized *largely at the behest of the client*. The professional is the expert who works within the client's brief, critical if it appears ethically — or technically — inappropriate, but not primarily motivated to rewrite it. The commitment is to service in "the best interests of the client" — a notion, we suggested, that could camouflage and sweeten the pressures the client could exert in their relationship.

Such a model, in fact, resembles that adopted by Tichy's (1974) A.F.T. ("Analysis for the top") change agents, who saw themselves as "expert advisors" with a "rather clear commitment to being hired to aid and advise the heads of systems" (p.178).

At first sight, it might appear that the adoption of this model of professionalism, rather than facilitating a value-led "matching" strategy for resolving the crises in evaluation, can only exacerbate the value crisis. For this model, as already argued, is supportive of conservative action, not reformist aspirations. If the roots of the value crisis lie in dissatisfaction with evaluation research's conservatism, how can adherence to such a model overcome this?

Put in these terms, of course it cannot. But, I suggest that a way forward is indicated, when we reconsider the paradoxes that have emerged throughout this discussion. It may be recalled that the following paradoxical speculations have been proposed:

(1) That positivistic designs prosper largely through acting as a rhetoric for an evaluation ritual whereby the lack of rationality of actual decision-making and the accountability and responsibility demanded of the idealized decision-maker are reconciled (Chapter 4).

(2) That interpretive designs may act as a rhetoric for an evaluation ritual whereby the appearance of democracy and non élitism serves to disguise the greater room for manoeuvre accorded to powerful decision-makers (Chapter 5).

(3) Decision-makers in theory want true information. In so far as they want it about human action rather than just behaviour, an interpretive design would appear to generate "truer" information than a positivistic one, as it recognizes that reality is not singular. But the information generated by an interpretive design is difficult to fashion into an input for decision-making unless it is treated according to positivistic assumptions. These assumptions deny the

view that reality is multiplex and hence deny the major ontological justification of an interpretive stance (Chapter 5).

(4) That the popular call for ethical codes is hardly surprising, as it may serve as a vehicle for reformist aspirations and as both a justification and mask for present conservative practice (Chapter 6).

(5) That the redefinition of utilization is highly functional for decision-makers as well as for evaluators because it provides them with a rhetoric through which to claim that they do utilize evaluation studies, if in ways that are not expressed in immediate action (Chapter 7).

In my view, a common thread unites these propositions: each has conservative implications. If this is the case, perhaps we have to accept that evaluation research, contrary to superficial appearances, cannot escape a functional and epistemological conservatism. In which case—and I recognize that my comments are highly speculative—the value crisis is best resolved by a different sort of matching process. Rather than the reformist evaluator being pressured to bring his values into line with those of his client (which would be stressful), or demanding that the client accept his values (which appears unrealistic) *matching might be achieved through appropriate selection and socialization policies*. In other words, if evaluation research is recognized to be inherently conservative, the profession might best enhance its effectiveness by recruiting those to whom such values are acceptable.

In these circumstances, the "trait" model of professionalism would appear a very appropriate route to take. The model allows that the guiding principle in an evaluator's relationship with his client should be to offer the best possible technical service to resolve his client's problem. That is, to provide data that will serve the evaluation functions sought by the latter, not those sought by other parties to the change programme. A "conservative" evaluator would have no value conflict with the implications of this assumption—that the evaluation functions of those who sponsored/funded the evaluation would automatically take precedence, while those of less powerful stakeholders would be ignored unless they happened to coincide. [Such was the experience of Tichy's (1974) "Analysis for the top" change agents, who, in marked contrast with his sample of organizational development change agents, reported no value/action incongruence.] Indeed, the argument that designing an evaluation around the requirements of those with power to get things changed facilitates utilization would provide ample justification for this position. The position is consistent, too, with using methods abstracted from their epistemological and ontological assumptions, as a tool-kit of techniques to be employed in the service of the client.

Conclusion

If this conclusion appears more like a whimper than a bang, it is not intended so. As suggested in Chapter 1, the evaluation of programmes of planned organizational and social change mediates the two great contradictions of the second half of the twentieth century and as such is an activity that will survive, crises or no. But these crises have been considered in order to assess the present status of such normative applied research, rhetoric apart, and the conclusions drawn may possibly be as unpopular as they are certainly speculative.

My final conclusions are these. Clearly the crisis in utilization must be resolved, because unless it is used, evaluation research lacks a *raison d'être*. Indeed, the very fact that at one level—that of rationalization and rhetoric—this crisis *has* been resolved (or swept under the carpet) is a reflection of its urgency, particularly at a time when almost all research budgets are under scrutiny. At another level, though, it has been suggested that utilization may be facilitated by a "matching" process, whereby the researcher "matches" the functions to be served with the methods that stand the best chance of generating data that will fulfil these functions. But, it would appear that as values permeate this process, the utilization crisis cannot be resolved at this level unless the value crisis is first alleviated. The way to do this may be by de-emphasizing the research orientation of the evaluator's role and by encouraging the adoption of a professionalism based on the "trait" model. Recognizing the inevitability of the conservative values that permeate the evaluation enterprise, the "profession" may be best advised to tailor its recruitment and socialization practices accordingly. In this way the crises in verification/methods, accreditation/values and utilization/functions may be overcome.

Notes

(1) Ironically, though, to formally evaluate whether these strategies would be successful presents us with another paradox. That is, it would involve the design and implementation of new evaluation procedures which could then only be formally tested by (a) those procedures they were designed to improve upon and replace, or (b) those "improved" procedures that constituted the subject of the evaluation. In the case of (a) it could be argued that to evaluate new evaluation approaches by procedures already hypothesized to be inadequate does not constitute a fair test. But, in the case of (b), it could be even more damagingly argued that such an evaluation would hardly constitute an independent test and must be self-validating. Formally evaluating strategies of evaluation would appear to be an endlessly regressive activity.
(2) The account of procedure (A) is largely drawn from an earlier publication (Gowler and Legge, 1979).

(3) Procedures from legal practice and art criticism respectively have provided inspiration for two relatively new approaches to evaluation design: namely, the "adversary" and the "connoisseurship and criticism" approaches.

Briefly, an adversary design is based on the legal model that the "truth" may best be arrived at through hearing evidence both for the defence and the prosecution. Accordingly, two researchers (or teams) are appointed, who first agree on the data collection procedures that will determine what constitutes "valid" evidence. On the toss of a coin, one is selected to make a case for the programme, and one to make a case against. Data collection, for example, via interviews may be jointly or separately conducted. Once the "cases" are assembled, the adversary evaluators argue their cases out in a quasi-court-room setting, presenting witnesses and evidence, with experts in the field acting as a jury or "blue ribbon" panel. The underlying assumptions, according to Owens and Owen (1981, p.100) are that evaluation researchers are subject to biases and partisanship that should be exposed by "honest opposition" charged with exploring the issue from another point of view; and that decision-makers should be exposed to various interpretations of both quantitative and qualitative data and to a range of value positions. (For examples and discussion of the use of this approach see Hiscox and Owens, 1975; Popham and Carlson, 1977; Owens, 1973; Owens and Hiscox, 1977; Owens and Owen, 1981; Wolf, 1975; Wolf and Tymitz, 1977; Worthen and Owens, 1978; Wright and Sachse, 1977.)

A "connoisseurship and criticism" approach, is based on the idea that a researcher can enhance his audiences' experiential understanding of a change programme by unfolding its essential form and style in a manner analogous to a wine connoisseur or art critic. Eisner (1979) is the chief exponent of this approach and his perspective is roughly as follows (I quote from the summary by Della-Piana, 1981, p.242):

> For Eisner connoisseurship is the art of appreciation and criticism of disclosure. More specifically, connoisseurship is the art of discerning the characteristics and qualities of whatever work (object, event) one has encountered. This discernment, says Eisner, requires an understanding of past forms, attention to the formal qualities of the work, understanding of the ideas that gave rise to the work, understanding of the socio cultural context in which the artist worked and the sources from which the artist drew, and the influence of the work upon the work of others. Criticism is the art of rendering in linguistic terms . . . what it is that one has encountered so that others not possessing the same level of connoisseurship can also experience the characteristics and quality of the work. [Applied to a change programme] criticism is the art of saying what is going on. The task is to provide a vivid rendering replete with metaphor, contrast, redundancy, and emphases so that others may see what transpires and experience the quality and character of the [change programme] so represented.

Such an approach implies no standard methodology, except a critical review, which may be accomplished through immersion and familiarity with the substantive context of the change programme, experience and apprenticeship to a recognized expert in the field in question. Stated as such this approach may seem to resemble interpretive research. In terms of some of the techniques used, such as immersion, this is so. But whereas the interpretive evaluator recognizes as significant those definitions and experiences which the actors in the change programme present to him as such, the evaluator as connoisseur, makes his own judgement about what is significant, and, as critic "renders" the situation in such a way as to point to its significant aspects. As such, rather than keeping data collection and values apart they become interwoven, although the values that imbue the connoisseurship and criticism are not always made explicit.

However, while no research is value-free, it is interesting the extent to which both these "professional" models present data collection as value-led.

References

Aaron, H. J. (1978). *Politics and the Professors: The Great Society in Perspective.* Washington D.C.: Brookings Institution.

Abelson, R. (1976). Script processing in attitude formation and decision-making. In J. Carol and J. Payne (eds), *Cognition and Social Behavior.* Hillsdale, N.J.: Lawrence Erlbaum Associates.

Aldrich, H. E. (1979). *Organization and Environments.* Englewood Cliffs, N.J.: Prentice-Hall.

Alkin, M. C., Daillak, R. H. and White, P. (1979). *Using Evaluations.* Beverly Hills: Sage.

Alwin, D. F. and Sullivan, M. J. (1976). Issues of design and analysis in evaluation research. In I. N. Bernstein (ed.), *Validity Issues in Evaluative Research.* Beverly Hills: Sage, 83–106.

Anderson, N. H. and Jacobson, A. (1965). Effect of stimulus inconsistency and discounting instructions in personality impression formation. *Journal of Personality and Social Psychology,* **2**, 4, 531–9.

Anderson, S. B. and Ball, S. (1978). *The Profession and Practice of Program Evaluation.* San Francisco: Jossey-Bass.

Angrist, S. (1975). Evaluation research: possibilities and limitations. *Journal of Applied Behavioral Science,* **11**, 75–91.

Argyle, M. (1978). An appraisal of the new approach to the study of social behaviour. In Michael Brenner, P. Marsh and Marilyn Brenner (eds), *The Social Contexts of Method.* London: Croom Helm, pp.237–55.

Argyris, C. (1970). *Intervention Theory and Method.* Reading, Mass.: Addison-Wesley.

Argyris, C. (1971). *Management and Organizational Development.* New York: McGraw-Hill.

Argyris, C. (1980). *Inner Contradictions of Rigorous Research.* London: Academic Press.

Argyris, C. and Schön, D. A. (1974). *Theory in Practice: Increasing Professional Effectiveness.* San Francisco: Jossey-Bass.

Argyris, C. and Schön, D. A. (1978). *Organizational Learning.* Reading, Mass.: Addison-Wesley.

Armenakis, A. A., Bedeian, A. G. and Pond III, S. B. (1983). Research issues in O.D. evaluation: past, present and future. *Academy of Management Review,* **8**, 2, 320–8.

Aronson, S. H. and Sherwood, C. C. (1967). Researcher versus practitioner: problems in social action research. *Social Work,* **12**, 4, 89–96.

Bachrach, P. and Baratz, M. S. (1962). Two faces of power. *American Political Science Review,* **56**, 947–52.

Baker, K. (1975). A new grantsmanship. *American Sociologist,* **10**, 206–19.

Bardach, E. (1976). Policy termination as a political process. *Policy Sciences,* **7**, 123–31.

Baritz, L. (1960). *The Servants of Power.* New York: Wiley.

Barnard, C. I. (1938). *The Functions of the Executive.* Cambridge, Mass.: Harvard University Press.

Baron, J. B. and Baron, R. M. (1980). In search of standards. In R. Perloff and E. Perloff (eds), *New Directions in Program Evaluation, No. 7: Values, Ethics, and Standards in Evaluation.* San Francisco: Jossey-Bass, pp.85–99.

Bate, P. and Mangham, I. L. (1981). *Exploring Participation.* Chichester: Wiley.

Bateson, G. (1973). *Steps to an Ecology of Mind.* London: Paladin.

Beckhard, R. (1969). *Organization Development: Strategies and Models.* Reading, Mass.: Addison-Wesley.

Beer, M. (1976). The technology of organization development. In M. D. Dunnette (ed.), *Handbook of Industrial and Organizational Psychology.* Chicago: Rand McNally, pp.937–93.

Beer, S. (1972). *Brain of the Firm: The Managerial Cybernetics of Organization.* London: Allen Lane.

Behn, R. D. (1978). How to terminate a public policy: a dozen hints for the would-be terminator. *Policy Analysis,* **4,** 393–413.

Bennis, W. G. (1966). *Changing Organizations.* New York: McGraw-Hill.

Bennis, W. G., Benne, K. D., Chin, R. and Corey, K. E. (eds). (1976). *The Planning of Change.* (3rd edn). New York: Holt, Rinehart and Winston.

Berg, P.-O. (1979). *Emotional Structures in Organizations: A Study of the Process of Change in a Swedish Company.* Lund: Studentlitteratur.

Berke, J. S. (1976). Policy-relevant research. Internal memorandum, October 27, Education Testing Service, Princeton, N.J.

Bernstein, A. (1977). Evaluating the evaluators. *Change,* **9,** 6, 8.

Bernstein, I. N., Bohrnstedt, G. W. and Borgatta, E. F. (1976). External validity and evaluation research. In I. N. Bernstein (ed.), *Validity Issues in Evaluation Research.* Beverly Hills: Sage, pp.107–34.

Bernstein, I. N. and Freeman, H. E. (1975). *Academic and Entrepreneurial Research: Consequences of Diversity in Federal Evaluation Studies.* New York: Russell Sage.

Berrill, K. (1983). *The Berrill Report.* London: Social Science Research Council.

Beyer, J. M. (1982). Introduction (to Special Issue, Part 1, The Utilization of Organizational Research). *Administrative Science Quarterly,* **27,** 588–90.

Beyer, J. M. and Trice, H. M. (1982). The utilization process: a conceptual framework and synthesis of empirical findings. *Administrative Science Quarterly,* **27,** 591–622.

Birchall, D. W., Carnall, C. A. and Wild, R. (1978). The development of group working in biscuit manufacture—a case. *Personnel Review,* **7,** 2, 40–9.

Blackler, F. H. M. (1982). Job redesign and social policies. In J. E. Kelly and C. W. Clegg (eds), *Autonomy and Control at the Workplace.* London: Croom Helm, pp.157–80.

Blackler, F. H. M. and Brown, C. A. (1975). The impending crisis in job redesign. *Journal of Occupational Psychology,* **48,** 185–93.

Blackler, F. H. M. and Brown, C. A. (1978a). *Job Redesign and Management Control.* Farnborough: Saxon House.

Blackler, F. H. M. and Brown, C. A. (1978b). Organizational psychology: good intentions and false promises. *Human Relations,* **31,** 333–51.

Blackler, F. H. M. and Brown, C. A. (1980). *Whatever Happened to Shell's New Philosophy of Management?: Lessons for the 1980s from a Major Socio-Technical Intervention of the 1960s.* Farnborough: Saxon House.

Blackler, F. H. M. and Brown, C. A. (1983). Qualitative research and paradigms of practice. *Journal of Management Studies,* **20,** 3, 349–65.

Blake, R. R. and Mouton, J. S. (1964). *The Managerial Grid*. Houston: Gulf.
Borgatta, E. (1955). Research: pure and applied. *Group Psychotherapy*, **9**, 3, 263–77.
Borgida, E. and Nisbett, R. E. (1977). The differential impact of abstract vs. concrete information on decisions. *Journal of Applied Social Psychology*, **7**, 3, 258–71.
Boruch, R. F. and Rindskopf, D. (1977). On randomized experiments, approximation to experiments, and data analysis. In L. Rutman (ed.), *Evaluation Research Methods: A Basic Guide*. Beverly Hills: Sage, pp.143–76.
Bowen, D. D. (1977). Value dilemmas in organization development. *Journal of Applied Behavioral Science*, **13**, 4, 543–56.
Bower, J. L. (1970). *Managing the Resource Allocation Process: A Study of Corporate Planning and Investment*. Boston: Harvard School of Business Administration.
Bowers, D. and Seashore, S. (1963). Changing the structure and functioning of an organization. Mimeograph No. 33, Ann Arbor: Survey Research Center, University of Michigan.
Bowey, A. M. (1982). Selecting a wage system. In A. M. Bowey (ed.), *Handbook of Salary and Wage Systems*. Aldershot: Gower Press, pp.349–62.
Bowles, S. and Gintis, H. (1972/3). I.Q. in the U.S. class structure. *Social Policy*, **3**, November-December, January-February, 65–96.
Bracht, G. H. and Glass, G. V. (1968). The external validity of experiments. *American Educational Research Journal*, **5**, 437–74.
Braskamp, L. A. and Brown, R. D. (eds). (1980). *New Directions for Program Evaluation, No. 5: Utilization of Evaluative Information*. San Francisco: Jossey-Bass.
Braybrooke, D. and Lindblom, C. E. (1963). *A Strategy of Decision*. New York: Free Press.
Brown, L. D. and Kaplan, R. E. (1981). Participative research in a factory. In P. Reason and J. Rowan (eds), *Human Inquiry*. Chichester: Wiley, pp.303–14.
Bruner, J. S. and Postman, L. J. (1949). On the perception of incongruity: a paradigm. *Journal of Personality*, **18**, 206–23.
Brunsson, N. (1982). The irrationality of action and action rationality: decisions, ideologies and organizational actions. *Journal of Management Studies*, **19**, 1, 29–44.
Brickell, H. M. (1976). The influence of external political factors on the role and methodology of evaluation. *Evaluation Comment*, **5**, 1, 1–6.
Buchanan, D. A. and Boddy, D. (1982). Advanced technology and the quality of working life: the effects of word processing on video typists. *Journal of Occupational Psychology*, **55**, 1, 1–11.
Buckley, W. (1967). *Sociology and Modern Systems Theory*. Englewood Cliffs, N.J.: Prentice-Hall.
Burgoyne, J. G. (1973). A new approach to evaluating management development programmes: some explanatory research. *Personnel Review*, **2**, 4, 40–4.
Burgoyne, J. G. and Cooper, C. L. (1975). Evaluation methodology. *Journal of Occupational Psychology*, **48**, 53–62.
Burns, T. and Stalker, G. M. (1961). *The Management of Innovation*. London: Tavistock.
Burrell, G. and Morgan, G. (1979). *Sociological Paradigms and Organisational Analysis*. London: Heinemann.
Camhis, M. (1979). *Planning Theory and Philosophy*. London: Tavistock.
Campbell, D. T. (1969). Reforms as experiments. *American Psychologist*, April, 228–42.

Campbell, D. T. (1974). Qualitative knowing in action research. Kurt Lewin Award Address, Society for the Psychological Study of Social Issues, meeting with the American Psychological Association, New Orleans, 1 September.

Campbell, D. T. and Erlebacher, A. (1970). How regression artifacts in quasi-experimental evaluations can mistakenly make compensatory education look harmful. In J. Hellmuth (ed.), *Disadvantaged Child. Vol. 3. Compensatory Education: A National Debate*. New York: Brunner/Mazel.

Campbell, D. T. and Stanley, J. C. (1963). Experimental and quasi-experimental designs for research on teaching. In N. L. Gage (ed.), *Handbook of Research on Teaching*. Chicago: Rand McNally.

Campbell, J. P., Dunnette, M. D., Lawler, E. E. and Weick, K. E. (1970). *Managerial Behavior, Performance and Effectiveness*. New York: McGraw-Hill.

Caplow, T. (1964). *Principles of Organization*. New York: Harcourt, Brace and World.

Carnall, C. A. (1979). The social context of work organization change. *Personnel Review*, **8**, 28–38.

Carnall, C. A. (1982). *The Evaluation of Organisational Change*. Aldershot: Gower.

Caro, F. G. (ed.). (1971). *Readings in Evaluation Research*. New York: Russell Sage.

Carter, R. K. (1971). Clients' resistance to negative findings and the latent conservative function of evaluation studies. *American Sociologist*, **6**, 118–24.

Cheng, J. L. C. and McKinley, W. (1983). Towards the integration of organization research and practice: a contingency study of bureaucratic control and performance in scientific settings. *Administrative Science Quarterly*, **28**, 1, 85–100.

Cherns, A. B. (ed.). (1972). *Papers on Social Science Utilization*. Loughborough: Centre for Utilization of Social Science Research.

Child, J. (1972). Organizational structure, environment and performance: the role of strategic choice. *Sociology*, **6**, 1–22.

Ciarlo, J. A. (ed.). (1981). *Utilizing Evaluation: Concepts and Measurement Techniques*. Beverly Hills: Sage.

Cicourel, A. (1964). *Method and Measurement in Sociology*. New York: Free Press.

Clark, P. A. (1972). *Action Research and Organizational Change*. London: Harper and Row.

Clegg, C. W. (1979). The process of job redesign: sign posts from a theoretical orphanage? *Human Relations*, **32**, 999–1022.

Clegg, C. W. (1982). Modelling the practice of job redesign. In J. E. Kelly and C. W. Clegg (eds), *Autonomy and Control at the Workplace: Contexts for Job Redesign*. London: Croom Helm.

Coch, L. and French, J. (1948). Overcoming resistance to change. *Human Relations*, **1**, 512–32.

Cohen, B. P. (1980). *Developing Sociological Knowledge*. Englewood Cliffs, N.J.: Prentice-Hall.

Cohen, D. and Weiss, J. (1977). Social science and social policy: schools and race. In C. H. Weiss (ed.), *Using Social Research in Public Policy Making*. Lexington, Mass.: Lexington Books/D.C. Heath.

Cohen, D. K. and Garet, M. (1975). Reforming educational policy with applied social research. *Harvard Educational Review*, **45**, 1, 17–43.

Cohen, J. (1969). *Statistical Power Analysis for the Behavioral Sciences*. New York: Academic Press.

Cohen, M. D. and March, J. G. (1974). *Leadership and Ambiguity: The American College President*. New York: McGraw-Hill.

Cohen, M. D., March, J. G. and Olsen, J. P. (1976). People, problems, solutions and the ambiguity of relevance. In J. G. March and J. P. Olsen, *Ambiguity and Choice in Organizations*. Bergen: Universitetsførlaget.

Coleman, J. S. *et al.* (1979). *Policy Issues and Research Design*. Chicago: National Opinion Research Center.

Conant, E. and Kilbridge, M. (1965). An interdisciplinary analysis of job enlargement: technology, costs and behavioral implications. *Industrial and Labor Relations Review*, **18**, 377–95.

Connor, R. F. (1980). Ethical issues in the use of control groups. In R. Perloff and E. Perloff (eds), *New Directions for Program Evaluation: No. 7, Values, Ethics and Standards in Evaluation*. San Francisco: Jossey-Bass, pp.63–75.

Cook, J. D., Hepworth, S. J., Wall, T. D. and Warr, P. B. (1981). *The Experience of Work. A Compendium and Review of 249 Measures and their Use*. London: Academic Press.

Cook, T. D., Cook, F. L. and Mark, M. M. (1977). Randomized and quasi-experimental designs in evaluation research: an introduction. In L. Rutman (ed.), *Evaluation Research Methods: A Basic Guide*. Beverly Hills: Sage, pp.103–39.

Cook, T. D., Levinson-Rose, J. and Pollard, W. E. (1980). The misutilization of evaluation research: some pitfalls of definition. *Knowledge: Creation, Diffusion, Utilization*, June, 477–98.

Cook, T. D. and Reichardt, C. S. (eds). (1979). *Qualitative and Quantitative Methods in Evaluation Research*. Beverly Hills: Sage.

Cooper, C. L. and Mangham, I. L. (1971). *T-Groups: A Survey of Research*. London: Wiley.

Corwin, R. G. and Louis, K. S. (1982). Organizational barriers to the utilization of research. *Administrative Science Quarterly*, **27**, 623–40.

Cronbach, L. J. (1975). Beyond the two disciplines of scientific psychology. *American Psychologist*, **30**, 116–27.

Cronbach, L. J. (1979). *Design of Evaluations*. Stanford: Stanford Evaluation Consortium.

Cronbach, L. J., Gleser, G. C., Nanda, N. and Rajaratnam, N. (1972). *The Dependability of Behavioral Measurements: Theory of Generalizability for Scores and Profiles*. New York: Wiley.

Cronbach, L. J. and Associates (1980). *Toward Reform of Program Evaluation*. San Francisco: Jossey-Bass.

Cummings, L. L. (1978). Toward organizational behavior. *Academy of Management Review*, **3**, 90–8.

Cummings, T. G., Molloy, E. S. and Glen, R. H. (1977). A methodological critique of fifty-eight selected work experiments. *Human Relations*, **30**, 8, 675–708.

Cummings, T. G. and Srivasta, S. (1977). The wheel line experiment: a case study of blue-collar work design. Chapter 9 in *Management of Work: A Socio-Technical Systems Approach*. Kent, Ohio: Comparative Administration Research Institute and Kent State University Press.

Cyert, R. M. and March, J. G. (1963). *A Behavioral Theory of the Firm*. Englewood Cliffs, N.J.: Prentice Hall.

Davidoff, P. and Reiner, T. A. (1960). A choice theory of planning. *Journal of American Institute of Planners*, May.

Davis, L. and Werling, R. (1960). Job design factors. *Occupational Psychology*, **34**, 109–32.

Dearborn, D. C. and Simon, H. A. (1958). Selective perception: a note on the departmental identification of executives. *Sociometry*, **21**, 2, 140–4.

Delbecq, A. L. and Van de Ven, A. H. (1971). A group process model for problem identification and program planning. *Journal of Applied Behavioral Science*, 7, 4, 466–92.

Della-Piana, G. M. (1981). Literary and film criticism. In N. L. Smith (ed.), *Metaphors for Evaluation, Sources of New Methods*. Beverly Hills: Sage, pp.211–46.

Deming, W. Edwards (1975). The logic of evaluation. In E. L. Struening and M. Guttentag (eds), *Handbook of Evaluation Research, Vol. 1*. Beverly Hills: Sage.

Denzin, N. K. (1970). *The Research Act: A Theoretical Introduction to Sociological Methods*. Chicago: Aldine.

Deutscher, I. (1976). Public issues or private troubles: is evaluation research sociological? *Sociological Focus*, 9, 231–8.

Dexter, L. A. (1966). Impressions about utility and wastefulness in applied social science studies. *American Behavioral Scientist*, 9, 6, 9–10.

Dror, Y. (1973). The planning process: a facet design. In A. Faludi (ed.), *A Reader in Planning Theory*. Oxford: Pergamon. First published in *International Review of Administrative Science*, 29, 1, 1963.

Duhem, P. (1954). *The Aim and Structure of Physical Theory*. Princeton, N.J.: Princeton University Press.

Dunbar, R. L. M. (1983). Toward an applied administrative science. *Administrative Science Quarterly*, 28, 129–44.

Duncan, K. D., Gruneberg, M. M. and Wallis, D. (eds.). (1980). *Changes in Working Life*. Chichester: Wiley.

Dunn, W. N. (1980). The two-communities metaphor and models of knowledge use. *Knowledge: Creation, Diffusion, Utilization*, 1, 515–36.

Dunn, W. N. (1981). Reforms as arguments. In B. Holzner *et al.* (eds), *The Political Realization of Knowledge: Towards New Scenarios*. West Germany: Physica-Verlag.

Edwards, P. K. and Scullion, H. (1982). *The Social Organization of Industrial Conflict*. Oxford: Blackwell.

Edwards, W., Guttentag, M. and Snapper, K. (1975). A decision-theoretic approach to evaluation research. In E. L. Struening and M. Guttentag (eds), *A Handbook of Evaluation Research, Vol. 1*. Beverly Hills: Sage.

Eisner, E. (1979). *The Educational Imagination*. New York: MacMillan.

Elinson, J. (1967). Effectiveness of social action programs in health and welfare. In *Assessing the Effectiveness of Child Health Services*. Report of the 56th Ross Conference on Pediatric Research. Columbus, Ohio: Ross Laboratories.

Emergy, F. E. and Trist, E. L. (1965). The causal texture of organizational environments. *Human Relations*, 8, 1, 21–32.

Etzioni, A. (1968). *The Active Society*. London and New York: Collier-MacMillan and Free Press.

Etzioni, A. (1973). Mixed-scanning: a "third" approach to decsion-making. In A. Faludi (ed.), *A Reader in Planning Theory*. Oxford: Pergamon Press. First published in *Public Administration Domain*, December 1967.

Evans, M. G. (1975). Opportunistic organizational research: The role of patch-up designs. *Academy of Management Journal*, 18, 1, 98–108.

Fairhurst, E. (1983). Organizational rules and the accomplishment of nursing work on geriatric wards. *Journal of Management Studies*, 20, 3, 315–32.

Faludi, A. (ed.). (1973). *A Reader in Planning Theory*. Oxford: Pergamon Press.

Feldman, M. S. and March, J. G. (1981). Information in organizations as signal and symbol. *Administrative Science Quarterly*, 26, 171–86.

Feyerabend, P. (1975). *Against Methods: Outline of an Anarchistic Theory of Knowledge*. London: N.L.B.

Fiedler, F. E. (1967). *A Theory of Leadership Effectiveness.* New York: McGraw-Hill.

Fineman, S. (1981). Funding research: practice and politics. In P. Reason and J. Rowan (eds), *Human Inquiry.* Chichester: Wiley, pp.473–84.

Fitter, M. J. (1982). Information systems and the organizational implications of job redesign. In J. E. Kelly and C. W. Clegg (eds), *Autonomy and Control at the Workplace: Contexts for Job Redesign.* London: Croom Helm, pp.129–56.

Ford, R. (1969). *Motivation through the Work Itself.* New York: American Management Association.

Foucault, M. (1970). *The Order of Things. An Archaeology of the Human Sciences.* London: Tavistock. (First published as *Le Mots et les Choses,* Editions Gallimard, 1966.)

Fox, A. (1966). *Industrial Sociology and Industrial Relations.* Research Paper 3, Royal Commission on Trade Unions and Employers' Associations. London: H.M.S.O.

Freidson, E. (1968). The impurity of professional authority. In H. S. Becker, B. Gear, D. Riesman and R. S. Weiss (eds), *Institutions and the Person.* Chicago: Aldine, pp.25–34.

Friedlander, F. and Brown, L. D. (1974). Organization development. *Annual Review of Psychology,* **25,** 313–41.

French, J., Israel, J. and As, D. (1960). Experiment on participation in a Norwegian factory. *Human Relations,* **13,** 1, 3–20.

French, W. L. and Bell, C. H. (1973). *Organization Development.* Englewood Cliffs, N. J.: Prentice-Hall.

Friedmann, J. and Hudson, B. (1974). Knowledge and action: a guide to planning theory. *Journal of American Institute of Planners,* January.

Friend, J. K. and Jessop, W. N. (1969). *Local Government and Strategic Choice.* London: Tavistock.

Galbraith, J. R. (1973). *Designing Complex Organizations.* Reading, Mass.: Addison-Wesley.

Geertz, C. (1973). Thick description: toward an interpretive theory of culture. In C. Geertz, *The Interpretation of Cultures.* New York: Basic Books.

Gellner, E. (1973). *Cause and Meaning in the Social Sciences.* London: Routledge and Kegan Paul.

Gillespie, A. (1973). *The Management of Wage Payment Systems.* London: Kogan Page.

Glaser, B. G. and Strauss, A. L. (1967). *The Discovery of Grounded Theory.* Chicago: Aldine.

Glennester, H. (1975). *Social Service Budgets and Social Policy.* London: George Allen and Unwin.

Goffman, E. (1959). *The Presentation of Self in Everyday Life.* Garden City, N.Y.: Doubleday.

Golembiewski, R. T. (1979). *Approaches to Planned Change. Parts 1 and 2.* New York: Marcel Dekker.

Goodman, P. S. (1979). *Assessing Organizational Change. The Rushton Quality of Work Experiment.* New York: Wiley-Interscience.

Goodman, P. S. and Pennings, J. M. (eds). (1977). *New Perspectives on Organizational Effectiveness.* San Francisco: Jossey-Bass.

Gordon, G. H. and Morse, E. V. (1975). Evaluation research. In A. Inkeles, J. Coleman and N. Smelser (eds), *Annual Review of Sociology.* Palo Alto, Calif.: Annual Reviews Inc., pp.339–61.

Gordon, M. E., Kleiman, L. S. and Hanie, C. A. (1978). Industrial-organizational psychology: open thy ears o house of Israel. *American Psychologist,* **33,** 893–905.

Gowler, D. and Legge, K. (1972). Occupational role development, Parts I and II. *Personnel Review*, **1**, 2 and 3, 12–27, 58–73.

Gowler, D. and Legge, K. (1979). The evaluation of planned organizational change: The necessary art of the possible? *Journal of Enterprise Management*, **1**, 201–12.

Gowler, D. and Legge, K. (1980). Evaluative practices as stressors in occupational settings. In C. L. Cooper and R. L. Payne (eds), *Current Concerns in Occupational Stress*. Chichester: Wiley, pp.213–42.

Gowler, D. and Legge, K. (1982). The integration of disciplinary perspectives and levels of analysis in problem-oriented organizational research. In N. Nicholson and T. D. Wall (eds), *The Theory and Practice of Organizational Psychology*. London: Academic Press, pp.69–101.

Greenwood, E. (1967). Attributes of a profession. *Social Work*, **2**, 45–55.

Greiner, L. E. (1967). Patterns of organization change. *Harvard Business Review*, **45**, 3, 119–30.

Guba, E. G. (1975). Problems in utilizing the results of evaluation. *Journal of Research and Development in Education*, **8**, 42–54.

Guba, E. G. (1981). Investigative reporting. In N. L. Smith (ed.), *Metaphors for Evaluation, Sources of New Methods*. Beverly Hills: Sage, pp.67–86.

Guba, E. G. and Lincoln, Y. S. (1981). *Effective Evaluation*. San Francisco: Jossey-Bass.

Gyllenhammer, P. G. (1977). *People at Work*. Reading, Mass.: Addison-Wesley.

Hackman, J. R. and Lawler, E. E. (1971). Employee reactions to job characteristics. *Journal of Applied Psychology*, **55**, 259–86.

Hackman, J. R. and Oldham, G. R. (1976). Motivation through the design of work: test of a theory. *Organizational Behavior and Human Performance*, **15**, 250–79.

Hage, J. (1974). *Communication and Organizational Control: Cybernetics in Health and Welfare Settings*. New York: Wiley-Interscience.

Hage, J. (1980). *Theories of Organizations: Form, Process, and Transformation*. New York: Wiley.

Hage, J. and Aiken, M. (1967). Program change and organizational properties: a comparative analysis. *American Journal of Sociology*, **72**, 503–19.

Hägg, I. (1977). *Review of Capital Investments*. Uppsala, Sweden: University of Uppsala, Department of Business Administration.

Hakel, M. D., Sorcher, M., Beer, M. and Moses, J. L. (1982). *Making It Happen—Designing Research with Implementation in Mind*. Beverly Hills: Sage.

Hall, P. (1974). *Urban and Regional Planning*. Harmondsworth: Penguin.

Hamblin, A. C. (1974). *Evaluation and Control of Training*. London: McGraw-Hill.

Hart, D. A. (1976). Planning as an iterative process. *Local Government Studies*, July.

Hayek, F. A. (1976). *Law, Legislation and Liberty, Vol. 2. The Mirage of Social Justice*. London: Routledge and Kegan Paul.

Herbst, P. G. (1976). *Alternatives to Hierarchies*. The Hague: Martinus Nijhoff.

Hill, P. (1971). *Towards a New Philosophy of Management*. Epping: Gower Press.

Hiscox, M. D. and Owens, T. R. (1975). Attempts at implementing an educational adversary model. Paper presented at the Third Annual Pacific Northwest Educational Research and Evaluation Conference, Seattle.

Hoffman, P. J. (1968). Cue-consistency and configurality in human judgment. In B. Kleinmetz (ed.), *Formal Representation of Human Judgment*. New York: Wiley.

Homans, G. (1961). *Social Behavior: Its Elementary Forms*. New York: Harcourt, Brace and World.

House, E. R. (1976). Justice in evaluation. In G. V. Glass (ed.), *Evaluation Studies Review Annual, Vol. I*. Beverly Hills: Sage.

House, E. R. (1980). *Evaluating with Validity*. Beverly Hills: Sage.

Hunt, D. E. and Hardt, R. H. (1969). The effect of Upward Bound programs on the attitudes, motivation and achievement of Negro students. *Journal of Social Times*, **25**, 117–29.

Ivancevich, J. M. (1974). Changes in performance in a management by objectives program. *Administrative Science Quarterly*, **19**, 563–77.

Jacoby, J. *et al.* (1976). Pre-purchase information acquisition: description of a process methodology, research paradigm, and pilot investigation. In B. B. Anderson (ed.), *Advances in Consumer Research, Vol. III*. Cincinnatti: Association for Consumer Research, pp.306–14.

Jenkins, W. L. (1978). *Policy Analysis: A Political and Organizational Perspective*. London: Martin Robertson.

Jick, T. D. (1979). Mixing qualitative and quantitative methods: triangulation in action. *Administrative Science Quarterly*, **24**, 602–11.

Johnson, E. J. (1978). Decision-making: what we know about process. Working paper, Department of Psychology, Carnegie-Mellon University, Pittsburgh.

Johnson, E. J. and Russo, J. E. (1978). The organization of product information in memory identified by recall times. In H. K. Hunt (ed.), *Advances in Consumer Research, Vol. V*. Chicago: Association for Consumer Research.

Johnson, T. J. (1972). *Professions and Power*. London: MacMillan.

Joyce, L. (1980). Developments in evaluation research. *Journal of Occupational Behavior*, **1**, 181–90.

Kahneman, D. and Tversky, A. (1972). Subjective probability: a judgment of representativeness. *Cognitive Psychology*, **3**, 430–54.

Kahneman, D. and Tversky, A. (1973). On the psychology of prediction. *Psychological Review*, **80**, 4, 237–51.

Katz, D. and Khan, R. L. (1966). *The Social Psychology of Organizations*. New York: Wiley.

Keeley, M. (1978). A social-justice approach to organizational evaluation. *Administrative Science Quarterly*, **23**, 272–92.

Kelly, J. E. and Clegg, C. W. (eds.). (1982). *Autonomy and Control at the Workplace*. London: Croom Helm.

Kilmann, R. H. (1979). On integrating knowledge utilization with knowledge development: the philosophy behind the MAPS design technology. *Academy of Management Review*, **4**, 417–26.

King-Taylor, L. (1972). *Not for Bread Alone: An Appreciation of Job Enrichment*. London: Business Books.

Kingdon, D. R. (1973). *Matrix Organisation*. London: Tavistock.

Klein, L. (1976). *A Social Scientist in Industry*. Epping: Gower Press.

Kluckhohn, C. *et al.* (1951). Value and value-orientations in the theory of action: an exploration in definition and classification. In T. Parsons and E. Shils (eds), *Towards a General Theory of Action*. Cambridge, Mass.: Harvard University Press.

Knight, K. (1967). A descriptive model of the intra-firm innovation process. *Journal of Business*, **40**, 478–96.

Knight, K. (ed.). (1977). *Matrix Management*. Farnborough: Gower Press.

Koestler, A. (1971). *The Case of the Midwife Toad*. London: Heinemann.

Komarovsky, M. (ed.). (1975). *Sociology and Public Policy*. New York: Elsevier.

Kotter, J. P. and Schlesinger, L. A. (1979). Choosing strategies for change. *Harvard Business Review*, **57**, 2, 111.

Kuhn, T. (1970). *The Structure of Scientific Revolutions* (second edition). Chicago: University of Chicago Press.

Lamont, W. D. (1955). *The Value Judgement*. Edinburgh: Edinburgh University Press.

Langer, S. K. (1942). *Philosophy in a New Key*. New York: Mentor.

Lawler, E. E. (1971). *Pay and Organizational Effectiveness: A Psychological View*. New York: McGraw-Hill.

Lawler, E. E. and Hackman, J. R. (1969). Impact of employee participation in the development of pay incentives. *Journal of Applied Psychology*, 53, 447–67.

Lawler, E. E., Hackman, J. and Kaufman, S. (1973). Effects of job redesign. A field experiment. *Journal of Applied Social Psychology*, 3, 49–62.

Lawrence, P. R. and Lorsch, J. W. (1967). *Organization and Environment: Managing Differentiation and Integration*. Cambridge, Mass.: Harvard University Press.

Lazarsfeld, P. F. and Thielens, Jr., W. (1958). *The Academic Mind*. New York: Free Press.

Leavitt, H. J. (1964). Applied organizational change in industry: structural, technical and human approaches. In W. W. Cooper, H. J. Leavitt and M. W. Shelly II (eds), *New Perspectives in Organization Research*. New York: Wiley.

Legge, K. (1978). *Power, Innovation, and Problem-Solving in Personnel Management*. London: McGraw-Hill.

Lewis, G. H. and Lewis, J. F. (1980). The dog in the night time: negative evidence in social research. *British Journal of Sociology*, 31, 4, 544–58.

Lindblom, C. E. (1959). The science of "muddling through". *Public Administration Review*, Spring.

Lindblom, C. E. and Cohen, D. K. (1979). *Usable Knowledge: Social Sciences and Social Problem Solving*. New Haven, C.T.: Yale University Press.

Lord, F. N. and Novick, M. R. (1968). *Statistical Theories of Mental Test Scores*. Reading, Mass.: Addison-Wesley.

Lukes, S. (1974). *Power—A Radical View*. London: MacMillan.

Lupton, T. and Bowey, A. M. (1974). *Wages and Salaries*. Harmondsworth: Penguin.

Lupton, T. and Gowler, D. (1969). *Selecting A Wage Payment System*. London: Kogan Page.

Lynn, Jr., L. E. (1973). A federal evaluation office? *Evaluation*, 1, 2, 56–9, 92, 96.

McCleery, R. H. (1957). *Policy Change in Prison Management*. East Lansing: Government Research Bureau, Michigan State University.

McDill, E. L., McDill, M. S. and Sprehe, J. T. (1969). *Strategies for Success in Compensatory Education: An Appraisal of Evaluation Research*. Baltimore: Johns Hopkins.

McGivern, C. (1983). Some facets of the relationship between consultants and clients in organizations. *Journal of Management Studies*, 20, 3, 367–86.

Mangham, I. L. (1978). *Interactions and Interventions in Organizations*. Chichester: Wiley.

Mangham, I. L. (1979). *The Politics of Organizational Change*. London: Associated Business Press.

Mann, F. C. and Williams, L. K. (1960). Observations on the dynamics of a change to electronic data processing equipment. *Administrative Science Quarterly*, 5, 217–56.

March, J. G. (1981). Footnotes to organizational change. *Administrative Science Quarterly*, 26, 563–77.

March, J. G. and Simon, H. A. (1958). *Organizations*. New York: Wiley.

Margulies, N. and Raia, A. P. (1972). *Organizational Development, Values, Process, and Technology*. New York: McGraw-Hill.

Marsh, P., Rosser, E. and Harré, R. (1978). *The Rules of Disorder*. London: Routledge and Kegan Paul.

Melio, N. (1971). Health care organizations and innovation. *Journal of Health and Social Behavior*, **12**, 163–73.

Merewitz, L. and Sosnick, S. H. (1971). *The Budget's New Clothes*. Chicago: Rand McNally.

Miller, E. J. and Rice, A. K. (1967). *Systems of Organisation*. London: Tavistock.

Miner, J. B. (1980). *Theories of Organizational Behavior*. Hinsdale, Ill.: Dryden Press.

Mintzberg, H. (1973). *The Nature of Managerial Work*. New York: Harper and Row.

Mitchell, G. D. (ed.). (1979). *A New Dictionary of Sociology*. London: Routledge and Kegan Paul.

Mitroff, I. I. and Kilmann, R. H. (1978). *Methodological Approaches to Social Science*. San Francisco: Jossey-Bass.

Mohr, L. B. (1973). The concept of organizational goal. *American Political Science Review*, **67**, 470–81.

Mohr, L. B. (1982). *Explaining Organizational Behavior*. San Francisco: Jossey-Bass.

Morgan, G. and Smircich, L. (1980). The case for qualitative research. *Academy of Management Review*, **5**, 4, 491–500.

Morris, J. and Burgoyne, J. G. (1973). *Developing Resourceful Managers*. London: Institute of Personnel Management.

Morse, N. and Reimer, E. (1956). The experimental change of a major organizational variable. *Journal of Abnormal and Social Psychology*, **52**, 120–9.

Mulkay, M. J. (1976). Norms and ideology in science. *Social Science Information*, **15**, 4/5, 637–56.

Mumford, E. (1972). *Job Satisfaction*. London: Longman.

Mumford, E. (1976). A strategy for the redesign of work. *Personnel Review*, **5**, 2, 33–9.

Mumford, E. (1981). *Values, Technology and Work*. The Hague: Martinus Nijhoff.

Mumford, E. and Banks, O. (1967). *The Computer and the Clerk*. London: Routledge and Kegan Paul.

Mumford, E. and Henshall, D. (1979). *A Participative Approach to Computer Systems Design*. London: Associated Business Press.

Nicholas, J. M. (1979). Evaluation research in organizational change interventions: considerations and some suggestions. *Journal of Applied Behavioral Science*, **15**, 23–40.

Nicholson, N. (1976). Management sanctions and absence control. *Human Relations*, **29**, 2, 139–51.

Nisbett, R. E. and Wilson, T. D. (1977). The halo effect: evidence for unconscious alteration of judgments. *Journal of Personality and Social Psychology*, **35**, 250–6.

Norris, C. (1982). *Deconstruction, Theory and Practice*. London: Methuen.

Nozick, R. (1974). *Anarchy, State and Utopia*. Oxford: Basil Blackwell.

Nunnally, J. C. (1967). *Psychometric Theory*. New York: McGraw-Hill.

Nurich, A. J. (1982). Participation in organizational change: a longitudinal field study. *Human Relations*, **35**, 5, 413–31.

Owens, T. R. (1973). Educational evaluation by adversary proceeding. In E. R. House (ed.), *School Evaluation: The Politics and Process*. Berkeley: McCutchan Publishing, pp.295–305.

Owens, T. R. and Hiscox, M. D. (1977). Alternative models of adversary evaluation: variations on a theme. Paper presented at the American Educational Research Association Annual Meeting, New York City, April.

Owens, T. R. and Owen, T. R. (1981). Law. In N. L. Smith (ed.), *Metaphors for Evaluation, Sources of New Methods*. Beverly Hills: Sage, pp.87–110.

Parlett, M. and Hamilton, D. (1972). Evaluation as illumination: a new approach to the study of innovatory programmes. Occasional paper, Centre for Research in the Education Sciences, University of Edinburgh.

Patton, M. Q. (1978). *Utilization—Focused Evaluation*. Beverly Hills: Sage.

Patton, M. W. *et al.* (1977). In search of impact: an analysis of the utilization of federal health evaluation research. In C. H. Weiss (ed.), *Using Social Research in Public Policy-Making*. Lexington, Mass.: Lexington Books/D.C. Heath, pp.141–64.

Paul, W. Robertson, B. and Herzberg, F. (1969). Job enrichment pays off. *Harvard Business Review*, **47**, 2, 61–78.

Payne, J. W. (1976). Task complexity and contingent processing in decision-making: an information search and protocol analysis. *Organizational Behavior and Human Performance*, **16**, 366–87.

Pelz, D. C. (1978). Some expanded perspectives on use of social science in public policy. In M. Yinger and S. J. Cutler (eds), *Major Social Issues: A Multidisciplinary View*. New York: Free Press, pp.346–57.

Perloff, R. and Perloff, E. (eds). (1980). *New Directions for Program Evaluation No. 7. Values, Ethics and Standards in Evaluation*. San Francisco: Jossey-Bass.

Perrow, C. (1961). The analysis of goals in complex organizations. *American Sociological Review*, **26**, 854–66.

Perrow, C. (1970). *Organisational Analysis*. London: Tavistock.

Peters, T. J. (1978). Symbols, patterns, and settings: an optimistic case for getting things done. *Organizational Dynamics*, **7**, 3–23. (Reprinted in the McKinsey Quarterly, Autumn 1978, under the title 'Change tools for chief executives', 21–45.)

Pfeffer, J. (1981). *Power in Organizations*. Boston: Pitman.

Pfeffer, J. and Salancik, G. R. (1974). Organizational decision-making as a political process: the case of the university budget. *Administrative Science Quarterly*, **19**, 135–51.

Pfeffer, J. and Salancik, G. R. (1978). *The External Control of Organizations: A Resource Dependence Perspective*. New York: Harper and Row.

Platt, J. (1976). *The Realities of Research*. London: University of Sussex Press.

Platt, J. R. (1964). Strong inference. *Science*, **146**, 3642, 347–52.

Pollner, M. (1970). *On the Foundations of Mundane Reasoning*. Unpublished doctoral thesis, University of California, Santa Barbara.

Popham, W. J. and Carlson, D. (1977). Deep, dark deficits of adversary evaluation. *Educational Researcher*, **6**, 3–6.

Popper, K. (1959). *The Logic of Scientific Discovery*. London: Routledge and Kegan Paul.

Pressman, J. L. and Wildavsky, A. B. (1973). *Implementation*. Berkeley: University of California Press.

Provus, M. (1971). *Discrepancy Evaluation*. Berkeley, Calif.: McCutchan.

Pugh, D. S. and Hickson, D. J. (1976). *Organisational Structure in its Context*. Farnborough: Saxon House and Lexington Books.

Purcell, J. (1982). Macho managers and the new industrial relations. *Employee Relations*, **4**, 1, 3–5.

Rawls, J. (1971). *A Theory of Justice*. Cambridge, Mass.: Harvard University Press.

Reason, P. and Rowan, J. (eds). (1981). *Human Inquiry*. Chichester: Wiley.

Reichardt, C. S. and Cook, T. D. (1979). Beyond qualitative *versus* quantitative methods. In T. D. Cook and C. S. Reichardt (eds), *Qualitative and Quantitative Methods in Evaluation Research*. Beverly Hills: Sage, pp.7–31.

Rein, M. (1976). *Social Science and Public Policy*. New York: Penguin.

Rice, A. K. (1958). Part III: The experimental reorganization of automatic weaving: the social organization of a technologically disturbed production system. In *Productivity and Social Organisation: The Ahmedabad Experiment.* London: Tavistock.

Rice, A. K. (1963). *The Enterprise and its Environment.* London: Tavistock.

Rich, R. F. (1979). Emerging issues for evaluators and evaluation users. In L.-E. Datta and R. Perloff (eds), *Improving Evaluations.* Beverly Hills: Sage, pp.245–56.

Riecken, H. W. and Boruch, R. F. (eds). (1974). *Social Experimentation.* New York: Academic Press.

Rivlin, A. M. (1974). Allocating resources for policy research: how can experiments be more useful? *American Economic Review,* **64,** 346–54.

Roberts, C. and Wood, S. (1982). Collective bargaining and job redesign. In J. E. Kelly and C. W. Clegg (eds), *Autonomy and Control at the Workplace.* London: Croom Helm, pp.63–84.

Roethlisberger, F. J. and Dickson, W. J. (1939). *Management and the Worker.* Cambridge, Mass.: Harvard University Press.

Rossi, P. H. (1972). Testing for success or failure in social action. In P. H. Rossi and W. Williams (eds), *Evaluating Social Programs.* New York: Seminar Press.

Rossi, P. H. (1979). Past, present and future prospects of evaluation research. In L.-E. Datta and R. Perloff (eds), *Improving Evaluations.* Beverly Hills: Sage, pp.17–33.

Rossi, P. H. and Wright, S. R. (1977). Evaluation research: an assessment of theory, practice and politics. *Evaluation Quarterly,* **1,** 5–52.

Rossi, P. H., Freeman, H. E. and Wright, S. R. (1979). *Evaluation, A Systematic Study.* Beverly Hills: Sage.

Rothschild (1982). *An Inquiry into the Social Science Research Council.* (Cmnd. 8554). London: H.M.S.O.

Rowan, J. (1981). A dialectial paradigm for research. In P. Rowan and J. Rowan (eds), *Human Inquiry.* Chichester: Wiley, pp.93–112.

Rush, H. M. R. and Wikstrom, W. S. (1969). The reception of behavioral science in industry. *The Conference Board Record,* **9,** 45–54.

Russo, J. E. *et al.* (1975). An effective display of unit price information. *Journal of Marketing,* **39,** 11–19.

Sabatier, P. (1978). The acquisition and utilization of technical information by administrative agencies. *Administrative Science Quarterly,* **23,** 396–416.

Sadler, P. and Barry, B. (1970). *Organisational Development.* London: Longman.

Salasin, S. (1980). The evaluator as agent of change. In R. Perloff and E. Perloff (eds), *New Directions for Program Evaluation, No. 7: Values, Ethics, and Standards in Evaluation.* San Francisco: Jossey-Bass, pp.1–9.

Sayles, L. R. and Chandler, M. R. (1971). *Managing Large Systems.* New York: Harper and Row.

Schmuck, R. and Miles, M. B. (1971). *Organization Development in Schools.* Palo Alto, Calif.: National Press.

Schön, D. A. (1971). *Beyond the Stable State.* New York: W. W. Norton.

Schön, D. A. (1979). Generative metaphor: a perspective of problem-setting in social policy. In A. Ortony (ed.), *Metaphor and Thought.* New York: Cambridge University Press.

Schutz, A. (1964). *Collected Papers, Vol.2.* The Hague: Martinus Nijhoff.

Scriven, M. (1967). The methodology of evaluation. In R. W. Tyler, R. M. Gagne and M. Scriven (eds), *Perspectives on Curriculum Evaluation.* Chicago: Rand McNally.

Scriven, M. (1972). Objectivity and subjectivity in educational research. In L. G. Thomas (ed.), *Philosophical Redirection of Educational Research*. Chicago: Chicago University Press.

Scriven, M. (1973). Goal-free evaluation. In E. R. House (ed.), *School Evaluation*. Berkeley: McCutchan.

Scriven, M. (1974). Evaluation perspectives and procedures. In W. J. Popham (ed.), *Evaluation in Education: Current Applications*. Berkeley, Calif.: McCutchan.

Sieber, J. E. (1980). Being ethical: professional and personal decisions in program evaluation. In R. Perloff and E. Perloff (eds), *New Directions for Program Evaluation, No. 7: Values, Ethics, and Standards in Evaluation*. San Francisco: Jossey-Bass, pp.5–61.

Silverman, D. (1970). *The Theory of Organisations*. London: Heinemann.

Simon, H. A. (1957). *Models of Man*. New York: Wiley.

Sjöberg, G. (1975). Politics, ethics and evaluation research. In M. Guttentag and E. L. Struening (eds), *Handbook of Evaluation Research, Vol. 2*. Beverly Hills: Sage, pp.29–51.

Slovic, P. (1966).Cue consistency and cue utilization in judgment. *American Journal of Psychology*, **79**, 427–34.

Slovic, P. *et al.* (1976). Cognitive processes and societal risk taking. In J. Curol and J. Payne (eds), *Cognitive and Social Behavior*. Hillsdale, N.J.: Lawrence Erlbaum Associates.

Smith, M. L., Gabriel, R., Schott, J. and Podia, W. L. (1976). Evaluation of the effects of Outward Bound. In G. V. Glass (ed.), *Evaluation Studies Review Annual, Vol. 1*. Beverly Hills: Sage, pp.400–21.

Smith, N. L. (1981). Developing evaluation methods. In N. L. Smith (ed.), *Metaphors for Evaluation, Sources of New Methods*. Beverly Hills: Sage, pp.17–49.

Spradley, J. P. and Mann, B. J. (1975). *The Cocktail Waitress*. New York: Wiley.

Sproull, L. (1977). *Management Attention in New Education Programs: A Micro-Behavioral Study of Program Implementation*. Unpublished doctoral thesis, Stanford University, California.

Sproull, L. (1978). Management attention patterns: a micro-behavioral analysis. Paper presented at A.E.R.A. annual meeting, Toronto.

Sproull, L. and Larkey, P. (1979). Managerial behavior and evaluator effectiveness. In H. C. Schulberg and J. M. Jerrell (eds), *The Evaluator and Management*. Beverly Hills: Sage.

Stake, R. E. (1974). Program evaluation, particularly responsive evaluation. Unpublished mimeograph.

Stake, R. E. (ed.). (1975). *Evaluating the Arts in Education: A Responsive Approach*. Columbus, Ohio: Merrill.

Stanton, A. H. and Schwartz, M. S. (1954). *The Mental Hospital. A Study of Institutional Participation in Psychiatric Illness and Treatment*. New York: Basic Books.

Steers, R. M. (1975). Problems in the measurement of organizational effectiveness. *Administrative Science Quarterly*, **20**, 546–58.

Steers, R. M. (1977). *Organizational Effectiveness, A Behavioral View*. Santa Monica, Calif.: Goodyear.

Stewart, R. (1967). *Managers and their Jobs*. London: MacMillan.

Stewart, R. (1976). *Contrasts in Management*. London: McGraw-Hill.

Stogdill, R. M. (1974). *Handbook of Leadership*. New York: Free Press.

Strauss, A. (1963). The hospital and its negotiated order. In E. Freidson (ed.), *The Hospital in Modern Society*. New York: Free Press.

Stufflebeam, D. L. (1968). *Evaluation as Enlightenment for Decision Making.* Monograph of Evaluation Center, College of Education. Columbus: Ohio State University.

Suchman, E. A. (1967). *Evaluation Research.* New York: Russell Sage Foundation.

Suchman, E. A. (1970). Action for what? A critique of evaluative research. In R. O'Toole (ed.), *The Organization, Management, and Tactics of Social Research.* Cambridge, Mass.: Schenkman.

Susman, G. I. and Evered, R. D. (1978). An assessment of the scientific merits of action research. *Administrative Science Quarterly,* **23,** 582–603.

Thomas, K. W. and Tymon, Jr., W. G. (1982). Necessary properties of relevant research: lessons from recent criticisms of the organizational sciences. *Academy of Management Review,* **7,** 345–52.

Thompson, J. D. and Tuden, A. (1959). Strategies, structures, and processes in organizational decision. In *Comparative Studies in Administration.* Pittsburgh: University of Pittsburgh Press.

Thompson, M. (1975). *Evaluation for Decision in Social Programs.* Lexington, Mass.: Lexington/D.C. Heath.

Tichy, N. M. (1974). Agents of planned social change: congruence of values, cognitions, and actions. *Administrative Science Quarterly,* **19,** 164–82.

Toffler, A. (1970). *Future Shock.* London: Bodley Head.

Trend, M. G. (1979). On the reconciliation of qualitative and quantitative analyses: a case study. In T. D. Cook and C. S. Reichardt (eds), *Qualitative and Quantitative Methods in Evaluation Research.* Beverly Hills: Sage, pp.68–86.

Trice, H. M., Belasco, J. and Alutto, J. (1969). The role of ceremonials in organizational behavior. *Industrial and Labor Relations Review,* **23,** 40–51.

Tversky, A. (1969). Intrasensitivity of preferences. *Psychological Review,* **76,** 31–48.

Tversky, A. (1972). Elimination by aspects: a theory of choice. *Psychological Review,* **79,** 281–99.

Tversky, A. and Kahneman, D. (1971). The belief in the 'law of small numbers'. *Psychological Bulletin,* **76,** 2, 105–10.

Tversky, A. and Kahneman, D. (1973). Availability: a heuristic for judging frequency and probability. *Cognitive Psychology,* **5,** 207–32.

Tversky, A. and Kahneman, D. (1974). Judgment under uncertainty: heuristics and biases. *Science,* **185,** 1124–31.

Van Beek, H. (1964). The influence of assembly-line organization on output, quality, morale. *Occupational Psychology,* **38,** 161–72.

Van Maanen, J. (1982). The boss: the American police sergeant at work. In M. Punch (ed.), *Controlling the Police.* Cambridge, Mass.: M.I.T. Press.

Van Maanen, J., Dabbs, Jr., J. M. and Faulkner, R. R. (1982). *Varieties of Qualitative Research. Studying Organizations, Innovations in Methodology,* **5.** Beverly Hills: Sage.

Van de Vall, M. (1975). Utilization and methodology of applied social research: four complementary models. *Journal of Applied Behavioral Science,* **11,** 14–38.

Van de Vall, M. and Boyas, C. (1981). A paradigm of social policy research in advanced systems: an empirical analysis. *International Review of Sociology,* **17,** 93–111.

Van de Vall, M., Bolas, C. and Kang, T. S. (1976). Applied social research in industrial organizations: an evaluation of functions, theory, and methods. *Journal of Applied Behavioral Science,* **12,** 158–77.

Vroom, V. H. and Yetton, P. W. (1973). *Leadership and Decision Making.* Pittsburgh: University of Pittsburgh Press.

Wagner, R. (1981). *The Invention of Culture* (Revised and Expanded Edition). Chicago: University of Chicago Press.

Wall, T. D. (1980). Group work redesign in context: a two-phase model. In K. Duncan, M. Gruneberg and D. Willis (eds), *Changes in Working Life*. London: Wiley.

Wall, T. D. and Clegg, C. W. (1981). A longitudinal field study of group work redesign. *Journal of Occupational Behavior*, **2**, 31–49.

Wall, T. D. and Lischeron, J. A. (1977). *Worker Participation: A Critique of the Literature and Some Fresh Evidence*. London: McGraw-Hill.

Walsh, D. (1972). Varieties of positivism. In P. Filmer, M. Phillipson, D. Silverman and D. Walsh, *New Directions in Sociological Theory*. London: Collier-MacMillan, pp.37–55.

Walton, R. E. and Warwick, D. P. (1973). The ethics of organization development. *Journal of Applied Behavioral Science*, **9**, 1, 681–98.

Ward, D. A. (1973). Evaluation research for corrections. In S. E. Ollin (ed.), *Prisoners in America*. Englewood Cliffs, N.J.: Prentice-Hall.

Ward, D. A. and Kassebaum, G. G. (1972). On biting the hand that feeds: some implications of sociological evaluations. In C. H. Weiss (ed.), *Evaluating Action Programs*. Boston: Allyn and Bacon.

Warmington, A., Lupton, T. and Gorfin, C. (1977). *Organizational Behaviour and Performance*. London: MacMillan.

Warr, P., Bird, M. and Rackham, N. (1970). *Evaluation of Management Training*. Epping: Gower Press.

Warr, P., Fineman, S., Nicholson, N. and Payne, R. (1978). *Developing Employee Relations*. Farnborough: Saxon House.

Warren, R. (1973). The social context of program evaluation research. Paper presented at Ohio State University Symposium on Evaluation in Human Science Programs, June.

Wason, P. C. (1960). On the failure to eliminate hypotheses in a conceptual task. *Quarterly Journal of Experimental Psychology*, **12**, 3, 129–40.

Waters, J. A., Salipante, P. F. and Notz, W. W. (1978). The experimenting organization: using the results of behavioral science research. *Academy of Management Review*, **3**, 483–92.

Watson, T. J. (1977). *The Personnel Managers: A Study in the Sociology of Work and Industry*. London: Routledge and Kegan Paul.

Wax, R. (1971). *Doing Fieldwork*. Chicago: University of Chicago Press.

Webb, E. J. *et al.* (1966). *Unobtrusive Measures*. Chicago: Rand McNally.

Webster, E. C. (1964). *Decision-Making in the Employment Interview*. Industrial Relations Center, McGill University, Montreal.

Weick, K. E. (1976). Educational organizations as loosely-coupled systems. *Administrative Science Quarterly*, **21**, 1, 1–19.

Weiss, C. H. (1972a). *Evaluation Research. Methods of Assessing Program Effectiveness*. Englewood Cliffs, N.J.: Prentice-Hall.

Weiss, C. H. (1972b). Evaluating educational and social action programs: a treeful of owls. In C. H. Weiss (ed.), *Evaluating Action Programs*. Boston: Allyn and Bacon, pp.3–27.

Weiss, C. H. (1972c). Utilization of evaluation: toward a comparative study. In C. H. Weiss (ed.), *Evaluating Action Programs*. Boston: Allyn and Bacon. (Reprint of a paper presented at the meeting of the American Sociological Association, Miami Beach, Florida, September 1966.)

Weiss, C. H. (1973). Organizational constraints on evaluation research. *Evaluation*, **1**, 2, 49–55. (Reprinted under the title 'Between the cup and lip')

Weiss, C. H. (1975). Evaluation research in the political context. In E. L. Struening and M. Guttentag (eds), *Handbook of Evaluation Research, Vol. I.* Beverly Hills: Sage, 13–26. (Paper presented at the annual meeting of the American Psychological Association, Montreal, August 30 1973. Also published as 'Where politics and evaluation research meet'. *Evaluation*, 1, 1, 37–45, 1973.)

Weiss, C. H. (1981). Use of social science research in organizations: the constrained repertoire theory. In H. Stein (ed.), *Organization and the Human Services.* Philadelphia: Temple University Press, pp.180–204.

Weiss, C. H. and Bucuvalas, M. J. (1977). The challenge of social research to decision-making. In C. H. Weiss (ed.), *Using Social Research in Public Policy Making.* Lexington, Mass.: Lexington Books/D.C. Heath.

Weiss, C. H. and Bucuvalas, M. J. (1980a). *Social Science Research and Decision-Making.* New York: Columbia University Press.

Weiss, C. H. and Bucuvalas, M. J. (1980b). Truth tests and utility tests: decision makers' frames of reference for social science research. *American Sociological Review*, 45, 2, 302–13. (Reproduced in H. E. Freeman and M. A. Solomon (eds), *Evaluation Studies Review Annual*, 1981, Beverly Hills: Sage, 695–706.)

Weiss, J. A. and Weiss, C. H. (1981). Social scientists and decision-makers look at the usefulness of mental health researches. *American Psychologist*, 36, 837–47.

Weiss, R. and Rein, M. (1970). The evaluation of broad-aims programs: a cautionary case and a moral. *Administrative Science Quarterly*, 15, 97–109.

White, S. E. and Mitchell, T. R. (1976). Organization development: a review of research content and research design. *Academy of Management Review*, 1, 2, 57–73.

Wholey, J., Scanlon, J. Duffy, H., Fukomoto, J. and Vogt, L. (1970). *Federal Evaluation Policy.* Washington, D.C.: The Urban Institute.

Wildavsky, A. B. (1975). *Budgeting, A Comparative Theory of the Budgeting Process.* Boston: Little, Brown.

Wilkinson, B. (1983). *The Shopfloor Politics of New Technology.* London: Heinemann Educational Books.

Williams, W. (1976). Implementation analysis and assessment. In W. Williams and R. F. Elmore (eds), *Social Program Implementation.* New York: Academic Press.

Williams, W. and Elmore, R. F. (eds). (1976). *Social Program Implementation.* New York: Academic Press.

Williams, W. and Evans, J. W. (1969). The problems of evaluation: the case of Head Start. *Annals of the American Academy of Political and Social Science*, 385, September.

Wolf, R. L. (1975). Trial by jury: a new evaluation method: 1. The process. *Phi Delta Kappan*, November, 185–7.

Wolf, R. L. and Tymitz, B. L. (1977). *Enhancing Policy Formulation through Naturalistic Judicial Inquiry Procedures: A Study of the Individual Education Program Component of Public Law 94-142.* Technical Report, Indiana Center for Evaluation, September.

Wood, S. (1979). A reappraisal of the contingency approach to organization. *Journal of Management Studies*, 16, 3, 334–54.

Woodward, J. (1965). *Industrial Organization: Theory and Practice.* London: Oxford University Press.

Woodward, J. (1970). *Industrial Organization: Behaviour and Control.* London: Oxford University Press.

Worthen, B. R. and Owens, T. R. (1978). Adversary evaluation and the school psychologist. *Journal of School Psychology*, 16, 334–45.

Wright, W. J. and Sachse, T. (1977). Payoffs of adversary evaluation. Paper presented at the American Educational Research Association annual meeting, New York City, April.

Yuchtman, E. and Seashore, S. E. (1967). A system resource approach to organizational effectiveness. *American Sociological Review*, **32**, 891–903.

Zaltman, G. and Deshpande, R. (1982). The use of market research: an exploratory study of manager and researcher perspectives. *Journal of Marketing Research*, February.

Zaltman, G., Duncan, R. and Holbek, J. (1973). *Innovations and Organizations*. New York: Wiley.

Zuckerman, H. (1977). Deviant behavior and social control in science. In E. Sagarin (ed.), *Deviance and Social Change*. Beverly Hills: Sage.

Zusman, J. (1976). Can program evaluation be saved from its enthusiasts? *American Journal of Psychiatry*, **133**, 1303–7.

Index

ORGANIZATIONAL AND OCCUPATIONAL PSYCHOLOGY

Series Editor: PETER WARR
MRC/ESRC Social and Applied Psychology Unit, Department of Psychology, The University, Sheffield, England

John E. Kelly
Scientific Management, Job Redesign & Work Performance, 1982

Kim S. Cameron and David A. Whetten (Editors)
Organizational Effectiveness: A Comparison of Multiple Models, 1982

Frank J. Landy and James L. Farr
The Measurement of Work Performance